The ICSA **Charity Trustee's Guide**

The ICSA
Charity Trustee's Guide

THIRD EDITION

Chris Priestley
Withers LLP

Published by ICSA Publishing Ltd, 16 Park Crescent, London, W1B 1AH

First edition published 2003
Second edition published 2008
This edition published 2012

Typeset in Sabon and ITC Franklin Gothic by
Hands Fotoset, Woodthorpe, Nottingham
Printed and bound in Great Britain by
Hobbs the Printers Ltd, Totton, Hampshire

British Library Cataloguing in Publication Data
A catalogue record for this book is available from the British Library.

ISBN 978-1-86072-490-9

To my wonderful parents Inez and John

Acknowledgements

ICSA Information & Training is indebted to Jane Arnott. Jane wrote the first edition of *The ICSA Charity Trustee's Guide* and she created an excellent base on which to publish subsequent editions.

The publishers would also like to thank Jane Ascroft for writing chapters 7 and 8: 'Accounting, financial management and control' and 'Taxation and other financial issues'. Jane is a Chartered Accountant with over 10 years' experience of the charity sector. Jane runs her own accountancy practice in County Durham and specialises in charity accounts and audit work.

Contents

1 Introduction

This chapter lays the foundations for the rest of the book. We will look at the definitions of charity and of trustees, the different terms used in the not-for-profit sector and their meanings. We will also consider the range of legal structures available for voluntary organisations and the legal framework for charities, including some of the wider legislation that impacts on the sector.

What is a charity?

The Charities Act 2011 (which consolidates a number of earlier Acts of Parliament dealing with charity law) provides a statutory definition of charity as an institution which is established for a charitable purpose that provides benefit to the public.

Public benefit

Charities must operate for the public benefit. The Charities Act 2011 reiterates this legal requirement for all charities in England and Wales. Earlier legislation removed the presumption of public benefit for religious, educational and poverty charities which had existed up until 2006.

The Charity Commission has published guidance on the public benefit requirement, which sets out the two key principles of public benefit. The first principle is that there must be an identifiable benefit or benefits which are clear, related to the charity's aims and be balanced against any detriment or harm. The second principle is that the benefit must be to the public or a section of the public. Charities must set out how they meet the public benefit requirement in their annual report.

Organisations which benefit a small section of the public can be charities, provided that the opportunity to benefit is not unreasonably restricted and the beneficiaries are appropriate to the aims. Certain charities offer benefits that are accessible to the public as a whole (e.g. Citizens' Advice Bureaux). An organisation providing services to people with a specific disability will only support a section of the public, which might be very small, for example, a medical charity relating to an extremely rare disease.

The Charity Commission's guidance on the public benefit requirement provides that the opportunity to benefit must not be unreasonably restricted by the ability to pay any fees charged, and that people in poverty must not be excluded from the opportunity to benefit. The Charity Commission has published specific guidance for fee-charging charities which sets out how they can meet the public benefit requirement.

It is possible that, in carrying out its activities, a charity will confer some private benefits. A degree of private benefit is acceptable, provided that it is incidental to the central purpose of the charity and does not undermine the benefit to the public. For example, the payment of salaries to charity staff for the work they do in order to achieve the charitable objects is an acceptable private benefit. In contrast, organisations which exist to distribute profit or benefits amongst their membership cannot be charitable, as the benefit is not available to the public as a whole or to a sufficient section of the community. Consequently, profit-distributing companies cannot be charitable, although they may undertake some charitable activities. In addition, certain clubs that exist principally to provide services or benefits to their members only (e.g. exclusive sport clubs) are also excluded.

The expectation that charities should operate for the public benefit is supported by the 'voluntary principle' of trusteeship, requiring that those responsible for governing charities should not benefit from the charity. This 'voluntary principle' determines that those with the responsibility for the charity hold that charity's assets and the organisation as a whole 'on trust' (hence the title 'trustees'), and must therefore act in the best interests of the charity.

In order to act in the charity's best interests, trustees must avoid any conflicts between their personal interests and those of the charity. The problems caused by conflicts of interest, and some suggestions of how such conflicts can be managed, are discussed in chapter 2.

Charities' independence

Conflicts of interest are not limited to the personal circumstances of trustees. Charitable bodies should act in the best interests of their

CASE EXAMPLE

An independent charity is founded by a company and receives a percentage of that company's profits as its sole source of income. The charity makes grants according to the objects identified in its governing document. The charity's objects clause identifies its principal areas of interest, which include advancing education, training, medical research and the provision of social welfare services in local communities. The objects clause makes no reference to the wishes of the sponsoring company in terms of the distribution of funds.

beneficiaries, and to do this they must, as far as is possible, be independent of external influence. Obviously, charities operate within a wider social and economic context; it can be difficult in some situations to find a balance between the needs of beneficiaries in the short term versus the longer term and the needs of the organisation itself. It is for trustees to find this balance, whilst avoiding external influence or control from other bodies, such as statutory agencies or commercial bodies. For example, although a charity funded by a local authority to provide services to the community may have to account to that authority for the quality and volume of the service provided under the funding, the charity itself should not be controlled by the local authority. Similarly a grant-making charity that is established by a company to distribute a proportion of its profits may operate to a broad grant-making framework or set of priorities that was determined by the company as part of the charity's inauguration, but it should not be controlled or directed by the company. Within its constitution, the trustees of the charity must determine the detail, exercising their independent control in deciding which applicants should receive a grant. Any more intrusive direction or control on the part of the originating company would fetter the discretion of the trustees and undermine the independence of the charity.

See chapter 4 for more information on governing documents.

Political activity

Charities may undertake some political activity (this is discussed in more detail in chapter 2) but may not be founded on political objectives. This principle is based on the premise that charities must operate for the public benefit and it is not for the courts (as the ultimate arbiters of charitable status) to determine whether a political purpose will benefit the public; rather, such arguments are the stuff of political debate and Parliamentary decision. Consequently, political bodies that exist to change law or policy are generally considered not to be charitable.

Charitable purposes

Not every organisation that appears to have philanthropic purposes can register as a charity. Charitable purposes were first defined by an Act of Parliament in 1601, but are now found in the Charities Act 2011. These are:

(a) the prevention or relief of poverty;

(b) the advancement of education;

(c) the advancement of religion;

(d) the advancement of health or the saving of lives;

(e) the advancement of citizenship or community development;

(f) the advancement of the arts, culture, heritage or science;

(g) the advancement of amateur sport;

(h) the advancement of human rights, conflict resolution or reconciliation or the promotion of religious or racial harmony or equality and diversity;

(i) the advancement of environmental protection or improvement;

(j) the relief of those in need by reason of youth, age, ill-health, disability, financial hardship or other disadvantage;

(k) the advancement of animal welfare; and

(l) the promotion of the efficiency of the armed forces of the Crown, or that of the police, fire and rescue services or ambulance services.

There is also a 'catch-all' clause which includes a purpose not within (a)–(l) but which is recognised as charitable under existing charity law (i.e. from case law or from Charity Commission decisions) or purposes that are analogous to, or within the spirit of, these purposes.

Prevention or relief of poverty

The relief of poverty has been interpreted widely over the years and is not restricted to absolute financial poverty, but may include relative financial poverty and those who do not have access to the normal things in life. Consequently, charities that assist particular groups of poor people, which relieve poverty in the UK and abroad and that provide debt management or financial advice often fall under this purpose, as well as charities for people with disabilities, refugees and other socially excluded groups. The relief of poverty was expanded by the Charities Act 2006 to include the prevention of poverty.

Advancement of education

Organisations which exist to promote education may be considered charitable. The education in question does not have to be formal and can include other means of training, development and research, but the subject of the education must have some merit. For research to be considered charitable it must be conducted in an objective and impartial manner and the public must have access to any useful results arising from the research. Even if access to the education itself is restricted (e.g. to those paying a fee) the organisation may still be considered charitable on this basis, provided that it provides sufficient public benefit.

Schools, colleges and universities, charities which provide apprenticeship schemes, museums, professional bodies and research projects may all come within this purpose.

Advancement of religion

The advancement of religion is considered charitable on the basis that spiritual well-being and the works of religious groups in society are beneficial to the public as a whole. Activities of charities falling under this head include running, staffing and maintaining places of worship and missionary work. The Charities Act 2006 broadened the definition of religion to include religions which do not involve a belief in a god.

Within this heading, distinctions are not made between different faiths, with major world religions such as Islam, Judaism, Christianity, Hinduism and Buddhism being included. Whilst the public benefit requirement can be met by a religion with very few followers, it will not be met where the activities of the organisation are entirely private (as in the example below) or where the religious beliefs in question contradict the common principles of religion or morality.

A number of organisations providing specific services, such as education, social care and overseas aid, are founded on religious principles and rooted within a particular faith but also fall under other charitable purposes because of the nature of their work.

CASE EXAMPLE

The Church of Scientology was refused charitable status by the Charity Commission on the basis that, although Scientologists believe in a supreme being, their activities did not constitute worship and were not beneficial to the public. The Church's practices of audit and training were considered to be more akin to counselling and study than veneration or reverence of a deity and, as such, did not represent worship. The limited access to the Church's activities and the private nature of the beneficial effects of the audit and training practices meant that the Church's application failed on both the advancement of religion head and the requirement for public benefit.

Advancement of health or the saving of lives

This purpose includes physical and mental health and curing ill-health and preventing it. Conventional as well as complementary, alternative or holistic methods can be included, provided that there is sufficient evidence of the efficacy of the method. Charities established for this purpose include hospitals, hospices, care homes and charities supporting their work, as well as bodies involved in the training of health professionals and medical research organisations. The saving of lives covers purposes such as the provision of lifeboats or relief from natural disasters.

Some health-related organisations, such as private hospitals, charge fees for their services, which can still be charitable on this basis, provided that sufficient public benefit is provided. Both direct public benefits and indirect public benefits, such as freeing-up of public health services, can be taken into account.

Advancement of citizenship or community development

A wide range of organisations come under this head, including organisations which are involved in rural or urban regeneration, promoting civic responsibility and volunteering, including Scout and Guide groups. Some of these activities have only been recognised as being charitable relatively recently.

Advancement of the arts, culture, heritage or science

There is an overlap between this purpose and the advancement of education. It encompasses organisations such as arts and drama groups, art festivals, museums, art galleries, cinemas, theatres, local history societies and scientific research projects.

Advancement of amateur sport

Sport is defined in the Charities Act 2011 as 'sports or games which promote health by involving physical or mental skill or exertion'. The emphasis on health-promoting effects means that sports such as snooker and motor racing have not been capable of being charitable. Public benefit requirements mean that sport is restricted to amateur sport, so organisations that are established for elite sport cannot be charities, but community amateur sports clubs can.

Advancement of human rights, conflict resolution or reconciliation or the promotion of religious or racial harmony or equality and diversity

These areas have been regarded as being charitable only relatively recently. Organisations involved in the promotion of human rights in the UK or abroad, such as relieving victims of human rights abuses and raising awareness of human rights issues, are capable of being recognised as charitable under this purpose, as well as organisations involved in conflict resolution or reconciliation, the promotion of religious or racial harmony, equality and diversity.

There are restrictions on the types of activities that such charities can carry out, because they can only be involved in limited political activity. For this reason, the work of Amnesty International is divided between Amnesty International Limited, a non-charitable company and the main Amnesty International Charity.

Advancement of environmental protection or improvement

This purpose includes the preservation and conservation of the natural environment and the promotion of sustainable development. This might involve the conservation of a particular animal or plant or wildlife, or the environment more generally. This can include a range of organisations from zoos and conservation bodies to botanic gardens and recycling groups.

Relief of those in need by reason of youth, age, ill-health, disability, financial hardship or other disadvantage

This includes running care homes for the elderly or children, providing services to people with disabilities, and housing associations. There is an overlap between this purpose and the advancement of health and education and also the prevention or relief of poverty.

Advancement of animal welfare

The nature of the benefit to the public of organisations which are established for this purpose is an indirect one, but it is accepted. It includes purposes directed towards the prevention of cruelty to animals or the relief of suffering of animals. Charities that promote kindness to animals or that provide veterinary care or treatment may come within this purpose.

Promotion of the efficiency of the armed forces of the Crown, or of the efficiency of the police, fire and rescue services or ambulance services

This is a long-accepted charitable purpose. The reason for it is that the armed forces defend the public and promoting their efficiency helps to ensure this. The police, fire and rescue services and ambulance services prevent or detect crime, preserve public order and protect the public.

Charities under this heading include organisations that promote the fitness of members of the services, provide sporting facilities, equipment and welfare to serving personnel and their dependants, and memorials.

Other charitable purposes

This 'catch-all' provision covers all existing charitable purposes and any purpose which is analogous to, or within the spirit of, any of the purposes. This ensures that other charitable purposes not mentioned in the list are still charitable and provides flexibility to allow further purposes to be added in future by analogy to existing purposes.

This could include a wide range of activities, such as the provision of facilities for recreation and other leisure-time occupations in the interests of social welfare, the relief of unemployment, the promotion of mental or moral improvement, the maintenance of public order and the rehabilitation of ex-offenders.

Organisations can fall under several different heads of charity or may be charitable if they meet just one of the criteria, *provided always* that they meet the public benefit requirement.

CASE EXAMPLE

Wikimedia UK's application for registration with the Charity Commission was approved in November 2011. The organisation, which promotes and supports public access to open-source content (including Wikipedia) first applied to the Charity Commission on the basis that it was an educational charity, but this was rejected. It made its successful second application on the grounds that it provided a public resource akin to a reading room or library, which case law from the nineteenth century established to be charitable. The Commission's approval was subject to the condition that the organisation has sufficient editorial and other quality content control procedures in place.

Not-for-profit organisations that are not charities

There are many not-for-profit organisations that are not charities. This may be because they confer some type of private benefit, as is the case with social enterprises and credit unions. Although these organisations may not have the strict profit-making motives of commercial bodies, the fact that the purpose of the organisation includes a significant element of personal gain or is not exclusively charitable excludes them from charitable status.

What is a trustee?

Historically, one of the significant problems of charity trusteeship was that many trustees were unaware of their legal responsibilities. The difficulty was often one of nomenclature, as there are many different titles used for the trustee board, such as management committee, council of management, executive committee, board of directors or board of trustees. Essentially, those with the ultimate responsibility for, and control of, the organisation are the trustees as they administer the organisation 'on trust' for the beneficiaries. This body should be defined in the governing document.

It is the trustees' function to govern the charity and, collectively, they form the governing body. They are responsible for determining the direction of the charity within the framework laid down by the governing document. Elements of this function include ensuring financial viability and the achievement of the charity's aims. The responsibility of trustees will be considered in more detail in chapter 2, but equivalents would be the non-executive director of a commercial company or a local authority councillor.

Legal framework

Legal structures

When looking at the legal basis of a charitable organisation, a common mistake is to confuse an organisation's legal structure with its charitable status. Organisation structure and charitable status are separate elements. Just because an organisation is unincorporated does not make it charitable. Just because an organisation is a company does not make it commercial in nature. Charitable status looks at the issues discussed at the beginning of this chapter – for example, is the organisation operating for the public benefit, does it fall within one of the charitable purposes, and so on? Charitable status is determined by the outward looking objects of the organisation as set out in its governing document. The legal structure of the organisation is concerned with its internal structure and functioning, particularly in relation to the governing body, and is determined by its governing document. Often, an organisation's legal status will be confirmed by registration with another regulator, e.g. limited companies will be registered at Companies House.

The table on pp. 11–13 below gives further information on the different legal structures available to charities.

Legal personality and limited liability

A charity may select any one of a number of available legal structures. The most appropriate structure for a particular charity will depend on a number of factors, the most common being the activities of the charity and the potential liability of its governing body. The key features that a charity should consider when selecting its legal structure are legal personality and limited liability.

Legal personality. All individuals over the age of 18 have 'legal personality'. This means that they can enter into contracts, sue and be sued. Not all organisations have legal personality. Where there is no legal personality, as in the case of unincorporated associations, it is the trustees as individuals who have to act on behalf of the organisation (e.g. by being party to contracts). In contrast, in incorporated bodies such as limited companies, it is the organisation that enjoys legal personality and can enter directly into contracts.

Limited liability. Legal personality determines the liability of trustees. Where the organisation has no legal personality and trustees must enter contracts on behalf of the organisation, the liability of the organisation, which is essentially the trustees, is unlimited. This leaves the trustees personally open to legal action (e.g. in the event of breach of contract or an act of negligence). In organisations that do have legal personality, it is the organisation itself, rather than the trustees, that can enter into contracts and be sued. Liability is limited to the assets of the organisation and the trustees generally are not personally liable unless they have acted wrongly or negligently.

The table below gives an overview of the principal legal structures available to not-for-profit organisations.

Legal structure	Governing document	Characteristics of the structure	Liability of trustees	Common examples
Trust	Trust Deed	Trusts are normally established to administer funds or property (e.g. following a bequest). The trustee board tends to be small in number and appointed rather than elected.	Unlimited	Grant-making bodies; organisations that manage a particular property (e.g. a community centre or playground).

Legal structure	Governing document	Characteristics of the structure	Liability of trustees	Common examples
Unincorporated association	Constitution or rules	A body of trustees appointed (and often elected) by a wider membership who are sympathetic to the objectives of the organisation.	Unlimited	Community organisations, traditional providers of welfare services, user groups and sports clubs.
Company limited by guarantee	Memorandum and articles of association	Run by a board of directors. Members must subscribe to the memorandum and guarantees of articles of association and their details are maintained in a register of members. Members guarantee to pay a nominal sum (often £1) towards the settlement of debts in the event of company insolvency. Guarantee companies are subject to the terms of the Companies Acts 1985–2006 and are regulated by Companies House.	Liability is limited to the assets of the company and the amount guaranteed by the members.	Larger organisations, especially those with extensive contractual relationships (e.g. for staffing, service provision or premises) or operating in high-risk arenas. This form of structure has become more popular as charities have taken on local authority contracts for services and trustees have grown more aware of their potential liabilities.

Legal structure	Governing document	Characteristics of the structure	Liability of trustees	Common examples
Incorporation by Royal Charter	Royal Charter and Bye-laws	This form of incorporation is, in effect, only available to well-established organisations of national significance. Royal Charters are the responsibility of the Privy Council.	Limited	Professional institutes (e.g. ICSA) and old established charities such as the British Red Cross Society. Organisations that have attained Royal Charters in recent years include the Prince's Trust and the Chartered Institute of Personnel and Development (CIPD).
Incorporation by Act of Parliament	Act of Parliament	Limited to quangos and similar organisations.	Limited	Universities, museums, galleries and organisations established for public purposes, such as distributors of lottery funds to good causes.
Industrial and Provident Societies	Rules	Organisations must have a community purpose, but often some form of member benefit is allowed (e.g. cooperatives).	Limited	Housing associations cooperatives, friendly societies such as building societies.

CAUTION?

Whatever the legal structure of the charity, the trustees' liability will not be limited if they act outside the law or their powers.

Any of the legal structures described above may be used by charitable organisations, but none of them were designed specifically for that purpose. Social, political and economic changes in the last century radically altered the nature of the nation's not-for-profit sector. Some charities are now multi-million pound bodies responsible for delivering mainstream public services, but none of the legal structures available are an ideal fit. Trustees, understandably keen to limit their personal liability, often select to incorporate as companies limited by guarantee, but this exposes registered charities to double (and inconsistent) regulation from the Charity Commission and Companies House. Details of new forms of incorporation for not-for-profit organisations are discussed in the box overleaf.

THE CHARITABLE INCORPORATED ORGANISATION

The Charities Act 2006 introduced the concept of the Charitable Incorporated Organisation (CIO), although this legal form may not be available until the latter part of 2012, subject to Parliamentary approval. The CIO will be a limited liability structure designed specifically for, and available only to, charities. It will have a structure which separates the role of members and trustees and provisions will be introduced to ease the transfer from existing legal structures into the CIO. The CIO structure will also be available in Scotland (the SCIO) and in Northern Ireland.

Trustees considering moving their charity to incorporated status should check the Office for Civil Society's implementation plan for CIOs and the information provided by the Charity Commission.

Community Interest Companies (CIC)

The CIC is a relatively new form, which cannot be used by charities. It is designed to be used for social enterprises. A CIC is a limited company which has an asset lock requirement and must meet a community interest test. It is useful for businesses which are run for community benefit and not just private advantage. CICs are regulated by the CIC Regulator.

Governing documents and breach of trust

The table above lists the range of governing documents that may be adopted by charities and the potential liabilities to trustees. Trustees are advised to pay careful attention to the governing document of their charity. It is the foundation on which the charity rests and it sets the framework within which the charity operates, including the determination of the trustees' powers. Trustees operating outside the governing document and the powers vested in them may be acting *ultra vires* (outside their powers) and/or in breach of trust. Depending on the exact circumstances of these actions, trustees may find that they are wholly and personally liable for any losses arising to the charity as a result.

For more information on preparing and using governing documents, see chapter 4.

Charity law

Charity law differs between the countries that make up the United Kingdom. The box below lists the different jurisdictions and the legislation that applies.

Requirement to register

The Charity Commission is the body established by statute to monitor charities operating in England and Wales and to ensure that charities are operating in accordance with the requirements of charity law. Organisations are required to register with the Charity Commission if they are set up in England and/or Wales for entirely charitable purposes and have an annual income of more than £5,000, and either:

- they are a company incorporated in England and Wales; and/or
- the majority of the charity trustees live in England and Wales; and/or
- the majority of their assets are in England and Wales.

Excepted and exempt charities

Certain charities, including some religious charities, the Scouts and Guides, have been excepted from registration with the Charity Commission on the basis that they are registered with other umbrella

JURISDICTIONS WITHIN THE UK

Charities in England and Wales are principally governed by the Charities Acts of 1992 and 2011. They are subject to regulation by the Charity Commission. This book focuses on this legal and regulatory framework.

Scottish charities are subject to the Charities and Trustee Investment (Scotland) Act 2005 and are regulated by the Office of the Scottish Charity Regulator (OSCR).

Charities in Northern Ireland are regulated by the Charities Act (Northern Ireland) 2008. Their regulator is the Charity Commission for Northern Ireland (CCNI). The CCNI has not yet started to register charities in Northern Ireland. This will work will begin when the 2008 legislation is amended – likely to be early in 2013.

English and Welsh charities operating in Scotland and Northern Ireland may need to also register there.

(Note that the legal requirements for Scottish and Northern Irish charities are not considered in this guide.)

bodies. They are still, however, regulated by the Charity Commission. The number of excepted charities is reducing because of changes introduced by the Charities Act 2006 which aimed to create a fairer and simpler system of registration with similar regulation for all charities. There is now a requirement for excepted charities to register if their gross income exceeds £100,000. It is intended that this income threshold will eventually be reduced over time.

Excepted charities may register voluntarily with the Charity Commission.

Historically, exempt charities have not been able to register with the Charity Commission, even on a voluntary basis, because they are usually subject to regulation by another body; however, they have always been bound by the general legal rules that apply to charities and certain statutory requirements. Exempt charities are listed in a Schedule to the Charities Act 2011 and include certain universities, named museums and galleries. Exempt charities that are found not to have an alternative regulator will be required to register with the Charity Commission if their income exceeds £100,000; those charities which remain exempt will need to comply with more general charity law requirements.

Charities with a gross income not exceeding £5,000 are not required to register, which is an increase from the threshold of £1,000 in the previous legislation. However, the Charities Act contemplates small charities being able to register voluntarily at some point once the excepted and exempt charities that are required to register have been registered.

Role of the Charity Commission

The Charity Commission is in the unenviable position of being both the friend and the regulator of charities in England and Wales. The essence of its role is to give the public confidence in the probity of charities. It seeks to do this by registering charities and supporting them through the provision of advice and information, monitoring charities through annual reporting arrangements and investigating those charities that appear to have acted improperly. The Charity Commission maintains the Register of Charities and members of the public can view information on the Register. The easiest way to do this is via the Charity Commission's website (www.charity-commission.gov.uk).

Where the Charity Commission discovers cases of abuse or negligence in charities, it can intervene in a number of ways. For example, it may step in to administer the charity until the situation can be rectified or the organisation is closed down. The Charity Commission has extensive powers under the Charities Act 2011 to regulate the sector, which includes the power to suspend or remove trustees and other personnel from membership of a charity and a very broad power to direct a charity to take action that the Charity Commission considers expedient.

What if the Charity Commission makes a mistake when exercising such powers? In the past, an appeal against a decision of the Charity Commission involved a High Court hearing, which could be an expensive and protracted exercise. The Charities Act 2006 introduced the Charity Tribunal, which opened for business on 18 March 2008. The suspension or removal of a charity trustee, the appointment of a receiver and manager for a charity, and a refusal to register a charity could all be appealed under the previous regime, and still are. There is now a right of appeal where there has been none before (e.g. against orders by the Charity Commission requiring the production of information or documents and for charity property to be applied in a particular way). Several matters which may be brought before the tribunal are 'reviewable' only and such a review has to be conducted on the same basis as a judicial review in the High Court. In other words, an appeal in respect of a reviewable matter is only likely to succeed if the decision under challenge is seriously flawed. The Tribunal may award costs against the Charity Commission or any other person.

Happily, most charities will never encounter the investigatory element of the Charity Commission's role. For the majority of charities, contact with the Charity Commission will be limited to annual reporting arrangements, occasional calls to the helpline and reference to the Charity Commission's advice booklets.

The Charity Commission is a statutory corporation and its strategic objectives are now set out in statute. They are:

- to increase public trust and confidence in charities;
- to promote awareness and understanding of the operation of the public benefit requirement;
- to promote compliance by charity trustees with their legal obligations in exercising control and management of the administration of their charities;
- to promote the effective use of charitable resources; and
- to enhance the accountability of charities to donors, charities and the general public.

The Charity Commission must publish an annual report, which will include the extent to which it believes its objectives have been met.

Overview of charity law requirements

Charity law has evolved through statute and precedent over the past 400 years. We have already considered the statutory list of charitable purposes and the need for charities to act for the benefit of the public. Other issues, such as reporting requirements, charity finance and fundraising will be considered in more detail in the later chapters of this book.

Company law

Charities that are incorporated as companies limited by guarantee are subject to company law in addition to charity law. Key requirements include regulations regarding the running of general meetings, maintenance of registers and reporting to Companies House are contained in the Companies Act 2006. Some aspects of the requirements for limited companies will be covered in the relevant chapters of this guide, but readers are also advised to refer to ICSA's *Best Practice Guide to*

Guarantee Companies and see Malcolm Leatherdale *How to Run Your Charity*.

Other legislation

All not-for-profit organisations need to be aware of the range of legislation that may be relevant to their work. For example, the requirements for Community Interest Companies are set out in the Community Interest Company Regulations 2005. Organisations will also be subject to any legislation that affects the work of their organisation. For example, organisations working with children and families will need to be familiar with the provisions of the Children Act 1989, the Safeguarding Vulnerable Groups Act 2006 and other family law legislation.

All organisations will be subject to general laws relating to issues such as health and safety, equal opportunities and employment, and these will be discussed further in the following chapters.

Section 73 of the Charities Act 2006 (now incorporated into the Charities Act 2011) required that the Act was reviewed within five years of the date that it was passed.

Lord Hodgson of Astley Abbotts was appointed in November 2011 to consider two main issues in relation to the Act. The first questions the operation and effectiveness of the Act; the second will assess what further changes need to be made to improve the legal and regulatory framework for charities.

Essentially, the scope of the review is to analyse how well the Act is operating in practice and whether it is fit for purpose. The review will take a broad approach and encompass three core areas:
- What is a charity and what is a charity's role?
- What do charities require in order to deliver those roles?
- How should the legal framework for charities look to help them meet their needs?

Other issues will also be considered including the need to preserve the public's trust and confidence in charities, the need to sustain independence and diversity throughout the charity sector, ensuring that there is sustainability and resilience in charities and allowing and encouraging advancement and development in the sector.

The 2006 Act specifically requires the review to investigate the public's confidence in charities; the current level of donations to charity; how willing people are to volunteer; charities that were 'excepted' but have had to register as a result of the Act; and, finally, the status of the Charity Commission as a non-ministerial department.

The review will also revisit the issue of trustee remuneration and the success (or otherwise) of self-regulation of charitable fundraising and the licensing regime for charitable collections.

The review will be independent and will gather evidence from representatives within the charities sector and interested bodies through a series of interviews which will be used to collate a report by summer 2012 with a consultation document being produced in 2013.

2 Responsibilities, risk and regulation

INTRODUCTION

As trustees have overall authority for their charity, they have wide-ranging responsibilities. In this chapter, we will consider these responsibilities, and the trustees' role in governing the charity and complying with relevant legislation and regulation. We will also deal with some of the other issues that trustees should consider, such as conflicts of interest and political activities.

Responsibilities

TRUSTEE DUTIES

Charity trustees are the people who serve on the governing body of a charity. Whether they are known as trustees, directors, committee members or board members, their main duties are the same. They have ultimate responsibility for running the charity and must ensure that it is well run, in accordance with its charitable purposes.

Duty of care

Trustees must act with integrity and use reasonable care and skill in their work to ensure that a charity is well run. This might mean obtaining external professional advice in some circumstances, particularly where there may be a material risk to the charity.

Trustees should make good use of all of their skills, knowledge and experience in all areas of the charity's work. There is a specific legal requirement for trustees that have any special knowledge or experience or act as trustees in the course of their job or profession to use reasonable skill and care in relation to their background experience in certain situations relating to financial management, including:

- investment (see chapter 8);
- acquiring land (see chapter 8);
- appointing agents, nominees and custodians (see chapter 8);
- insurance; and
- auditing (see chapter 7).

Duty of prudence

The trustees must ensure that the charity is solvent, complies with the law (see below) and that charitable funds and assets are used reasonably and only in furtherance of the charity's objects. They must avoid activities that might place the charity's assets or reputation at undue risk and should take special care when investing the funds of the charity, or borrowing funds for the charity.

Compliance responsibilities

The trustees must ensure that the charity complies with legislation, in particular charity law, and also the requirements of relevant regulators such as the Charity Commission and Companies House (if the charity is also a company) including preparing and filing annual reports and annual returns.

Governance

The governance role of trustees is complex and wide ranging, so the following examples are illustrative, rather than exhaustive. It involves:
- keeping the charity true to its objects and to the governing document;
- ensuring the organisation's probity;
- being accountable for the charity;
- planning for the future of the organisation; and
- monitoring activities and outcomes against objectives.

How trustees fulfil this role will vary from one charity to another and, within a charity, may change over time. In some organisations, particularly smaller groups with few or no paid staff, trustees may be heavily involved in the daily administration of the organisation; in others they may work purely on the 'high level' basis of directing policy and ensuring the charity's efficacy.

Accountability

As a charity's governing body with legal responsibility for the organisation, the trustees are accountable for the charity as a whole. Whether the charity is being questioned in law, or by the public, donors, beneficiaries or anyone else, it is the trustees who will ultimately be held to account. Many charities emphasise the trustees' governance and accountability functions by appointing trustees through direct election, voted by the charity's members (where a charity has members).

Policy/strategy

One of the governance functions of trustees is to determine the route that the organisation should take in seeking to achieve its constitutional objects. Obviously the direction and approach taken by a charity will change over time, subject both to internal and external influences. It is the function of the trustees to monitor such influences and decide on the best approach for the future of the organisation and the needs of its beneficiaries. Commonly, trustees achieve this through developing plans, such as business or strategy plans, for implementation by staff and volunteers.

BUSINESS PLANNING

Why?

Used in the corporate sector as a means of convincing banks to invest in a company, business plans have now become common in the voluntary sector for largely the same reason – many funders require them. Properly prepared and implemented, business plans are a valuable means by which voluntary organisations may determine and achieve their goals.

Charities exist in a constantly shifting environment and the voluntary sector often prides itself on its flexibility and its swift response to change and social need. In this context it can be easy for charities to drift off course, perhaps to meet a newly emerging need or to pursue a readily accessible source of funds. However, it can also be easy for charities to take the course of least resistance, for example by continuing to deliver the same services using the same method for many years. Business planning provides a framework within which charities can take a step back and thoroughly review how they operate, their activities, and the influences of the external environment. On the

---

BUSINESS PLANNING continued

basis of such a review and taking their constitutional purpose as a foundation, charities can determine their direction, in terms of how its charitable objects can best be achieved.

What?

A business plan should serve a dual purpose as a planning document for the charity itself and as a means of convincing potential funders to support the charity. As such, a business plan may cover the following areas.

1 **The starting point** – an analysis of the charity as it currently stands, including its constitutional purpose, its track record and its activities and services.

2 **The external environment** – this could include changing social needs, the prevailing economic climate, competition from other organisations and new opportunities.

3 **The strategy** – what is the ultimate goal and how does the charity intend to get there? The business plan should consider the overall aims of the organisation and, within those aims, any subsidiary objectives. The plan should explain the relationship between the different objectives and identify priorities. The strategy may also define areas of work that the charity does not intend to undertake.

4 **Resources** – the business plan should also consider how the charity intends to resource its plan, including staffing implications, premises and financial projections. The financial aspect of the business plan should include budgeted expenditure and income predictions together with cash flow forecasts. Financial planning is discussed in detail in chapter 7.

5 **Implementation and monitoring** – business plans should be 'living' documents which are updated regularly and the plan itself should contain information as to how it will be implemented. Risks that may prevent the charity from delivering the plan's objectives should also be addressed and the plan should also explain how its implementation will be monitored. Many charities plan on a three-to-five year basis, although a longer period may be appropriate, particularly for organisations undertaking large-scale capital projects. To be most effective, plans should be reviewed on a regular basis to take account of progress and changing circumstances. Monitoring and evaluation criteria and systems for the services and activities delivered under the business plan and their impact should be established at the outset and

BUSINESS PLANNING continued

included in the plan. Monitoring and evaluation are discussed in detail in chapter 10.

6 *Capacity* – charities should demonstrate, for their own benefit and that of funders, that they have the capacity to deliver the business plan's objectives. This may include details of the skills and experience of the trustees and key staff, as well as any plans for further increasing organisational capacity.

How?

The process of business planning can be as valuable as the final plan itself. It is important to establish a baseline for the plan and, as a starting point, the organisation should consider its purpose. Agreeing a mission statement based on the charity's legal objects set out in its governing document can be a useful way of reaching a shared understanding of the purpose of the organisation and communicating this to all stakeholders. To review existing activities and to consider the impact of external factors, it will be necessary to collect a range of information. This may include internal monitoring and evaluation reports, external studies and user surveys. Organisations should also undertake an analysis of their strengths and weaknesses, the opportunities available to them and any threats facing the organisation (known as a SWOT analysis).

From the base of the agreed mission statement and the analysis of internal and external pressures and trends, the charity can build its strategy. Once the trustees have decided what the charity is to achieve and how, they can then consider if it has the capacity to achieve its objectives and how these will be resourced. This is likely to be an iterative process and different elements of the plan may need to be revised and revisited to achieve a realistic, cohesive plan.

Who?

In order for business plans to function as working documents it is important that those affected by them should have a sense of ownership of, and commitment to, the end result. It is therefore important for the planning process to involve stakeholders as well as the trustees. As a minimum, the trustees should be involved in discussions regarding the mission statement, strategy, priorities and resource implications and must have ultimate approval in these areas. They should also actively monitor the implementation of the plan.

In organisations with professional staff, the staff will normally manage the business planning process and all charities should

BUSINESS PLANNING continued

seek the input of staff and volunteers. This is essential in relation to those elements of the plan that impact on their work. It may also be advisable to seek the views of users and other stakeholders, perhaps through a formal consultation exercise.

Business planning is an important part of the trustee's role and the box below gives an overview of the process and content of typical business plans.

Running parallel to the business plan should be policies and procedures appropriate to the charity's work. These may be items that stand in their own right, separate from the business plan (e.g. disciplinary and grievance procedures for staff and conflict of interests policies, or they may be an integral part of the plan and the objectives it seeks to achieve). For example, an organisation seeking to increase the number of service users from black and minority ethnic groups could include an equal opportunities policy as part of its business plan. It is the function of trustees to be involved in the development of policies, to approve the agreed policies and to monitor their implementation.

CASE EXAMPLE

A council for voluntary service had taken on a number of activities at the request of the local authority. All the activities involved the provision of services to individuals in the community and as such were not directly related to the organisation's key role of supporting the local voluntary sector. The board of trustees became concerned that the work involved in delivering direct services was detracting from the charity's core function and so included in its business plan the express provision that the organisation would not take on any more activities of this nature.

Monitoring and evaluation criteria should be integral to the development of business plans. This is also true of any policies, procedures and internal changes to the organisation. Implementation of internal changes, the impact of services, and the impact of any changes to services, should be assessed against the original aims. It is the responsibility of trustees to set the criteria against which activities will be evaluated, to identify the data necessary for evaluation to take place and to ensure that systems are established to collect and record the necessary data. Monitoring and evaluation are covered in more detail in chapter 10.

CASE EXAMPLE Marketing vs operational objectives

A large charity working with a wide range of beneficiaries ran several projects providing services for young people leaving social services care ('care leavers'). The marketing and PR department of the charity saw great opportunities for media coverage (and potential fundraising rewards) in human interest stories about care leavers. Without consulting the project workers, the marketing and PR department launched a campaign that portrayed the care leavers in simplistic terms. It implied that all care leavers were completely cut off from their families, unable to care for themselves adequately and unsupported by statutory agencies.

The reality was somewhat different and care leavers started to complain.

Many of the care leavers still had contact with their families, but these relationships were fragile and the media coverage had only served to increase tensions. Statutory agencies who were actively working with (and often funding) the projects to improve services for care leavers also objected.

The campaign had failed to improve understanding of the complex issues affecting care leavers and subsequently involved operational staff in extensive work to rebuild relationships with clients and partner agencies.

The trustees had approved the campaign following presentations from the PR director. They had not sought the opinion of operational staff and so had failed in their obligation to act in the best interests of the organisation as a whole.

In staffed organisations, employees often play a key role in developing plans and policies. It is entirely appropriate that those involved in service delivery should have an input into organisational development, as they will have a more practical understanding of the needs of beneficiaries and the methodology of service delivery than many trustees; however, it remains the ultimate responsibility of trustees to steer the organisation in the right direction. Whilst staff input should be welcomed, information and suggestions presented by staff should be carefully examined and thoroughly debated within the wider context of the trustees' vision and ideas. The final decisions must be actively made by the trustees, not directed by staff.

Chapter 6 looks at the boundaries between the roles of the trustees and staff in more detail.

Finance

Trustees are responsible for the financial health of the organisation. Although the detailed requirements of bookkeeping and accounting may be delegated to staff or appropriate professionals, it is the trustees who bear ultimate responsibility for ensuring that charitable funds are spent on charitable purposes. Trustees' responsibilities also include the more prosaic requirements of financial reporting, budgeting and securing sufficient income to run the organisation.

Another element of this financial responsibility is to maximise the income available from assets and investments held by the charity. This will include decision making regarding, for example, investments, trading activities and the use of property.

Financial management and reporting, fundraising and other financial issues are considered in detail in chapters 7 to 9.

Employment

If an unincorporated organisation such as a trust employs staff, the trustees themselves are employers. In the case of an unincorporated association, this responsibility rests directly with the individual trustees. In charitable companies, the company is the employer. Trustees may delegate some responsibility to employees, but cannot delegate their overall responsibility and it is important to be clear as to the extent of the responsibility that has been delegated. Many charities also take on consultants.

There are many issues relating to the employment of staff, and staffing issues will be discussed in more detail in chapter 6.

Marketing and communications

A good reputation is crucial to a charity for fundraising, the recruitment of staff and volunteers, and gaining the trust of the beneficiaries. Consequently, it is important that trustees oversee the charity's marketing and communication strategy. The trustees should determine both the purpose of the organisation's marketing and communication strategy and the image of the charity and the charity's beneficiaries that any advertising or publicity campaign seeks to convey. A communication and marketing strategy can have several aims, including:

- increasing the charity's income;
- raising awareness of an issue;
- raising the profile of the organisation; and
- establishing 'market' prominence for the charity to ensure that people choose to donate to it, rather than to another charity.

It is particularly important for trustees to consider both operational and marketing demands and the fact that they are responsible for ensuring that the image communicated is mutually beneficial for both the organisation and the users of its services.

Trustees are also responsible for ensuring that the cost of any marketing or communication campaign can be justified against the planned benefits. Trustees should always be alert to cost–benefit considerations, but this is particularly important in relation to marketing and communication where costs can be very high and the benefits difficult to quantify. For this reason, the measurable benefits which it is hoped will accrue from any campaign should be clearly defined at the outset.

As a charity depends on its reputation, any damage to that reputation can present a very real risk to the charity. Damage to the reputation of the charity, whether based on reality, rumour or perception, can be very hard to repair. Trustees need to be alert to the risk of damage and manage it appropriately. It may be worth developing a contingency plan to deal with the effect of such damage, should it occur. This may include building up a list of named media contacts and ensuring that the charity has ready access to communication experts. Such a plan will be particularly valuable if the charity has a high profile, works in a politically sensitive field, or undertakes inherently risky activities such as working with children and/or vulnerable adults, medical care or disaster relief.

tip

One of the ways to reduce the risk of damage to your charity's reputation is to take the 'tabloid test'. This involves analysing your organisation's activities and considering them through the eyes of the tabloid press. For example, how would a tabloid newspaper report a decision to make a grant to a repeat offender? Asking this question need not stop you from making the grant, or undertaking any other potentially controversial activity, but it may help you to plan how to counteract any adverse publicity that may follow.

Risk management

Risk management is a crucial element of trustees' work, and the opportunities available need to be balanced against the risk, cost or potential negative impact of those opportunities. Although many risks have a financial implication, they are often presented in terms of threats to other aspects of the organisation and its function, such as its reputation, operation, achievement and personal safety. The following sections on regulatory issues and risk have a bearing on trustees' responsibilities in terms of risk management. Financial risk management is discussed in chapter 7.

Trustees must assess the level of risk and decide on the appropriate action to take to prevent damaging eventualities occurring and to mitigate the effect if they do. To do this, the trustees should begin by looking at the organisation from a variety of angles, which will help to identify the full range of risks faced by the charity. It is useful to go beyond the board of trustees to draw on the experience of staff and volunteers who are involved with the everyday activities of the organisation. They will be able to identify operational risks. Third parties, such as funders and users, may be able to help identify some of the external and environmental risks. It can be helpful to manage this process by dividing the risks into different categories, for example:

- governance (e.g. conflicts of interest for trustees);
- operational (e.g. staff shortages);
- financial (e.g. poor cashflow);
- environmental or external (e.g. damage to a charity's reputation); and
- compliance with law and regulation (e.g. being sued, fined or being the subject of enforcement action).

When dealing with risk, trustees need to achieve a proper balance. Too much emphasis on risk may constrain the work of the charity unnecessarily, but real risks must be considered carefully. Once a risk has been identified, there are two issues for trustees to evaluate:

- the probability that the risk will occur; and
- the impact of the risk, should it happen.

The following table may be a helpful tool in assessing risk and achieving the right balance between paralysis and laissez-faire and identifying those risks that require most active management. By grading both the probability and the impact of a risk as high, medium or low, risks can be placed in priority order. Allocating a numerical value to the grades helps to further define priorities, so scores of 1, 2 and 3 are awarded for low, medium and high probability or impact. Multiplying the two scores creates a 'risk total' with the highest scoring risk becoming the top priority.

Likelihood of risk occurring		Impact of risk, should it occur		Score
High	3	High	3	9
Medium	2	High	3	6
Low	1	High	3	3
High	3	Medium	2	6
Medium	2	Medium	2	4
Low	1	Medium	2	2
High	3	Low	1	3
Medium	2	Low	1	2
Low	1	Low	1	1

The nature of the risk, its probability and its potential impact will determine how trustees should respond to it. High scoring risks are likely to need countermeasures as a means of managing and mitigating the risk. This could be:

- *prevention* of the risk happening (e.g. by stopping the activity);
- *reduction* of the probability or impact of the risk (e.g. by increasing security or implementing risk reducing procedures); or
- *transferring* the risk elsewhere (e.g. by taking out insurance which transfers some financial risk from the insured to the insurer).

Trustees may decide to accept low scoring risks. Although these risks should not be ignored completely, they are unlikely to require much active management. Trustees may also decide that some of the preventative or risk reduction measures required to combat higher scoring risks are unacceptable and so accept the reduced measure of protection. For example, placing bars on windows reduces the risk of break-ins, but can also create an unwelcoming atmosphere and may impede fire safety. In deciding not to install window bars, a reduced level of protection against burglaries is accepted.

It may be necessary to develop a contingency plan to deal with the effect of an identified risk should it arise. This approach is particularly suitable for risks that would have a high impact.

As well as dealing with individual risks, risk management processes can inform the strategic approach of the organisation as a whole. By identifying and categorising all the risks facing the charity, a clear picture of the balance of risk within the organisation can be developed – this is known as a 'risk profile'. A risk profile showing a large volume of high-risk activities may indicate that certain areas of the charity's work or function should be reviewed. Similarly, a proliferation of low-risk activities may imply that the organisation is being unduly conservative. The process may also help trustees to determine their 'risk tolerance' (i.e. the level of risk that they are prepared to accept). This will vary between and within charities. For example, a charity with a stable funding base may be prepared to take a high financial risk in developing a new service, but be very cautious about protecting its reputation.

Risk management should be subject to regular monitoring to ensure that any changing risks are properly managed and that countermeasures are in place and continue to be appropriate. This process is best supported by a risk register. The register records the risk, its probability, its potential impact and the controls that are in place to manage it. The register should also record the name of the person responsible for managing the risk and the frequency of the risk management review (e.g. monthly, quarterly or annually).

Money laundering

Charities are involved in handling money and, as such, should be alert to the risks of money laundering and terrorist financing. They should ensure that they have appropriate governance and operational systems in place to guard against any risk. Legislation is in force which makes it difficult for the proceeds of crime to filter into the legitimate financial system. It is an offence for anyone to acquire, use, or possess criminal property, or do anything to help conceal criminal property.

It is important that staff employed by a charity are aware of the possible problems, have appropriate policies on donor identification and ensure that there is a system in place for staff and trustees to report suspicions. The Charity Commission has published helpful guidance for charities and trustees on this issue which can be found in its '*Compliance*

Toolkit: Protecting Charities from Harm' which can be found on its website.

Where there is knowledge or suspicion of money laundering, this should be reported to the Serious and Organised Crime Agency. Failure to comply with this could have serious consequences, including criminal liability for the charity and its staff.

A charity should look particularly carefully at any unusual transactions. Even where it might stand to benefit a great deal from a donation, this might be the price for a criminal of transferring the proceeds of crime into the legitimate economy. Suspicious circumstances may include, amongst other things:

- donations that are conditional on part of the donation being repaid to the donor;
- gifts that involve currency swaps; and
- a donor having 'second thoughts' about their gift to a charity and asking for their money back.

Bribery

The Bribery Act 2010 (the Act) came into force on 1 July 2011. It simplifies and expands the range of bribery-related offences for which organisations and individuals can be prosecuted.

The offences are:

- *Giving bribes* ('active offence') – to promise, offer or give a bribe (whether directly or through a third party).
- *Receiving bribes* ('passive offence') – to request, receive or agree to receive a bribe.
- *Bribery of a foreign public official* ('public offence') – to bribe a foreign public official (the definition of a foreign public official covers both foreign government officials and individuals working for international organisations).
- *Failure of commercial organisations to prevent bribery* ('corporate offence') – a commercial organisation may be guilty of an offence if someone acting on its behalf commits an active offence or a public offence.

In addition, a senior officer of a corporate body will be personally guilty of an offence if he or she consents to, or connives in, an active, passive, or public offence by the organisation.

The concept of a 'bribe' is broad. It can mean any financial or other advantage which is intended to induce or reward the improper performance of a business activity or public function. Improper performance is performance (or non-performance) that breaches the expectation of good faith or impartiality, or breaches a position of trust.

Implications for charities

The first three offences could be committed by any person, which would include charity employees, trustees, an incorporated charity or a charity's subsidiary trading company.

In the Ministry of Justice's guidance on the Act (the Guidance), the Secretary of State for Justice writes that:

> ... combating the risks of bribery is largely about common sense, not burdensome procedures. The core principle [the Guidance] sets out is proportionality.

Given the scope of the Act, charities should, in particular, analyse their current activities to establish whether there are any particular risk areas and to assess the strength of measures they have in place to prevent bribery.

Hospitality

In most circumstances it seems very unlikely that the hospitality offered by a charity would constitute a bribe.

The Guidance is clear that:

> bona fide hospitality and promotional, or other business expenditure which seeks to improve the image of a commercial organisation, better to present products and services or establish cordial relations, is recognised as an established and important part of doing business and it is not the intention of the Act to criminalise such behaviour.

For a charity to commit an offence under the Act in relation to hospitality, the charity would probably need to do something that it should not be doing anyway, for example:

- giving an extra benefit to a decision maker during the tender process, above what can be legitimately offered; or
- offering lavish hospitality either to public officials to help win public funding or contracts, or to donors who may be considering making a gift to the organisation.

Facilitation payments

Offences under the Act can be committed abroad – in the case of the first three offences, provided that the person committing them has a close connection to the UK, such as a British national or a body incorporated in the UK. The requirement for a close connection to the UK does not apply to the corporate offence.

Facilitation payments are small payments which may be made to public officials in certain countries as a way of ensuring that duties are properly or promptly performed. The Guidance is clear that the Act does *not* provide an exemption for facilitation payments.

There may be circumstances in which charities working internationally are faced with difficult situations where such a payment may be requested – the Guidance provides that:

> It is recognised that there are circumstances in which individuals are left with no alternative, but to make payments in order to protect against loss of life, limb, or liberty.

and

> In cases where hospitality, promotional expenditure or facilitation payments do, on their fact, trigger the provisions of the Act, prosecutors will consider very carefully what is in the public interest before deciding whether to prosecute. The operation of prosecutorial discretion provides a degree of flexibility which is helpful to ensure the just and fair operation of the Act.

Application of the corporate offence to charities

The introduction of the corporate offence is a significant departure from the current law.

The offence of 'failure of commercial organisations to prevent bribery' could be committed by *incorporated* charities.

The offence could be committed by charitable companies (e.g. companies limited by guarantee, Royal Charter bodies and statutory corporations), but it could not be committed by unincorporated charities (e.g. charitable trusts and unincorporated associations).

To commit this offence, the charity would need to be carrying on a 'business' but this term is not defined. If there is any doubt, charities should take a cautious approach and assume that this offence might apply.

The offence will be committed where:

- the bribery is committed by a person performing services on behalf of the commercial organisation;
- the person performing services intends to secure a business advantage for the organisation; and
- the bribery is either an active offence (giving bribes) or a public offence (bribing a foreign public official). This offence does not apply where the individual commits a passive offence (i.e. requests, or receives, a bribe).

The scope of this offence is wide. The person committing the bribery may be an employee, agent or subsidiary of the charity, or of any third party who performs services for the charity on its behalf. The person need not be prosecuted successfully for the corporate offence to apply.

The only defence available to a charity is to prove on the balance of probabilities that it had *adequate procedures* in place designed to prevent bribery from being committed by those performing services on its behalf.

The Guidance gives more information about adequate procedures.

The steps taken to prevent bribery will vary from charity to charity, but a charity may consider the following to ensure that it has adequate procedures in place:

Risk assessment and due diligence

Consider whether any relationships with third parties, including joint ventures, need to be reviewed and whether the organisation's anti-bribery policies should be notified to the third parties.

When entering into new relationships, consideration should be given to what contractual protections should be included in any written agreement. These might include, where the arrangements are perceived to carry a degree of risk, a requirement for the other party to certify annually that it has complied with agreed form undertakings regarding compliance with anti-bribery policies.

Senior/responsible officers

The scope of the Bribery Act should be understood by the charity's senior management team and trustees of charity, who should take responsibility for implementing effective anti-bribery measures. The Guidance states that: 'Those at the top of an organisation are in the best position to foster a culture of integrity where bribery is unacceptable.' It may be appropriate to designate somebody to oversee and monitor compliance with the anti-bribery measures.

Anti-bribery policy and employment contracts

Put in place an anti-bribery policy (or review any existing policy) which covers bribery generally as well as concerns specific to the charity (including rules on gifts, entertainment, expenses, sponsorship and charitable donations) and monitor compliance with the policy.

Emphasise that compliance is mandatory and set out actions that are prohibited, but also address the question of what to do if an individual comes across bribery within the charity.

Ensure the anti-bribery policy is communicated and readily available to all employees at all levels (e.g. by e-mail, in the appropriate section of a staff handbook and/or on an intranet) and that it is endorsed and promoted from the highest levels in the organisation.

Ensure employees are aware that breach of the policy may give rise to disciplinary action (including possible summary dismissal). The policy must also be communicated to everyone else who performs services for or on behalf of the charity, including consultants, contractors and agency staff.

Whistleblowing procedure

Ensure there is an adequate whistleblowing procedure in place (and readily available), so that staff feel confident that they can report bribery, or suspected bribery, safely and confidentially.

It is important that staff members are encouraged not only to avoid participating in bribery, but also to report bribery by others. Contracts with staff, contractors and consultants should, if possible, impose a general obligation to report wrongdoing.

Implementation, induction and training

An anti-bribery policy should be an integral part of any induction process and training. Training, appropriate to the organisation's size and the extent of bribery risk, should be given to all staff where appropriate, not just new joiners.

Business dealings in certain countries

Charities doing business in countries which have a low rating according to Transparency International's Annual Corruption Perceptions Index should review areas such as dealings with state enterprises and dealings through agents. Any subsidiaries or other controlled organisations should adopt the same anti-bribery measures.

Trading subsidiaries

Where a charity has a trading subsidiary, this company will fall within the definition of 'relevant commercial organisations' and will fall within the scope of the corporate offence in its own right.

Trading subsidiaries will therefore need to be included in any policy and procedural changes made.

Regulatory issues

Insurance

Appropriate insurance is a key part of financial risk management and, in some areas, is compulsory. Trustees should look at the full range of their charity's activities and identify areas of risk when deciding which insurance is optional but necessary and which is legally required. For example, charities employing staff are legally required to have employer's liability insurance and should display the appropriate insurance certificate. Those working with volunteers and beneficiaries should have public liability insurance. Where the charity provides transport or requires staff and volunteers to use their own cars on charity business, trustees need to be sure that at least third-party cover is taken out in respect of each driver and that this cover is valid for charity business. Some insurance companies include cover for the use of the insured's car for volunteering or work within their standard policies, but others require an additional premium for this type of cover.

Organisations occupying premises require buildings and contents insurance. Where an organisation owns and occupies property, it is responsible for all insurance relating to the property. Where property is let, either to or from another party, insurance requirements are usually specified by the terms of the lease agreement. For example, the landlord may be responsible for insuring the fabric of the building, with tenants arranging their own insurance for possessions kept on the property.

Those running advice services should take out professional indemnity insurance to protect them against claims for losses arising from poor advice.

The activities of the charity will determine if further insurance cover is necessary. As with all insurance policies, it is important to inform insurers of the full range of charitable activities that are carried out to ensure that all necessary policies are valid and in place.

Trustees may also seek to protect themselves against actions arising out of their trusteeship through trustee indemnity insurance. As with all policies, trustees should consider the level of risk against the cover offered by the insurance to justify the cost. Trustee indemnity insurance is a trustee benefit and trustees must be satisfied that buying it will be in the best interests of the charity. The Charities Act 2011 allows trustees to purchase trustee indemnity insurance even if a charity's governing document contains a general prohibition on trustees receiving personal benefits (although not if there is a specific prohibition on taking out trustee indemnity insurance). Trustees need not arrange insurance cover themselves – this task may be delegated to staff – but should ensure that appropriate cover has been secured and is maintained (e.g. by viewing insurance certificates). Copies of insurance documentation should be kept off site.

The following checklist summarises the areas trustees should consider in relation to insurance.

CHECKLIST

✓	What policies are required by law?	e.g. employer's liability, third-party vehicle cover
✓	What policies are required under the charity's contracts?	e.g. buildings insurance
✓	What policies are needed in relation to the charity's activities (both permanent and ad hoc)?	e.g. professional indemnity, public liability
✓	What policies are needed in relation to the charity's assets?	e.g. buildings insurance, contents insurance
✓	What other policies might be needed?	e.g. trustee indemnity insurance
✓	Who has responsibility for arranging insurance?	Ensure that this is documented and clearly communicated to the individual concerned
✓	Are all policies current?	Check all certificates at regular intervals
✓	Do all policies represent good value for money?	Is the cover worth the premium, or could you get better value with a different insurer?
✓	Where are policy documents kept?	This should be clearly recorded and should be off site

Health and safety

Trustees are responsible for health and safety within the organisation. This includes the health and safety of any staff, volunteers and those using any service that the charity provides. If the charity employs staff, the health and safety law poster (available from the Health and Safety Executive) should be displayed. A health and safety policy may also be required.

The need to develop a health and safety policy is not exclusive to organisations undertaking high-risk activities, such as providing adventure holidays for young people, or working with people with challenging behaviour. All organisations must have a written health and safety policy – this is a legal requirement for those with five or more employees. Nor is the policy restricted to the occupation of premises (e.g. groups undertaking outreach, home visits or detached work must pay particular attention to the personal safety of volunteers and staff where the interaction with beneficiaries may be unpredictable). The policy should consider the activities undertaken by the organisation, the working environment and the nature of the client group.

All employers (and self-employed people) are required to assess risks from work activities. Where there are five or more employees, any significant findings of the risk assessment must be recorded, so the health and safety policy should discuss those risks and identify the means of minimising risk and addressing problems as they arise. Regular health and safety audits, preferably by an external body, are also advisable to ensure that the policy is being followed and that the working environment is safe.

The sorts of issues that should be covered by a health and safety policy are discussed below. However, this is not a comprehensive list. Some organisations will need to consider a wider range of issues and many of the points covered will not be relevant to some charities.

Trustees are advised to physically protect their staff, volunteers and beneficiaries and to financially protect themselves by developing and implementing an appropriate health and safety policy and ensuring that those affected by it receive the appropriate information and training.

Appropriate arrangements should be made to deal with any accidents or emergencies that do occur at work. This includes first aid provision in the form of suitably trained individuals and the necessary equipment. Such provision should be used to cope with minor injuries and to manage more serious cases until medical help arrives.

All accidents and emergencies should be recorded and many organisations keep an accident book for this purpose. By law you are required to report certain injuries and diseases to the Health and Safety Executive or the environmental health department of your local authority. These include death, major injury (including certain fractures and dislocations), 'over three day' injuries (i.e. the employee cannot do his or her normal job for three or more days as a result of the injury) and certain work-related diseases. Dangerous occurrences that could have led to a reportable injury must also be reported.

Work-related stress can be a serious problem in voluntary organisations and trustees of charities that employ staff have a legal obligation to address this issue (e.g. by reviewing workloads and giving employees sufficient autonomy regarding the planning of their work and time).

Trustees are advised to seek specialist advice on health and safety issues. In particular, they should be aware that this area of law is currently under review and substantial simplification and consolidation of the existing law is expected in the coming years. The Health and Safety Executive provides an extensive range of free information in relation to health and safety obligations (see the Directory for details) and will provide information about forthcoming changes to the law.

Area of work	Issues to consider
Premises	Alarms and evacuation procedures, including use of fire extinguishers, access to fire exits and emergency assembly points; corridors and stairs to be unobstructed; tripping and slipping hazards (e.g. trailing cables, loose carpets, wet floors etc.); adequate lighting; adequate heating/cooling systems and ventilation; safe noise levels; safe electrical equipment, gas appliances, kitchen equipment etc.; manual handling (e.g. lifting or moving equipment or furniture); security of the building and personal safety issues such as policies on lone working and office hours.
Work stations and VDU use	Lighting that ensures adequate illumination whilst minimising glare; ensure set up of desk, chair and computer minimises risk of back strain or repetitive strain injury; ensure adequate breaks from VDU use and make vouchers available for sight tests and prescriptions.
Working away from the office	Travel arrangements that maximise personal safety (e.g. use of own vehicle versus public transport or travelling in pairs); office-based records covering issues such as destination, expected time of return and emergency contact numbers; mobile phones and attack alarms; identity cards for staff; arrangements for working in the evening/overnight.
Working with the public	Guidance on lone working; training on identifying and dealing with risk situations; electing whether to visit a client in their own home or an alternative venue; ensuring that staff maintain clear escape routes; advice on manual handling (e.g. if providing personal care to clients).

Area of work	Issues to consider
Outings, centre-based and residential activities	Ratio of staff and volunteers to clients; vetting and criminal record checks on staff and volunteers; appropriate training for staff and volunteers; parental consent for activities involving people under 18 years old; risk assessment; policies regarding substance misuse (e.g. refusing admission to people under the influence of alcohol or non-prescription drugs); policies regarding administration of medication and self-medication; information regarding any medical conditions; emergency procedures; emergency contact numbers.

Corporate manslaughter

The Corporate Manslaughter and Corporate Homicide Act deals with the criminal liability of organisations where serious failures in the management of health and safety result in a fatality. The Act provides for the criminal offence of corporate manslaughter.

The offence only applies to 'organisations', which could include charitable companies.

While the Act does not apply to individuals, such as trustees or managers, individuals can still be prosecuted at common law for manslaughter by gross negligence or under existing health and safety regulations, and an individual trustee of a charitable company (or director of a trading subsidiary) can be charged with the criminal offence of manslaughter when he or she causes death through gross negligence.

What constitutes an offence?

An organisation will be guilty of an offence if the way in which its activities are managed or organised:
- causes a person's death; and
- amounts to a gross breach of a relevant duty of care owed to that person.

Who are senior management?

An organisation cannot be convicted of the new offence unless the prosecution can prove that a substantial element of the breach lies in the way the organisation's senior management managed or organised its activities.

It is therefore important to clarify who is considered to be 'senior management'. Under the Act, 'senior management' is defined as those persons who play significant roles in:

- the making of decisions about how the whole or a substantial part of an organisation's activities are to be managed or organised; or
- actually managing or organising those activities.

Whether the role of senior managers is significant is a question of fact, but the intention is to capture those whose role is decisive or influential. As the Act is concerned with the way an activity is managed or organised, the offence cannot be avoided by senior management delegating responsibility for health and safety.

What constitutes gross breach?

Gross breach means conduct that falls far below what can reasonably be expected of the organisation in the circumstances. The Act sets out certain factors that a jury must take into account when deciding whether an organisation is guilty of the offence:

- whether the organisation failed to comply with any health and safety legislation;
- how serious that failure was; and
- how much of a risk of death it posed.

What are the consequences of breaching the Act?

An organisation committing the offence will be subject to a trial in the Crown Court by judge and jury. The maximum penalty is an unlimited fine. In addition, the court may make:

- a remedial order requiring the organisation to remedy the management failure that caused the death;
- a publicity order requiring the organisation to publicise the conviction; and
- a compensation order to pay compensation to the victim's family.

What can be done to reduce the risk of health and safety incidents and prosecution under the Act?

- ensure that health and safety leadership within the organisation is appropriate to the scale and risk profile of the organisation;

- consider whether safety management systems have been successful to date and whether improvements can be made;
- consider carrying out an independent audit of health and safety management systems and health and safety compliance;
- develop an incident response plan; and
- consider ways to strengthen the health and safety culture within the organisation, so that everyone takes responsibility for improving health and safety.

Data protection

The Data Protection Act 1998 (the Act) controls the way in which organisations, including charities, manage any information they hold that relates to individuals.

Personal data

'Personal data' is data relating to living individuals who can be identified from that data, or from the data and other information which is in the possession of, or is likely to come into the possession of, the data controller (see explanation below). It includes any expression of opinion about the individual and any indication of the intention of the data controller or any other person in respect of the individual. Therefore, information/feedback captured on a 360° appraisal will be personal data, which has to be safeguarded and is capable of release to the individual concerned by means of a subject access request.

'Personal data' will also include, for example, names, addresses, telephone numbers, job titles and dates of birth. The information does not have to be confidential. A simple list of clients on a computer will constitute personal data under the Act. The Act applies only to data which relates to individuals and so will not apply to data relating to companies or other legal entities. To be personal data, the information must:

(a) identify the individual;
(b) relate to the individual in a way which might be such as to affect his privacy; and
(c) must have the individual as its focus and be information of a biographical nature.

The legislation covers computerised data and any manual records held as part of a 'relevant filing system' (i.e. one which is organised so that personal data is readily accessible). In practice, the law will apply equally to most paper and all electronic filing systems.

Sensitive personal data

Within personal data, there is a further subset of personal information which is the subject of more rigorous levels of protection – 'sensitive personal data'. This includes data relating to race, sexual orientation, political opinion, health, religious and other beliefs, trade union membership and criminal records. Some of this information is the sort likely to be held by human resource departments, or departments responsible for recruitment. It is of particular relevance for not-for-profit organisations, as many will require volunteers to undertake a Criminal Records Bureau check prior to permitting a volunteer to be involved with the organisation, and the results of this are sensitive personal data.

The key data protection principles

Not-for-profit organisations that retain information on individuals, whether they be staff, volunteers, trustees, beneficiaries, members or donors, are subject to the legislation and trustees are responsible for ensuring that the law is complied with. The principles central to the legislation include the following:

- Data must be processed fairly and lawfully: this means that there must be a legitimate basis for processing the data and that the processing must be fair. The 'fair processing code' considers the ways in which data is obtained. This includes the requirement that the identity of the data controller (i.e. the organisation holding the information) and the purposes for which the data is being processed should be available to the individual, together with any other information necessary to ensure fairness. Many charities manage this requirement by providing an explanation of the ways in which any data will be used, offering individuals an opportunity to opt out of these uses by ticking a box. Data may be processed without consent in order to protect the vital interests of the individual (i.e. life or death situations).

- Individuals must be informed if their data is to be disclosed to third parties for marketing purposes and be at least permitted the opportunity to opt out of this disclosure. Ideally, for third-party marketing, the individuals concerned should be asked to 'opt-in' rather than opt-out. They must also be informed of their right to access and rectify data held by a data controller.
- Sensitive personal data will only be processed fairly and lawfully in accordance with the Act if certain restrictive conditions are met; for example, at least one of the following conditions is satisfied: (i) the individual has given his explicit consent to the processing; or (ii) it is necessary to protect the vital interests of the individual in circumstances where consent cannot reasonably be obtained; or (iii) where processing is carried out by certain non-profit organisations.
- Data kept on individuals should be accurate and, where necessary, kept up to date. Where information is obtained from a third party, reasonable steps must be taken to ensure the accuracy of the data.
- Personal data should be processed in accordance with the rights of individuals. This means that individuals can request access to their personal information by means of a subject access request addressed to the relevant organisation; they can request the prevention of data processing that is likely to cause damage or distress or will be used for direct marketing. Organisations can charge £10 to individuals for access to information held on them and must respond within 40 days of the subject access request. Telephone and fax 'preference services' have been established so that people can register their objection to receiving unsolicited calls and faxes.

Security measures

Those holding data as data controllers or data processors are expected to take appropriate technical and organisational security measures to ensure that data is not unlawfully processed, lost or damaged. This obligation to safeguard personal data continues where the data controller wishes to make data available to a third party to process information on another's behalf. Such third parties must agree to implement equivalent data protection safeguards to those adopted by the data controller. Here, the security of data should be integral to the contractual relationship between the two parties and should be expressly provided for in any contract which will involve personal data.

International transfer of data

Data cannot be transferred outside of the European Economic Area ('EEA') unless the destination country or territory ensures an adequate level of protection. Very few non-EEA countries have been assessed by the European Union (EU) as offering an adequate level of protection. Transfer of personal information to the United States of America is of particular importance in this regard, and the EU has a set of guidelines which must be followed before data can be transferred outside the EEA and, in partic-ular, to the US. Sensitive personal data requires further levels of protection and it is therefore usual that explicit consent is sought from the individual prior to the transfer of sensitive personal data outside the EEA. This prin-ciple will be relevant to international not-for-profit organisations. These data transfer issues apply even to transfers between branches of the same organisation or group companies.

Notification requirements

Organisations are required to notify the Information Commissioner that they hold personal information. Notification is subject to an annual charge (currently £35) and applications for notification must be made on a form that is available from the Commissioner's office and on the ICO's website. Exemptions from notification are available for the main-tenance of a public register and for processing data for organisational administration (e.g. staff records). Trustees should consider whether notification is required for their organisation. Even those organisations exempt from notification must still comply with the principles listed above.

Websites

Use of a website may also have data protection implications, and care should be taken to ensure that all users are aware of the organisation's data protection and privacy policy governing use made of personal data submitted to a website if they are required to register. In particular, users need to be made aware of any use made by the organisation of cookies to store information about their visit to a website.

Direct marketing by telephone, e-mail or SMS

There is also relevant European legislation to consider relating to marketing activities, restricting a marketer's ability to contact potential customers and setting out a framework for certain forms of marketing. Organisations wishing to send marketing communications by e-mail, fax, SMS or automated calling machine messages must obtain the prior actual consent of the intended recipient (i.e. a positive 'opt-in'). The only exception is the so-called 'soft opt-in' (i.e. the marketing is being done by the business that has obtained the recipient's contact details in the context of a previous sale or negotiations for sale of a product or service). The recipient in this case must be given the opportunity, free of charge, to opt out (or unsubscribe) from receiving further marketing communications, both at the time of collection of the data and in every subsequent communication. All marketing communications must make it clear that that is what they are, identify the sender organisation, contain a valid return address to which the recipient may send a request to cease further communications and must explicitly mention the recipient's right to opt out of receiving further communications.

Data protection: summary

The nature of trustees' responsibility for their organisations' activities and administration means that it is in their interests to ensure compliance with data protection requirements. The Information Commissioner can issue an enforcement notice in the event of non-compliance and may prosecute organisations that breach such notices. Failure to comply with such notices constitutes a criminal offence. In addition, individuals may claim compensation if damage or distress has been caused or if organisations are unable to prove that adequate care has been taken in processing data. Non-compliance with the Act may lead to the Commissioner imposing a fine of up to £5,000.

The following checklist highlights the key points that voluntary organisations should consider. Further information is available on the Information Commissioner's website at www.ico.gov.uk.

CHECKLIST

- [✓] Is there a legitimate reason for processing the data, including the collection of such data in the first place?

- [✓] Is your organisation's identity as the data controller and the purposes for which the data is being processed available to the individual?

- [✓] Are individuals able to opt out of the processing?

- [✓] Does the organisation process sensitive personal data? If so, is the information adequately safeguarded?

- [✓] If you process data without the subject's consent, is this necessary to protect the vital interests of the individual?

- [✓] Is data accurate and up to date? How can you be confident of this?

- [✓] How do you ensure the accuracy of data obtained from a third party?

- [✓] What security measures are in place to protect data? Are these included in any contracts with those who process data on your behalf?

- [✓] Is notification with the Information Commissioner necessary or is the organisation exempt?

- [✓] Are any direct marketing activities carried out by the organisation? If so, is the organisation in compliance with the relevant direct marketing legislation?

- [✓] Does the website contain suitable terms and conditions of use, which are accessible to users, setting out the user's rights in relation to personal data collected by the organisation?

Conflict of interest

Trustees must act in the best interests of the charity and should not benefit from their trusteeship. As such, trustees are required to avoid any conflict between their own interests and those of the charity. A conflict of interest may take many different forms, as illustrated by the table opposite.

A conflict of interest damages the ability of the board to make decisions that are in the best interests of the charity and can undermine board cohesion if board members feel that one of their number is seeking to influence decisions to his or her own advantage. Even where trustees have acted appropriately, if there appears to have been a conflict of interest, the reputation of the charity can be severely damaged. Consequently it is important for charities to identify potential conflicts of interest and prevent or manage any that arise. A register of trustees' external interests may be kept and regularly updated and trustees may be asked to sign a commitment to declare any interests that arise in the course of a charity's business. When such interests do arise, trustees should withdraw, not only from the decision making, but also from the discussion, to ensure that they are not in a position to influence the final outcome. In addition, the organisation should not send any sensitive information to the affected trustee in relation to the item in conflict. In these circumstances, even if the remaining trustees do make a decision to the advantage of the interested trustee, they can at least establish that the decision has been made properly and the conflict has been properly managed.

Situations may well arise where a decision which is in the interest of a trustee is also the best decision for the charity. In seeking to manage the conflict appropriately, charities should consider the 'tabloid test' discussed earlier in this chapter (i.e. 'How would this situation appear if reported in a tabloid newspaper?').

Type of conflict	Description	Examples
Direct financial interest	A trustee's financial interest in an issue related to the charity is the most easily recognisable form of conflicting interest as it runs directly counter to the principle that trustees must not benefit from the charity. Here trustees will directly benefit from their trusteeship and this financial benefit is likely to affect objective trustee decision making.	– The payment of salary or professional fees to a trustee by the charity. – The award of a contract to a company of which a trustee is a director. – The sale of property to a trustee at below market value.
Indirect financial interest	This occurs when a close relative of a trustee benefits from the charity. Here trustees will benefit indirectly if their financial affairs are bound with those of the relative in question through the legal concept of 'joint purse', as would be the case if the relative were the spouse, partner or dependent child of the trustee.	– Awarding an employment contract to a trustee's spouse. – Making a grant to a trustee's dependent child.

Type of conflict	Description	Examples
Non-financial or personal conflicts	Here trustees receive no financial benefit but continue to be influenced by external factors. Conflicts of loyalty fall within this category.	– Trustees influencing board decisions on service provision to their own advantage, perhaps because they use the charity's service themselves or care for someone who does. – Awarding contracts to friends of a trustee. – Making a decision in favour of another organisation of which a trustee is a member, trustee or in some other way involved.

Remuneration

The duty of trustees to act in the charity's best interests is intertwined with the 'voluntary principle' of trusteeship (i.e. that trustees should not be paid). The basic principle is that trustees must not put themselves in a position where there may be a conflict between the charity's interests and those of the trustees.

However, the level of responsibility carried by trustees, the amount of work involved in trusteeship and the difficulty of recruiting trustees of sufficient number and suitable quality means that, in certain circumstances, trustees can be paid. In all cases, the conflict of interest must be managed when deciding to make any type of payment to a trustee and the charity's governing document must permit it.

- Trustees can have reasonable *expenses* met from the funds of the charity, such as travelling expenses when on trustee business.
- The Charities Act 2011 contains a power for charities to pay their trustees (or a person connected to a trustee) for *services* provided to the charity, even if the governing document contains no express power which allows this, provided that the governing document does not expressly prohibit this. This power might be used to pay a fee to a trustee who has legal or financial skills and is undertaking a specific piece of work for the charity (such as negotiating contracts)

or a trustee who is a builder (for repairing the charity's premises). There are safeguards as to how this power can be used: there must be an agreement in writing which sets out the services that will be provided and the sum that will be paid; the amount must not exceed what is reasonable in the circumstances for the provision by the particular person of the services in question; and, immediately after the agreement is entered into, the total number of trustees to which such an agreement relates must be in a minority. The power does *not* cover payment for acting as a trustee, nor does it allow trustees to be paid as employees of the charity.

- A trustee may be paid for *serving as a trustee,* but only in very limited circumstances and where a governing document allows it or the permission of the Charity Commission has been obtained. Paying a trustee in this way would only be appropriate where it is clearly in the best interests of the charity to do so and provides a clear and significant advantage over other options.

Charities must disclose any payment to trustees in its accounts and it is particularly important to review the performance of any trustee that is receiving any payment from the charity.

Ultra vires/breach of trust

The role of trustee is defined by charity law and the individual organisation's governing document. Acting appropriately within their legally defined roles provides trustees with an element of protection from legal action against them. Once trustees step outside the legal boundaries they may be acting *ultra vires* (i.e. outside their powers) or in breach of trust. In such circumstances, the level of protection available diminishes and trustees become much more vulnerable to legal action and personal liability. One of the defences available is to have acted in breach of trust but 'honest mistake', rather than negligence or wilful breach. However, trustees are advised to be familiar with the scope and limitations of their governing document and to act within it.

Campaigning and political activities

Although organisations that are established to pursue political purposes cannot be charities, a charity can engage in campaigning and political activities in the context of fulfilling its charitable purpose. The Charity Commission provides detailed guidance on its website on the extent to which charities can engage in campaigning.

'Campaigning' is a broad term that can include raising public awareness and education, or seeking to influence and change public attitudes. Provided that it is an effective means of furthering the purposes of the charity and is done to an extent justified by the resources applied, a charity may choose to devote all of its resources to non-political campaigning to further its purposes so long as the activities are permitted under the governing document. Where the campaign is of a political nature, charity trustees must ensure that these activities do not become the dominant means by which they carry out the purposes of the charity. What is 'dominant' is a question of scope and degree upon which trustees must make a judgement and, in exercising their discretion, the trustees must weigh up whether the chances of the political activity furthering the charitable purposes justify the resources used and the exclusion of any alternative activities.

POLITICAL ACTIVITY

Subject to the basic principles discussed above, the following **are** acceptable political activities to be undertaken by charities:

- ✓ commenting on public issues;
- ✓ dialogue with government;
- ✓ publication of views expressed to government;
- ✓ providing information to the public in support of a campaign;
- ✓ supporting particular policies which will contribute to the delivery of its charitable purposes;
- ✓ providing information on the way in which MPs or parties have voted;
- ✓ providing supporters with information and material to send to MPs and others;
- ✓ conducting petitions;
- ✓ responding to possible changes in law or government policy, including support or opposition for the passage of a Bill;
- ✓ supplying MPs and members of the House of Lords with information for use in debate;
- ✓ affiliating to campaigning alliances, provided the alliance undertakes only those activities that the charity could undertake itself;
- ✓ employing Parliamentary staff and lobbying agencies;

POLITICAL ACTIVITY continued

✓ commenting during elections (but particular care must be taken to ensure political neutrality);	✗ seeking to influence public opinion in support or opposition of a political party;
✓ seeking MPs' support for grants; and	✗ organising or participating in party political demonstrations;
✓ promoting or participating in lawful demonstrations and direct action which is limited to the promotion of reasoned argument and education (e.g. through speeches and leaflet distribution).	✗ participating in demonstrations and direct action outside the promotion of reasoned argument and education (e.g. marches);
	✗ claiming evidence of public support on a political issue without adequate justification; and
The following activities **are not** acceptable:	✗ seeking to influence electoral voting.

As with any activity a charity undertakes, trustees must ensure that their charity's strategy for undertaking campaigning and political activities furthers its objects and is in the overall best interests of the charity and its beneficiaries. Trustees will also need to consider the impact of any campaigning or political activities for the charity's reputation.

Charities must act independently of political parties and the government and they may not undertake any activities which support or oppose a particular party or politician or the government. Where a charity's opinion is in sympathy with, or in opposition to, a particular party, the charity should assert the independence of its opinion. The table opposite lists some acceptable and unacceptable political activities for charities.

Any powers to undertake political activities will be vested in the trustees by the governing document and it is the trustees who are responsible for ensuring that campaigns are within the terms of the governing document and the wider legal framework. Activities outside of these limitations could represent a misuse of charitable funds for which the trustees could be liable. This could involve the trustees being personally required to reimburse these funds together with any tax relief gained against them. The reputation of a charity and public support for that charity may also be damaged by improper political activities.

Wrongful trading

Trustees often choose a company limited by guarantee as the appropriate legal form for their charity because it limits their personal liability. However, incorporation offers no protection in cases of wrongful trading. This arises when an organisation continues to operate and enter financial arrangements even though it has inadequate assets to meet its liabilities (i.e. it is technically insolvent) for example, if a charity enters into a contract to lease office space but cannot afford to continue operating or to pay the rent. Trustees' liability is not limited in these circumstances, so trustees must be fully aware of the organisation's financial health at all times.

Insurance is available to underwrite trustees' liabilities in the event of wrongful trading. As with all insurance policies, trustees should consider the risk against the cost and level of cover offered by the policy.

3 Recruitment, appointment and induction of trustees

INTRODUCTION

Given the function of trustees, it is important to make sure that the initial stages of any trusteeship lay a solid foundation for the task ahead, ensuring that trustees fully understand their role and responsibilities, relating both to the concept of trusteeship and their specific work within the charity. This can be achieved through an effective recruitment, appointment and induction process, which has the added advantage of helping new trustees to adapt quickly to their new role, thus enabling them to play a full part in the governance of the charity at an early stage. This process is clearly an issue of governance rather than management and, as such, should be led by the board itself.

This chapter looks at the recruitment, appointment and induction process. Issues such as the composition and diversity of the board, periods of trusteeship and the turnover of board membership are discussed in chapter 4.

Recruitment

The combination of high workloads, significant responsibilities and lack of recognition or financial compensation can discourage people from becoming trustees. In a society where people have heavy commitments to both work and family, the idea of taking on an additional role can be unattractive.

The current Coalition Government is committed to encouraging volunteering and a number of initiatives are being launched under the 'Big Society' policy banner to help achieve this.

Charities still face real difficulties when seeking to recruit adequate numbers of trustees to meet their constitutional requirements, let alone achieve a sufficient number and variety of individuals to deliver the skills, experience and capacity to run a complex modern voluntary organisation.

In fact, the last research undertaken by the Charity Commission on this issue found that 39% of charities experienced difficulties (at least sometimes) in filling vacancies on the trustee board. The problem is more acute with large charities, with 66% of respondents reporting that they found it difficult to attract trustees with the right skills. The research also found that most charities still rely on a very limited range of recruitment techniques, and the Commission reiterated that if charities employed a wider variety of methods, difficulties in recruiting new trustees would be reduced.

The 'Good Governance Code for the Voluntary and Community Sector' (which can be found on the Charity Commission's website) provides helpful information about the recruitment of charity trustees. In particular, the Code's third principle provides that a productive board of charity trustees will provide good governance and leadership by working effectively both as individuals and as a team.

The Code goes on to provide that trustee boards should have a range of appropriate policies and procedures, knowledge, attitudes and behaviours to enable both individuals and the board to work effectively. These will include:

- finding and recruiting new board members to meet the organisation's changing needs in relation to skills, experience and diversity;
- providing suitable induction for new board members;
- providing all board members with opportunities for training and development according to their needs; and
- periodically reviewing their performance both as individuals and as a team.

Charities are required to report on trustee selection methods in the Trustees' Annual Report.

Methods of recruitment

- *Word of mouth*. Historically, charities have tended to recruit new trustees by word of mouth. Depending on the nature and reputation of the charity, this can be an effective means of recruiting a sufficient number of trustees, but risks resulting in a board of people from similar professional and personal backgrounds, lacking the diversity of skill or experience that can be so beneficial for board debate. It may lay the charity open to charges of cronyism.

- *Networking with other charities.* The not-for-profit sector can be very incestuous, with staff, volunteers and trustees moving between charities. Charities in search of trustees may seek recommendations and references from other charities operating in the same geographical region or area of work.

- *Trustee brokerage agencies.* There are a number of options for charities wishing to recruit beyond the current trustees' immediate circle of friends and acquaintances. There is now a range of local and national trustee brokerage agencies, working rather like recruitment agencies and volunteer bureaux. These agencies link individuals who are keen to take on a trusteeship with charities looking for new trustees. Services may be geographically based (e.g. many local volunteer bureaux have potential trustees amongst their volunteers). Alternatively, services may be focused on a particular board role (e.g. treasurer or company secretary) or they may be more general. Charities recruiting through these means will often be required to give the agency some information about the organisation, the frequency and venue etc of board meetings and any particular requirements relating to the vacancies (e.g. skills required or any restrictions on appointments). The agency will then link the charity to a possible trustee, giving both the charity and the trustee an opportunity to accept or reject the match.

- *Employee volunteering.* The recognition of employee volunteering as part of a business corporate social responsibility strategy and as a valuable means of staff development has provided charities with another source of trustees, as companies may nominate a member of staff to serve as a trustee as a means of training and developing the skills of that staff member.

- *Advertising.* Another option now frequently used by large charities is to advertise for new trustees as they would advertise to fill staff vacancies. This includes placing advertisements in the national press. This route is also available for smaller charities through the free or reduced cost advertising space available for voluntary groups in some local papers and websites.

- *Succession planning.* Many organisations are very aware of the difficulties inherent in recruiting new board members and have developed structures within the charity to ensure an adequate succession of trustees, particularly honorary officers. This may take the form of a dedicated sub-committee (frequently referred to as a nominations and governance committee) the function of which is the recruitment, selection and training of new trustees. More commonly, charities may use sub-committees, consultations, policy development or evaluation mechanisms as a means of drawing a range of people, often members of the organisation into the governance of the organisation, who may later go on to join the board. For example, members or service users may be invited to sit on a sub-committee considering different aspects of service development. Such individuals may, through this experience, develop an interest in the governance of the organisation or become more confident about participating in formal meetings and subsequently decide to join the board.

Whatever the method of recruitment, charities should prepare appropriate information for prospective trustees and adopt a selection procedure to filter out those who, for whatever reason, would be better employed elsewhere in the organisation. Before appointment, potential trustees should be aware of the legal responsibility and the scale of the workload that they will be adopting. The charity should be confident that the prospective trustee is eligible to act as a charity trustee and can therefore be validly appointed to make a useful contribution to the board. In particular, the charity should identify any skills or experience that are lacking from the current board (e.g. a trustee with a business background or operational experience) and should consider the dynamic of the board. The Charity Commission recommends that trustees undertake a skills audit of the board to identify any gaps in the essential skills required.

Charities should, however, be wary of adopting a tokenistic approach to board recruitment by selecting, say one lawyer, one accountant, one personnel expert, etc. Rather they should aim to recruit a mix of trustees who will work well as a team, with every member making a useful contribution. One of the ways that charities can provide information to potential trustees is through seminars or workshops for candidates on the role of the trustee in general and within the organisation. This may have the additional benefit of helping trustees to identify any potential conflicts of interest prior to appointment. Job descriptions and codes of conduct also serve to clarify the scope and responsibilities of the role.

tip

Participation workshops. Hold participation workshops for members, users and others who may be interested in joining the board. Use the workshop to discuss the structure of the charity and the function of different groups within the charity, looking at the role of the board, any sub-committees and volunteers.

Make the workshop a real and positive experience by inviting existing trustees, committee members and volunteers to give presentations about their work and achievements. Include discussion about responsibilities, time commitments and the level of support available for trustees, committee members and volunteers, encouraging people to decide which role best suits them. Those keen to see instant results may be better involved as volunteers rather than on the board, where it can take some time for decisions to filter through implementation to end results.

The session should be timed before nominations are required for the relevant meeting dealing with the election of the board, but not so far in advance that potential trustees get distracted by other issues and lose interest.

Open board meetings. Hold an open board meeting so that members and potential trustees can see how the board functions. Alternatively, invite potential trustees to attend a normal board meeting.

Appointment

Not everybody can serve as a trustee and the charity and the existing trustees should ensure that all potential trustees are legally entitled to hold that role prior to appointment.

Disqualification

Some people are disqualified from serving as charity trustees. People in the following circumstances cannot serve:

1 Those under the age of 18 (only if the charity is a charitable trust or unincorporated association – those aged 16 or over can be a company director and a charity trustee of a charitable company).
2 Undischarged bankrupts.
3 Those who have made compositions or arrangements with creditors that have not been discharged.

4 Those who have been removed from the office of charity trustee or trustee for a charity by an Order of the Charity Commission or by an Order made by the High Court, on the grounds of any misconduct or mismanagement in the administration of the charity, for which he or she was responsible or was privy or which he or she by his or her conduct contributed to or facilitated.

5 Those with unspent convictions for offences involving deception or dishonesty (this includes convictions for theft and fraud).

6 Those who, due to misconduct, have been removed from a trusteeship by the Charity Commission, Office of the Scottish Charity Regulator or a court in England, Wales or Scotland.

Under the Company Directors Disqualification Act 1986 (CDDA), orders may be made disqualifying the people from becoming a company director or taking part in the formation, promotion or management of a company for a fixed disqualification period. Disqualification under the CDDA can be for one of a number of reasons including:

- a conviction for an indictable offence involving the promotion, formation or management of a company;
- repeated breaches of requirements to provide information to the Registrar of Companies;
- acting fraudulently in winding up a company;
- wrongful trading; and
- being considered unfit to serve as a director (e.g. following an investigation or when a director's conduct with an insolvent company renders the director unfit).

It is an offence for an undischarged bankrupt to serve as a company director.

Disqualification under the CDDA or under the Insolvency Act 1986 (for failing to pay under a county court order) is relevant to all charities because, under the Charities Act, an individual who is disqualified under such an order from acting as a company director cannot serve as a charity trustee, regardless of whether or not the charity has the legal form of a company. It is also relevant to companies limited by guarantee which are not registered charities.

It is an offence to act as a trustee whilst disqualified. Those disqualified from acting as trustees should not seek appointment to charity boards and, if they become disqualified whilst serving as a trustee, must resign their membership of the charity's governing body. Charities are advised to alert potential trustees to the requirements in terms of disqualification. Existing trustees who are knowingly involved in the appointment of a disqualified trustee are likely to be acting in breach of trust. New trustees should be asked to sign a declaration that they are not disqualified.

A person disqualified from trusteeship under the Charities Act may, in certain circumstances, apply to the Charity Commission for a waiver, which will allow him or her to serve as a trustee of a charity.

Children's charities should also be aware of child protection restrictions. If a person has been convicted of an offence against a child and is disqualified from working with children, it is an offence to apply for a post as a trustee of a children's charity. The Charity Commission cannot grant a waiver allowing someone disqualified from working with children to serve as trustee of a children's charity. Trustees must have a Criminal Records Bureau (CRB) check carried out where there is a legal requirement to do so, such as for prospective governors of schools, trustees of child care organisations or charities that work with vulnerable adults and personally provide care for them.

The governing document may also impose requirements in relation to eligibility to stand or be appointed as a trustee. For local charities, the constitution often requires that the trustees should live or work within the charity's area of benefit. User organisations may require that all trustees are users of the charity's services.

Election or appointment?

Governing documents usually determine whether trustees become a trustee through election or appointment. In some organisations, election is neither appropriate nor possible (e.g. where there is no membership, or where the members and the trustees are one and the same).

Although election is often the preferred method of appointment, especially in charities with a large membership, it can present problems in filling identified gaps in the board, whether these are related to a skills shortage or lack of demographic diversity. Charities often seek to address these problems by informing the electorate of the gaps and trusting them to make appropriate appointments. It may also be possible to 'pre-screen' candidates before they are put to the membership for election via some form of nomination committee. If a nomination committee is used, it is important that it has clear terms of reference. If this method is not used, or is not useful, most governing documents allow boards to co-opt a number of trustees, often with full voting rights.

Where the only available method of bringing in new trustees is appointment, it may be beneficial for a body other than the existing trustees to be able to make a small proportion of the appointments, provided that this will not undermine the charity's independence. Boards solely appointed by the existing trustees run the risk of perpetuating inequalities or a lack of diversity on the board, particularly where trustees recruit in their own image. At best, such appointment systems may foster cronyism; at worst they may allow trustees to appoint others who will collude in any ongoing impropriety.

Many boards include reserved places for nominated or 'representative' trustees, such as those appointed by a local authority or user group. Such trustees, the board as a whole and, most importantly, the nominating or represented body must understand that, as a matter of charity law, all trustees must at all times act in the best interests of the charity, rather than the body which they represent or were nominated by. All trustees should be clearly informed of their responsibilities before appointment, but it is particularly important in this case as new trustees may soon find themselves in a position of conflicting loyalties, which they will need to manage as a conflict of interest.

CHECKLIST – PROSPECTIVE TRUSTEES

Prior to appointment, trustees should be aware of:

- [✓] charity trustees' responsibilities, both general and legal: (the Charity Commission's publication; 'The Essential Trustee: What you need to know' and its summary publication; 'Being a Trustee' are very useful sources of guidance and information to which to refer prospective trustees);
- [✓] the job description for the role of trustee;
- [✓] any additional job description for the specific role (e.g. treasurer or secretary);
- [✓] limitations on eligibility for appointment and term of office;
- [✓] the level of commitment required by the charity (e.g. a Trustee's Code of Conduct);
- [✓] details of the charity's conflicts of interest policy;
- [✓] the charity's governing document/constitution;

☑ the charity's expenses policy;

☑ the frequency, timing of and venue for board meetings; and

☑ the activities of the charity and the key issues it faces in the coming year. It is helpful to send prospective trustees a copy of the charity's most recent annual review and accounts.

It is good practice for charities to confirm the appointment of new trustees and to ask trustees to literally 'sign up' to the charity. This may include signing any code of conduct that may have been developed by the charity for the trustee board; signing the organisation's confidentiality and/or equal opportunities policy; and completing a declaration of interests.

tip

Trustees' Code of Conduct

New trustees may be required by the charity to sign up to a code of conduct. This may include:

- a commitment to act in the best interests of the charity;
- adherence to internal policies, such as confidentiality, equal opportunities and health and safety;
- a commitment to attend a minimum number of board meetings per year;
- a commitment to devote sufficient time to the role ensuring adequate preparation for board and committee meetings including (as a minimum) reading all meeting papers;
- the conduct expected during board meetings;
- a commitment not to bring the organisation into disrepute; and
- a declaration of interests and a commitment to declare any interests that arise in future.

Where the charity has the legal form of a company, Companies House must be informed of the appointment of new directors within 14 days of the appointment. Forms are available from Companies House for this purpose. Details of newly appointed directors must be added to the company's register of directors and, if the director has any interests in the company's contracts, these should be declared to the other directors by updating the charity's register of trustees' interests. All trustees should have regard to the Charity Commission's guidance on dealing with potential conflicts of interest. A charity should have open and transparent guidelines on declaring interests and excluding trustees from the decision-making process on matters subject to a conflict of interest.

Induction

All organisations should provide a structured induction programme
for new trustees, even if extensive preparatory work was undertaken
prior to appointment, or an individual has served as a trustee before.
The purpose of the induction is to ensure (a) that trustees have a basic
competence in all areas of their role and (b) that they understand the
activities and structure of the charity and their function within the
charity. It also supports trustees in adapting to their role and helps them
to play an active part in the organisation's governance from an early
stage in their trusteeship.

The induction process should cover the following key areas:

- a brief history of the charity and the context in which it currently
  operates;
- the organisation's legal structure, including a copy of the governing
  document, information on key areas of interest for trustees and
  copies of any by-laws or standing orders;
- information on the role and responsibilities of trustees generally and
  in relation to the charity;
- details of the governance, management and staffing structure,
  including contact details for all trustees and key staff;
- information on trustee meetings, including frequency, format,
  content, copies of minutes for the last few meetings and dates for
  future meetings;
- the latest set of annual accounts and the annual report;
- the latest management accounts, an overview of the charity's
  financial situation, suitable training in understanding the accounts
  and guidance on the key points to be mindful of when reviewing
  accounts;
- any relevant policies of the charity (e.g. equal opportunities, confidentiality etc);
- a thorough overview of the activities of the charity;
- any recent monitoring or evaluation reports; and
- a digest of key issues facing the charity.

Obviously a lot of this information will be paper-based, but giving a new
trustee a huge file of paperwork is not an adequate form of induction.
There is no guarantee that trustees will read or understand the papers and
it is not the most engaging way of communicating information. However,

appropriate documents, such as the governing document, list of other trustees, accounts etc. should be supplied as 'compulsory reading' with access to further information for reference purposes and to support other methods of induction.

Given the volume of information to be communicated to new trustees, it may be desirable to use a variety of methods in different sessions so that trustees remain engaged and are active participants in the process, retaining the information communicated.

Many charities run induction days for new trustees. These may include presentations on the trustees' role and the charity's work. Such sessions provide opportunities for new trustees to meet existing trustees, key staff, volunteers and service users. It can also be useful to bring in external speakers to cover areas such as the role of trustees, finance training or the wider context within which the organisation exists. Alternatively, any internal induction could be complemented by sending trustees on external courses many of which are provided free of charge by professional services firms as a well as umbrella groups in the third sector.

For larger charities and those providing direct services, it can be very useful for trustees to visit different premises or activities of the charity to see the charity in action. This may be arranged as part of a trustee's ongoing training as well as his or her induction as it helps to emphasise the end result of the trustee's work and to build a connection between the trustees and the service users and operational staff.

Once the initial introductory stage of induction has been completed, charities may wish to offer continuing support to new trustees (e.g. by pairing a new trustee with a more experienced trustee who will be available to explain procedures and documentation or fill in background information and answer questions if necessary). This form of 'buddying' could be time limited or ongoing, but charities should be aware of the risk that prolonged buddying or mentoring relationships can develop or perpetuate factions in the board. An alternative may be to have one board member (e.g. the vice-chair or secretary) who takes responsibility for the induction of all new trustees. Whoever takes on this support role, it is essential that all the existing trustees have a clear understanding of the charity's purpose and their role as trustees, so that misconceptions are not perpetuated in the new generation of board members.

Induction logs

Give each new trustee an induction log. This may take the form of a checklist on a sheet of paper or a more detailed folder.

The log should include a list of all the areas you expect trustees to cover during the induction period. Trustees should sign and date each item as it is completed. Ideally, space should be provided for trustees to comment on the different elements of the induction programme. These comments can then be used to adapt any future induction programmes to better suit the needs of new trustees.

Induction logs should also provide space for trustees to list any outstanding or future training requirements and identify areas of concern.

The chair of the board should be available to meet with all trustees on an individual basis to address any concerns and identify any future training needs. This is particularly important in the early stages of trusteeship and regular meetings should be scheduled.

Support for trustees should not end after the induction period. Ongoing training and support is crucial to ensure that trustees have a good understanding of current issues and do not become stale. Such training will help trustees to fulfil their roles effectively and remain engaged with the charity, in turn supporting the retention of board members.

The checklist below may prove useful in supporting new trustees.

CHECKLIST – TRUSTEE INDUCTION

- [✓] Does the trustee have a list of forthcoming meetings, including venue details?
- [✓] Has the trustee been given all essential paperwork (e.g. governing document, annual report, business plan, mission statement, papers for the last and next board meetings, including management accounts)?
- [✓] Does the trustee have access to other paperwork that may be needed for reference?
- [✓] Does the trustee have contact details for other board members and key staff?
- [✓] Has the trustee attended a trustee induction session?
- [✓] Does the trustee understand his or her responsibilities as a trustee?
- [✓] Have critical issues affecting the charity been discussed with the trustee (e.g. funding applications, confidentiality requirements)?

✓ Has the trustee visited the premises and met key staff and volunteers?

✓ Has the trustee attended finance training?

✓ Has the trustee signed any required documents (e.g. code of practice, confidentiality policy)?

✓ Has the trustee identified his or her future training needs and have arrangements been made to meet these needs?

✓ Has the trustee met with the chair, following induction, to feedback on the induction process?

Representative trustees and user and carer trustees

Trustees who represent a particular organisation or constituency and those who use the organisation's services or care for a service user may face particular problems when discussing certain issues on the board agenda.

Conflict of loyalty and interests

Where trustees have been nominated by a section of the charity or an external organisation or elected by a constituency of the organisation's members they often, understandably, feel that their primary allegiance is to that nominating body or constituency. However the law is clear: a trustee's primary responsibility is to act in the best interests of the charity. This means that such trustees must make decisions in the interest of the charity as whole, even where this may contradict the interests of their nominating body. The same is the case for user and carer trustees. As with all trustees, they must not make decisions in their own interest or disregard the interests of the charity.

In some cases for user and carer trustees, there may be a clear, direct and personal conflict of interest (e.g. if the level of service provision to an individual is under discussion). Here appropriate action should be taken to prevent trustees operating under conflicting interests (i.e. the trustee in question should withdraw from the discussion and the decision). However, there will be many other cases where the trustee is affected as one of a group of users or carers and these can be more difficult to manage. For this reason it is important that user, carer or representative trustees are clearly informed prior to appointment and during induction of their obligation to act in the charity's best interest and that this interest extends beyond immediate concerns to include care for the future health of the organisation.

Where it is impossible to reconcile the interests of the charity with those of the users, for example where a charge for services is being considered, some innovative solutions for managing the conflict may have to be considered. This is especially true where the board is user led and it is simply not possible for all those with conflicting interests to withdraw, as the meeting would no longer be quorate. Solutions include undertaking a thorough appraisal of the options to be considered and using this as the foundation for discussion. Such an appraisal may be conducted by an independent agency and should consider the impact on the users and the organisation, financially and otherwise, immediate and long term, of each option. This information may help the trustees to make an objective decision. Another solution may be to draw on the skills of an independent, external facilitator to chair a difficult debate. These options help trustees both to make decisions that are truly in the best interest of the charity and also to demonstrate that they have done so, thus minimising the appearance of a conflict of interest.

Confidentiality

Another issue that can prove difficult for representative, user, and carer trustees is confidentiality. Often, during the course of trusteeship, trustees will gain information that is confidential to the charity. The nature of this confidentiality may be commercial (i.e. it relates to the work of the charity) or it may be personal information regarding another trustee, a member of staff, volunteer, service user or carer. All trustees should treat such information as confidential; this is an area that should be covered on induction. Trustees may even be asked to sign a confidentiality agrement. It can be a particularly difficult issue for those who are closely involved in the operational aspects of the charity and may have a direct connection with the issue at hand. It is essential that such trustees are mindful to act in the best interests of the charity in these circumstances.

The Charity Commission produces useful guidance on this issue – see 'Users on Board: Beneficiaries who become Trustees'.

Reviewing the process

There is little value in implementing a comprehensive recruitment, appointment and induction process if you do not consider its effectiveness. The board as a whole should regularly review the process to test whether it has met its required objectives, be they recruiting a certain number of trustees, or gaining specific skills or diversity within the board.

See chapter 10 for detailed information on monitoring and evaluation.

4 Governance structure

INTRODUCTION

Just as a charity will develop in response to its environment, so too should the board. The board's form should fit its function, being appropriately structured to meet the changing demands of the charity's circumstances. This does not mean that boards should be ever-changing, as there needs to be a degree of stability and continuity in the organisation's governance, but trustees of charities should from time to time review whether the charity's governance structure is meeting its needs. This chapter looks at some issues to consider when determining and reviewing the governance of your organisation.

Overall structure

Governing document

The governing document often prescribes the key elements of the board's structure, including the size of the board (most often in the form of maximum and minimum sizes), quorum and method of appointment. This should be the first reference point when considering the governance structure. Governing documents can be changed, but before changes are made, it is important to consider the reasoning behind the structure set out in the organisation's constitution. For example, there may have been prevailing circumstances at the time the document was drafted that led to the board being drawn from regional or divisional groups. The trustees should consider whether the circumstances have changed sufficiently to warrant a change to the board structure.

Determining the governance structure

When considering whether the current governance structure is right for your charity, you should consider a number of factors, including the scope of the charity's work, whether there are different regions, projects or client groups catered for that should be represented on your board, whether particular skills are required by the type of work done by the charity, and whether there is a membership that should be able to appoint board members.

Size of board

When considering the structure of the board, one of the key elements to determine is the ideal size of board for your charity. A board that is too large can be cumbersome, slowing the decision-making process and making a unity of approach and outlook difficult to maintain; factions may then arise. Members of a board that is too large might not feel that they are personally involved, which may lead to poor attendance at board meetings. A board that is too small may not include trustees with an adequate range of skills and experience and there may be insufficient debate on important issues. A small board may make it more likely that the trustees will (consciously or unconsciously) collude in acting in their own interests rather than those of the charity. The Charity Commission recommends a minimum of three trustees, to help reduce the risk of collusion or deadlock.

Trustees should consider the activity of the board, particularly in relation to the size and constituency of the organisation and the amount of work delegated to staff, and create a board where its size fits its function. A board of between eight and 12 people would be appropriate for many charities, providing a balance between the extremes discussed above – providing an adequate range of skills and experience to promote debate and good decision making, and a group which is small enough to work cohesively in governing the charity.

Appointment of trustees

There is a range of ways in which trustees may be appointed. Some charities use one of the methods set out below, others use a combination of these methods.

Once appointed, a trustee's duty is to act in the interests of the charity; he or she is not a representative or agent of his or her appointor. Where a conflict arises between the interests of the charity and the interests of the appointor of a trustee, the trustee must act in the interests of the charity; where it is not possible for them to do this, they must not take part in the discussion of the issue in question.

The governing document of some charities provides that new trustees will be appointed by the current trustees. Sometimes the governing document will require a trustee to be appointed by a unanimous decision of the trustees. In some cases, the member or members of the charity will have the power to veto the appointment of a particular trustee. Appointment by the existing trustees is often appropriate where the charity is small, or the trustees and the members are the same people and there are no other interested parties that wish to take part in the appointment of trustees.

The trustees of some charities are appointed by a resolution of the members of the charity as a body, either at a meeting or in writing. In some charities the candidates for appointment as a trustee will be nominated by the trustees, in others by the members and in others both members and trustees will have the right to nominate trustees. In cases where the trustees of a charity are appointed by the members, there will often be a provision permitting the current trustees to co-opt a person to serve as a trustee until the following meeting of the members, at which point he or she may be appointed by the members. This provision is useful where a position becomes vacant on the board, or it becomes necessary to recruit a trustee with particular expertise, between members' meetings. This method of appointment is common where a charity has a large number of members who are not trustees.

Where the individual members of a charity have a specific and particular interest in the charity, the articles may provide that each member will have the right to appoint and remove a specified number of trustees. This is particularly common where the members of a charity are, or are appointed by, interested parties as described above.

Where there are a number of parties that have an interest in the charity, the articles of the charity sometimes provide that each interested party or group may appoint a number of trustees.

Diversity and skills

The Charity Commission's guidance on the selection of trustees and the Code of Good Governance for the Voluntary and Community Sector emphasise the importance of appointing trustees from diverse race, gender, age, disability and professional and social backgrounds, and appointing trustees that represent the community, the beneficiaries and other stakeholders in the charity. Diverse boards can be extremely beneficial to a charity, as the variety of backgrounds and experience enriches debate. Diversity may also help to establish credibility with certain stakeholders, especially funders and beneficiaries. However, it is important to note that a tokenistic approach of appointing, for example, a lawyer, an accountant, someone with a disability, someone from a minority ethnic group etc. will not, of itself, create a good board.

The guidance also highlights the importance of ensuring that the board provides the right skills and experience needed to govern the charity effectively. Necessary skills include management experience, financial aptitude and an understanding of the issues with which the charity works. Depending on the nature of the charity, further skills, such as fundraising or public relations, may be valuable. The Charity Commission suggests that charities undertake a skills audit to analyse the full range of skills and experience of existing board members (many of whom may have hidden talents) and to identify any gaps.

Recruitment of trustees with specific skills or backgrounds can be extremely difficult. Targeting advertising or direct approaches to relevant professional bodies, companies or other organisations are all viable options. The situation is more difficult still for charities with elected boards, as there are no guarantees that the membership will elect the candidates most suited to complement the existing board. One approach used by charities in these circumstances is to inform the members of the skills or experience needed on the board and trust them to vote accordingly. The nature of democracy means that this is a far from certain exercise and co-option of trustees can be used effectively to supplement elected posts.

CHECKLIST – DIVERSITY ON THE BOARD

A 'box-ticking' approach is not suited to ensuring appropriate board diversity or a cohesive governing body. The following list looks at the issues you should consider to achieve a balanced board within the context of your location and functions.

 Race. Does your board reflect the racial mix of your community and/or users or beneficiaries?

✓ *Age.* Does your board include a spread of appropriate ages for balance and succession? This is particularly important where the organisation provides age-related services (e.g. organisations that exist to provide assistance for older people would be expected to have representatives of that age group on the board). Where a charity provides services for people below the age of 16, who are too young to be charity trustees, they may be represented in an advisory group that discusses issues with the board.

✓ *Gender.* Is the board mixed and does it need to be? There are cases where a single-gender board may be appropriate (e.g. women's centres, or support groups for male survivors of sexual abuse).

✓ *Socio-economic group.* Does the board reflect the balance of the users and/or beneficiaries?

✓ *Users.* Does the board have real experience of the needs of the users of the charity's services (e.g. through user trustees)?

✓ *Disability.* Do the arrangements for board meetings facilitate or prevent people with disabilities from participating? Consider issues such as wheel-chair access, provision of induction loops etc.

✓ *Professional experience.* Do board members have the necessary skills and experience to run the organisation? If not, do they appreciate the limitations of their skills and have access to external advice where necessary?

Continuity versus new ideas

Working in an ever-changing social context, charities need a degree of stability on their boards to ensure that the past history of the charity is not forgotten and that organisations are not perpetually buffeted by internal change. Boards can, however, be too stable, becoming stale due to a settled group dynamic and lack of fresh ideas. Board appointment processes can be structured to strike a balance between achieving conti-nuity and bringing in new skills. Such structures also offer the additional benefit of supporting succession to honorary officer posts on the board as there is a gradual turnover of board membership. Often such boards are structured on a three-year cycle, with a third of the board appointed each year and each board member being appointed for a three-year term. This means that, at any point in time, only one-third of board members will have less than one year's experience.

Board members can usually serve a number of successive terms, subject to an upper limit, at which point they may be required to retire from the board for a period of at least 12 months before being considered eligible for re-election or reappointment unless there is some exceptional reason to retain a particular individual (and this is permitted under the charity's governing document).

Underlying documents

In addition to the governing document, charities need further guidance for the operation of the board and the relationship between the charity and its membership. These documents, be they procedures, policies, standing orders or bye-laws, should fill in the gaps left by the governing document. Although the governing document sets the overall framework for the governance of the organisation, the trustees may need more detailed guidance or a more adaptable approach in some areas. These documents serve to supplement the governing document and, as such, are easier to amend to suit the changing needs of the charity. They may include: a conflict of interest or confidentiality policy; a procedure for dealing with disputes within the board; bye-laws regarding the conduct of elections; and standing orders regarding membership issues.

Such documents should be valuable at all times, but come into their own at times of uncertainty or dispute by offering a clear, predetermined and fair course of action.

CASE EXAMPLE

A charity which supported those with disabilities was going through a period of internal conflict. Tensions ran high between the long-standing trustees and those users who wanted greater input into the charity's governance. The different factions each nominated candidates for board elections, and both users and trustees drew staff into the conflict. The bye-laws provided for board elections to be administered by an independent organisation with confidential postal voting. This allowed all members to vote freely and included those who would not have been able to attend the AGM. The process ensured that members, users, and trustees could be confident that the electoral process had been fair and ensured that they respected the final result. This allowed the charity to move forward following the conflict.

Sub-committees

Sub-committees provide opportunities for charities to consider a wide range of issues in more detail than can be covered in trustees' meetings, but there is a risk that the number of sub-committees may multiply and the trustees may lose control of the charity as the sub-committees take on more and more of the board's work. There are a number of ways to use sub-committees positively to contribute towards the governance of the charity without undermining the role of the board and creating undue levels of administration in servicing the sub-groups.

Terms of reference. Every sub-committee should have written terms of reference. The broad areas covered by the terms should be common to all the sub-committees and some details should be consistent across all of them. For example, terms of reference should cover the following areas:

- purpose of the committee and anticipated end result or output;
- duration of committee (i.e. standing committee or time or task limited);
- level and scope of delegated authority (e.g. can the committee make decisions and take action in its own right or does it have to refer all recommendations to the board for decision?). Does the committee have any delegated budgetary authority and what are the controls on this?
- the composition of the committee (the charity may agree a standard requirement for all sub-committees (e.g. 'the sub-committee must have a minimum of three people and a maximum of eight, of whom the simple majority/at least two members must be trustees of the charity'));
- reporting requirements to the full board. This may be another standard detail (e.g. 'every sub-committee must provide a written report to each board meeting or the board meeting immediately after each sub-committee meeting').

Clearly stated terms of reference relating to the purpose, delegated authority, composition and reporting requirements of sub-committees will help to prevent the proliferation of such committees and avoid the potential slipping of power from trustees to committees.

Many charities have a sub-committee to focus on financial and administrative issues (e.g. the presentation of accounts, appointment of staff etc). Depending on the charity's work, other sub-committees may be necessary (e.g. charities providing medical or health care may need a sub-committee to focus on quality and safety issues).

The number of standing sub-committees should be kept to a minimum, with their purpose and authority clearly defined. There is a risk, particularly with finance sub-committees, that the majority of trustees' power vests with the sub-committee rather than the full board. In such circumstances, it may be better for the terms of reference to define the activities of the sub-committee in addition to the purpose (e.g. 'the sub-committee will produce budgets and management accounts for discussion and approval by the board of trustees').

Additional sub-committees may be established on a task-focused or time-limited basis (e.g. for the appointment of a new member of staff or the production of a funding application).

Sub-committees do provide an opportunity for charities to draw on a wider range of skills than may be present on the board and to identify and develop the skills of potential future board members. They enable a more detailed consideration of particular matters or functions.

Advisory and reference groups

Charities working in a complex environment may wish to draw on a wider range of skills than is available on the board, but to do this in an *ad hoc* way, rather than through a formal sub-committee. One option is to set up a body of advisers or a reference group that can be called upon either individually or collectively as and when needed. This can be particularly effective for organisations working in scientific or politically complex fields (e.g. environmental organisations or charities campaigning for welfare rights). This can also be a useful way of recognising the skills and contributions of former board members, especially when making the transition from a large to a small board.

Governing documents

People who wish to establish a new charity, or radically restructure an existing charity, may wish to consider the model governing documents for trusts, unincorporated associations, companies limited by guarantee and (soon to be available) charitable incorporated organisations that are available from both the Charity Commission and the Charity Law Association.

These models are useful to all not-for-profit organisations. Those with charitable purposes are advised to use the model documents as a starting point, as this will ease the process of applying for Charity Commission registration – particularly if the model documents are adopted without amendments (apart from the insertion of the objects and selection of clauses where the model gives alternatives).

The Charity Commission models include all relevant sections of the governing document, so specimen wording has not been included in this guide. However, the models should not just be adopted as they stand. The models are just that – models – and charities should consider what they require from their governing document before finalising its terms. Some areas of the Charity Commission models are blank, as the exact terms are to be decided by the individual charities themselves. It may also be useful to refer to the governing documents of similar groups for suggestions regarding common constitutional elements.

Here we will consider the key areas to be considered, whether writing your organisation's first constitution, or revising an existing document.

Basic principles

Usefulness. Before you start work on your governing document and throughout drafting you should keep in mind the purpose of the document as the framework for the charity's governance, the foundation upon which it rests. It should be a useful document that can be referred to in order to answer questions regarding governance – rather like a guidebook for the trustees and the charity's secretary. As such, it should be well structured and written in clear and accessible language.

Flexibility. Although governing documents can be changed, frequent alterations create uncertainty as well as being administratively burdensome. It is advisable to develop a governing document that has the flexibility to cope with developments in the charity without being so vague as to be meaningless. When drafting the document, consider potential developments within the charity over the next five to ten years. Does the document facilitate or prevent such changes? You should be particularly conscious of whether the area of benefit, objects and powers allow for the expansion of the charity's activities.

Practicality. The terms of the governing document should be realistically achievable. This is particularly important when it comes to issues such as the required number of trustees or the quorum for meetings and, again, those drafting the document should consider the potential expansion of the charity in future. Clauses that may seem reasonable now (e.g. a quorum for members' meetings of 10% of members out of a current membership of 100) may be completely impractical should the membership grow to 2,000 people.

Again, a balance is required. In ensuring that the provisions are practical, do not make requirements so easy to fulfil that they leave the charity open to abuse (e.g. a quorum for members' meetings which is too low (one or two people where there is a much wider membership)).

Relationship between the governing document and legislation

Charity and company law establish the foundations on which charities that have the legal form of a company must run – the default position. Governing documents may require higher, but not lower, standards. This relationship should be considered when drafting the governing document. If the document's requirements are less stringent than the prevailing legislative position then, generally speaking, the law will apply; however, if the governing document specifies a higher standard, this must be followed. This can present particular difficulties for charities in relation to, for example, financial reporting requirements, as the legal position may change or the organisation may pass between different thresholds. In this area, some charities have addressed the problem by drafting the relevant clauses to state that the charity will comply with the prevailing legal requirements.

Key clauses of the governing document

Name of the charity. The governing document should be in the full name of the charity. This is often given in the first clause. If the charity is to operate under an acronym or different name, give it here.

Area of benefit. Most charities operate within a defined geographical area or 'area of benefit'. When drafting this clause, bear in mind that local authority boundaries may change in future and that if the charity operates outside the area defined by its governing document it will be acting *ultra vires*. Many charities resolve this by avoiding reference to a local authority and instead describe their area of benefit as a certain location and the surrounding area.

Purpose or objects. This is the most important element of the governing document. For organisations seeking charity registration, the wording of this clause will be one of the key determinants of charitable status, as the objects described must fall within the statutory list of charitable purposes as described in chapter 1.

The objects clause cannot be changed without the prior written consent of the Charity Commission so, ideally, it should describe the purpose of the charity throughout its existence. As such, it should be broadly worded to describe the overall aims of the organisation rather than the methods of achieving those aims, as these are likely to change during the life of the charity. For example, the objects could be simply to promote the welfare of those suffering from a particular type of illness. Sometimes the objects and area of benefit clause may be combined (e.g. 'to promote the welfare of people with mental ill-health living or working in Greater Manchester and the surrounding area').

Charities may have multiple purposes and the objects clause can be much more detailed than the example given above.

When an organisation is committed to a particular model of work and this is part of the purpose of the charity (as is the case with user groups) this may be included within the objects clause.

The objects clauses of registered charities can be viewed on the Register of Charities via the Charity Commission website at www.charity-commission.gov.uk. This can provide useful examples of suitable objects clauses which may be adapted by new charities. The Charity Commission also provides sample objects at www.charitycommission.gov.uk/.

Powers. This section of the document defines the things that the charity can do in order to achieve the objects. It is usually separate from the objects clause and should not focus on the activities of the charity but on the broad authorities given to trustees and should include (where appropriate):

- power to employ staff;
- power to own or lease property;
- power to raise funds;
- power to borrow money; and
- power to invest funds.

Trusts and unincorporated associations should also include a power to change the organisation's name. This is not necessary for companies limited by guarantee as changes can be made by members' resolutions.

Again, it is important to be forward looking when determining the powers. Powers that may seem superfluous now could be essential in future years.

If seeking charitable status, be careful not to include powers that are not charitable, such as the distribution of profits to members.

The powers should also contain a general provision allowing the charity to do anything lawful that is necessary or incidental to the furtherance of its objects.

Membership. If the charity is to have a membership, this should be described in the governing document. This is essential in the case of a company limited by guarantee, as it is the membership that provides the guarantee.

The governing document should explain how people are admitted into and removed from membership, any different classes of members, voting rights and, if appropriate, the maximum number of members. All companies must have at least one member. Restrictions may be placed on eligibility for membership, but these should not be discriminatory and should be appropriate to the charity. It would, for example, be acceptable to restrict membership to those living in the area of benefit or those affected by the illness that is the focus of the charity's work.

There may also be a clause limiting the extent to which members may benefit from the charity (e.g. 'members may not receive a share in any surplus').

Board of trustees. As has been discussed elsewhere in this chapter, the structure of the governing body should be determined by the governing document. This should include the number of trustees, the method of appointment and retirement, removal or resignation, the minimum number of meetings per year and the procedures and quorum for trustees meetings. The number of trustees is normally expressed as minimum and maximum with the quorum (i.e. the minimum number of trustees that must be present for a meeting to be valid) described as a proportion of the board or a minimum number, whichever is greater. The governing document should also include arrangements for the resignation of trustees, including the minimum number that can remain after resignations (i.e. a trustee can only resign if there are at least x trustees remaining). As a matter of good practice, the minimum number of trustees, the quorum and the minimum remaining trustees should not be less than three. Maintaining a minimum of three trustees reduces the opportunities for abuse. If less than three trustees remain, their powers should be limited to appointing sufficient trustees to restore the minimum number and calling a members' meeting.

Requirements for the retirement and rotation of trustees may also be included. Indefinite appointments make for stale boards, whereas annual elections offer little continuity. Many charities operate on a retirement-by-rotation principle, with three-year appointments for trustees and one-third of the board retiring each year as discussed above. Governing documents may also include any restrictions on the number of consecutive terms that trustees may serve before being obliged to stand down.

The provisions relating to trustees should also describe the level of benefit that trustees can receive from the charity. As has been discussed in previous chapters, the usual requirement is that none of the trustees should benefit and this should be clearly stated in the governing document. Where payment to trustees for professional services is allowed, this should be specifically included in the governing document, as should any arrangements for the payment of trustee indemnity insurance premiums from charity funds. The Charities Act 2011 allows charities to pay trustees for services provided that certain conditions are met. However, it does not allow a trustee to be paid simply for being a trustee; nor does it allow trustees to be paid as an employee of the charity. If either of these scenarios are envisaged, then the specific prior consent of the Charity Commission must be obtained.

Members' meetings. Under the Companies Act 2006, private companies (which include charitable companies limited by guarantee) are not required to hold Annual General Meetings (AGMs) unless they are required to do so by their governing documents. However, this does not prevent charitable companies holding annual members' meetings (often referred to as 'general meetings') and many charities may choose to keep the requirement to hold an AGM. This will depend largely on the structure of the charity: if all the members are trustees, an AGM is less useful than if there is a large body of members who are not trustees. Whether or not the governing document requires the organisation to hold an AGM it should set out provisions for how members' meetings are to be held (e.g. the frequency of these meetings and the amount of notice to be given).

Accounts. Governing documents should give instructions on the control of the charity's bank account and require annual accounts to be produced. This is an area that charities should be wary of when drafting governing documents as reporting requirements change and charities move between reporting thresholds. Charities may find that their governing document requires an audit, whereas the statutory requirement may be for a less onerous independent examination, but the higher constitutional standard will apply. Charities are advised to draft the clause so that it requires compliance with the prevailing legislation, rather than specifying the method of examination.

Changes to the governing documents. The governing document should describe the process by which it can be amended. Certain changes to the governing documents of registered charities require the Charity Commission's *prior* written approval. These are changes to the objects, amendment and dissolution arrangements, and any provisions authorising trustee benefits, extending investment powers or spending permanent endowments. Charities must seek Commission approval prior to any of these amendments being made or agree amendments specifying that they are subject to the Commission's approval.

Charitable companies do not need to include an amendment clause as companies legislation lays down the procedure for changing articles of association.

If the governing documents of unincorporated organisations do not include any power or provision to make amendments, registered charities may apply to the Charity Commission for an order that is called a 'scheme'. The Charity Commission can make an order to give trustees administrative powers that are not currently available in the governing document if it believes it is in the best interests of the charity to do so. This can be done quite swiftly. In contrast, a scheme directly changes the constitution. This is a time-consuming process involving, in certain cases, periods of public notice of the constitutional change. Clearly it is preferable for charities to include an appropriate amendment clause. Organisations which are not registered may have no alternative but to wind up, establish a new group and transfer the assets across.

Dissolution. Governing documents should include provision for the winding up of the charity. This may occur if the charity has achieved its purpose, become redundant due to social, political or economic change, has inadequate support to operate, or is no longer financially viable. The governing document should describe the process of closing the charity down and the distribution of any funds remaining once liabilities have been met. The normal requirement is for the remaining assets to be passed to another organisation or multiple organisations with similar objects to the closing charity being wound up or used in furtherance of the objects.

Group structures

Many charities in England and Wales are classified by the Charity Commission as branches or subsidiaries of another charity; many other not-for-profit organisations operate within some kind of group structure. Such collaboration affects the role of trustees and should be taken into account when reviewing the governance structure of the charity.

Different types of group structure

Informal groups of charities. Sometimes charities may work together on a particular project or issue or to share information without formally establishing how the group will operate.

Formalised groups of charities. Sometimes a group of charities will establish a formal group (e.g. local charities may be the legal members of a council for voluntary service, or charities may pay affiliation fees to an umbrella body). Sometimes charities will enter into contracts with each other to carry out a particular project as a 'joint or collaborative venture'.

Linked charities. Charities with similar objectives may be brought together by what is known as a 'uniting direction' of the Charity Commission. Such charities will share a registered number and have prepared a single set of accounts. The provisions in the Charities Act 2011 governing the merger of charities are now more straightforward and many charities which were formally linked have merged to form single charities.

Independent branches. Branches may be established as independent charities with their own governing documents, boards of trustees and accounts. Although independent, they will usually be required to operate within a framework or affiliation arrangement determined by the parent body in order to use its name and logo.

Where charities work together, it is important to establish clearly which organisations and individuals are responsible for making particular decisions or taking particular actions.

5 Running the board

INTRODUCTION

One of the most common reasons for difficulties within charities is the poor functioning and performance of the board. This may happen for a variety of reasons, such as trustees not fully understanding their role or not working effectively together. Although such problems are often attributed to personality clashes, conducting meetings effectively can do much to overcome the trickier elements of group dynamics and ensure that all board members are able to participate fully.

Why meet?

Negative experiences of meetings can leave some people feeling that they are a fruitless inconvenience that interrupt the 'real' work. Yet meetings are crucial for charity trustees as they provide the principal means for collectively governing the charity. Without board meetings, charities could be victim to unilateral decision making by the chair or another member of the board, or receive mixed instructions from individual trustees. Although a degree of governance can be conducted by phone, letter and e-mail, individual communication does not generate the same level of debate as meeting as a group. Collective discussion allows people to bounce ideas off each other and develop arguments. As all trustees are bound by board decisions, it is preferable for these to be made by consensus rather than a majority view; on contentious issues, meetings are essential to come to a decision with which all board members are comfortable.

Often charities have many different stakeholders and a high level of public interest and, as such, making governance decisions through meetings ensures a level of confidence in the integrity of the board and provides opportunities for greater openness. For example, interested parties can be invited to attend or contribute to board meetings and minutes (or extracts from them where confidential matters have been discussed) can be circulated to staff.

Structure and protocol of board meetings

The governing document and supporting papers are the foundations that determine, for example, the frequency of meetings and rules regarding non-attendance. They may also lay down a framework structure for board meetings or specify items, such as financial reports, that must be considered. These documents represent the minimum standard and trustees should increase the frequency of meetings where necessary.

Structure is essential to make a meeting worthwhile and this may be shaped to suit the objectives of the meeting and the culture of the board. This may take the form of a predetermined agenda, bullet points on a flip chart agreed at the beginning of the meeting, or discussion of a single issue at a specially convened or 'extraordinary' meeting.

Boards may move between different structures at different stages of development or for different purposes. For example, a planning meeting or board away day might be very informal to allow the group to gel and to give them the opportunity to think freely. In contrast, a trustee meeting following the award of a new grant should be formal and very structured to focus on the development of new work funded by the grant and to move ahead as swiftly as possible. Without structure, meetings are likely to run off course and become unproductive.

The Code of Good Governance for the Voluntary and Community Sector provides a helpful pointer on this aspect of ensuring board effectiveness. It advises that trustees should ensure that: the board meets often enough to be effective; board members are well-prepared and committed to attending all meetings and contributing constructively; and board meetings have a well-structured agenda and good chairmanship.

Different types of board

Boards operate in different ways. For the sake of illustration, the following section will look at two fictitious caricatures at either end of the spectrum. The extremely formal 'Madam Chairman' board and, at the opposite end, the highly informal 'jeans and trainers' board.

Protocol, like structure, is likely to depend on the culture of the board and the purpose of the meeting. It is common for boards to direct comments through the chair, but some organisations work on a very formal 'Madam Chairman' basis whilst others are very much on first-name terms. Similarly, although some boards will vote on all decisions, others will simply get a sense of consensus, confirm the decision and move on. Boards will also have different approaches to discussing agenda items, from formally presented papers, through workshop-type sessions to informal discussion. Again the most appropriate format will depend on the item and board culture. 'Madam Chairman' boards will feel no more comfortable sitting on the floor with a flip chart pad than a 'jeans and trainers' board will feel at home with men in suits giving PowerPoint presentations.

Of course, 'Madam Chairman' and 'jeans and trainers' boards are extremes; most occupy the middle ground. Although some tend more to formality and others to informality, boards will adopt different styles depending on the size of the organisation or of the board, the item under discussion and the culture set by the chair or the history of the charity.

BOARD EXAMPLES – TWO EXTREMES

'Madam Chairman'

Looks like: Smartly dressed board members, consisting of the great and the good. Refer to fellow trustees by their titles, either personal or role-related (i.e. Dr Smith, Madam Chairman, etc). Meetings stick rigidly to a pre-determined agenda and are extremely businesslike. Trustees sit around a board table with Madam Chairman at the top, the secretary on one side and treasurer on the other. Discussion is very formal and the board takes a very conservative approach.

Most frequently found: Long-standing charities, usually with lots of money.

'Jeans and trainers'

Looks like: Casually dressed individuals. Board members on first name terms only, often with no defined roles within the board, instead functioning on a cooperative basis. Members sit wherever they like and debate issues passionately, but as there is no agenda, discussion is frequently at a tangent to board business. Tend to be innovative and creative.

Most frequently found: Student unions, embryonic groups.

Membership of the 'Madam Chairman' board is unlikely to be particularly creative or innovative, whilst the jeans and trainers board may be cripplingly unproductive. The ideal balance for most organisations is to have enough formality to identify the tasks in hand and get the job done, together with sufficient informality to allow people to relax and contribute to the discussion, to foster wide thinking and to allow them to enjoy their roles.

Planning meetings

Agendas

Whether it consists of bullet points on a flip chart or a formal list sent out a week or more in advance, every board meeting must have an agenda. Agendas are crucial to ensuring that each board member knows and shares the purpose of the meeting and that decisions are made on the issues that are most pressing for the charity at that point in time. Every board member should also be able to contribute items to the agenda, usually by identifying items to the chair or secretary in advance of the meeting or failing that under a standing 'any other business' item. Agendas that are distributed before the meeting allow trustees the opportunity to prepare for the meeting and consult others where necessary thereby improving debate and increasing the value and effectiveness of the meeting.

As well as structuring the meeting, well-designed agendas send out important messages about the relative importance of the issues facing the charity. Most agendas include standard items such as approving the minutes of the last meeting, discussing any matters arising from those minutes and financial reports. The remainder of the agenda is usually determined by the board and the sequence of those items on the agenda can indicate the importance of the issues. Some charities dispense with the routine issues first and leave key items towards the end of the meeting. Whilst there is a degree of logic in this approach, in that it allows simple questions to be swiftly dealt with, it can mean that later agenda items are not fully discussed. This is particularly the case where timing for the meeting is tight, where some of the trustees have to leave early, or where the meeting takes place in the evening. As a result, trustee numbers may be dwindling and the remaining trustees tiring just as critical issues come up for discussion. Possible solutions may either be to place the crucial item higher on the agenda, arrange a dedicated meeting to discuss that one question, or dispense with routine items until a later meeting. The board secretary and the chair should consider the relative importance of the agenda items. Which is more important to a charity facing an immediate funding or staffing crisis – addressing the crisis and maintaining the existence and activities of the charity, or agreeing the minutes of the last meeting?

A useful tool is to include a meeting timetable as an integral part of the agenda. As well as focusing the mind and helping to keep the meeting on track, including a timescale for each agenda item indicates the relative importance of that agenda item. Ideally, meetings should last no longer than two hours. Although concentration levels can drop long before this point, after two hours fatigue generally sets in.

The starting point is to determine the anticipated length of the meeting. If it is likely to continue for more than two hours, include a break for refreshments and time for a change of environment before resuming.

SAMPLE AGENDA

Anycounty Children and Families Forum
Board of Trustees
13.5.20XX
7pm at Anycounty CVS, Anytown
Agenda

1	Welcome	5 min (standard item)
2	Apologies for absence	5 min (standard item)
3	Minutes of last meeting (15.3.20XX) – papers enclosed	5 min (standard item)
4	Matters arising	5 min (standard item)
5	Local authority plans for charging policy papers enclosed	30 min
6	Gaps in childcare provision – papers enclosed	30 min
7	Development of new family support service progress report – papers enclosed	10 min
8	Finance report – papers enclosed	10 min (standard item)
9	Sub-committee reports – papers enclosed	10 min (standard item)
10	Any other business	5 min (standard item)
11	Date of next meeting – 17.7.20XX	5 min (standard item)

Within your anticipated timescale, break down the meeting into timed chunks for each item. Standard items such as apologies and the minutes of the last meeting should be brief, whereas discussion of key issues such as a new project, a funding application, or policy development may require 30 minutes to an hour. Timing may be described by the actual time you expect to start and finish each topic or, as in the sample agenda, in terms of the number of minutes for each item.

Papers

As can be seen from the sample agenda, the discussion of many items will be based around papers circulated before the meeting. Some papers may be for information only, intended to generate discussion without necessarily expecting any conclusions or decisions at the meeting. The paper should clearly specify on its front cover who its author is; who has been consulted in its preparation; and if it is for information only, or for a decision by the board.

Where a decision is needed, papers should describe the issues for discussion, the options available for decision and the implications (particularly the financial implications) of each decision, with a recommended course of action for the board. Such papers help to direct discussion and ensure that an actual decision is made.

Papers should be circulated in advance of the meeting to give trustees time to read them and consider the issues raised; formulate any further questions they may have; and identify any options not considered in the paper. In exceptional cases, where there is a good reason for this not being possible, papers can be tabled at the meeting, but this should only be used as a last resort.

Timing

On a large or diverse board, it will be very difficult to plan meetings at a time to suit everyone, but it is important to arrange meetings that can accommodate as many board members as possible and do not leave individuals marginalised. When arranging meetings, consider both the professional and domestic responsibilities of board members, as well as their personal circumstances. If trustees have full-time jobs, plan meetings around their working hours and travelling time. Those with young children may prefer meetings during the school day or later in the evening when they can arrange childcare. People with disabilities or suffering from ill-health may need to fit meetings around domiciliary care or medication requirements, or may wish to schedule meetings for the time of day when they feel at their best.

Evening meetings often suit trustees who work during the day, but may not be ideal as the trustees are likely to be tired. If evening meetings are essential, they should be kept to an agreed time limit. Another issue to consider with evening meetings is the transport arrangements for trustees and their personal safety when travelling to and from the meeting.

Venue

The venue should be accessible to trustees, both in terms of geographic location and access into and within the building, particularly if the trustees include people with disabilities. Geographic location is particularly important for charities covering a large or rural area. It can be a source of friction within boards if the meeting venue continually favours one group of trustees over others, so it is desirable to seek a central venue or one with good transport links so that access is easy for all trustees. Alternatively, meetings may be rotated between a number of different venues. This is useful if the charity operates from a number of sites as it allows the trustees to view the different elements of the charity's work and to meet staff and volunteers.

The venue should be physically accessible to wheelchair users and include appropriate adaptations for other disabilities (e.g. induction loops) to ensure that all those who currently serve on the board or those who wish to do so in future will be able to participate fully in meetings.

Meeting venues should also be comfortable and appropriate for board meetings. There should be adequate space for board members to sit around a table, with separate rooms for refreshments or break-out groups if necessary. Rooms should be well-lit, warm and ventilated.

Running the meeting

It is the role of the chair to ensure that the meeting is productive. Many problems within board meetings are due to poor chairing. It may be that the chair rules the meeting and stifles debate, allows others to dominate, or fails to keep the meeting to the agenda. Keeping control of the meeting means ensuring that everybody is able to contribute to the debate equally, without individuals or a small group dominating to the exclusion of others. The chair should also ensure that the debate is relevant to the item at hand and that discussion is not diverted to superfluous issues.

Chairs of charity boards need to be particularly aware of the 'lowest common denominator effect'. This involves trustees debating the minutiae of an agenda item, such as what colour to paint the office walls, whilst missing the bigger, more difficult issues, such as the development of the charity following the refurbishment. This often happens because trustees feel overwhelmed by the volume or complexity of issues facing them, so find it difficult to prioritise or grasp the more complex challenges. As a result they focus on the details that they can all understand – the lowest common denominator. It is the chair's role to ensure that the big picture is not lost, for example by arranging for complex issues to be explained in a way that is comprehensible to all trustees.

Other difficulties are ensuring participation and dealing with disputes. It only takes a few strong personalities on a board for other trustees to feel unable to contribute and the objective of considered collective decision making is lost. Trustees may be silent to avoid a dispute, because they feel that they have nothing to add, or because they are wary of asking a stupid question. Some boards adopt the philosophy that 'there are no stupid questions', reflecting the fact that the supposed 'stupid question' is frequently the one that everybody else was thinking but did not dare to ask! Again it is the function of the chair to ensure participation. This may be done by establishing ground rules that underpin every meeting, or by actively asking those who have not yet contributed to the debate for their views. Some chairs do this by asking each trustee in turn if they have anything to add, others by specifically addressing the silent trustees and asking for their comments.

Significant disputes within boards are less common than lack of participation, but harder to deal with. Again the chair has a crucial role to play in ensuring that all views are heard, that the opinions expressed are relevant to the item under discussion and that the dispute does not get out of hand. Ground rules can be useful for dealing with disputes, but pain-free resolution is largely dependent upon the agitated trustee's respect for the authority of the chair, as only the chair can draw an item to its close. Where disputed items are not subject to time pressures, a cooling-off period may be allowed, deferring the issue to a subsequent meeting to allow for greater investigation of all views expressed. On some issues it may also be appropriate to consult with a wider group (e.g. service users or volunteers) to see if fresh opinions can aid consensus.

As board decisions are binding on all trustees, it is preferable to reach consensus decisions wherever possible. Ensuring consensus, rather than making majority decisions, can take more time, but it does mean that issues are fully debated.

The Charity Commission produces helpful guidance (in association with ICSA) entitled; 'Charities and Meetings' which can be found on the Charity Commission website.

Board roles

The classic board structure involves at least three dedicated posts: chair, secretary and treasurer. Many boards have an additional role of vice or deputy chair. Collectively these are the honorary officers of the charity. Each has a very distinct function and some charities have developed job descriptions for each role. This both assists potential honorary officers in understanding the post and provides guidance for those trustees in officer roles.

Chair. Several aspects of the chair's role are discussed in the sections in this chapter relating to running the meeting as this is, essentially, the chair's function. The chair is the first among equals on the board. This leadership role includes responsibility for determining the agenda (usually in partnership with the secretary) and steering the meeting to achieve the agenda's objectives. This involves introducing the agenda item, stimulating debate, keeping discussion to the item at hand, ensuring participation, dealing with disputes, offering suggestions and ensuring consensus. Where consensus cannot be reached and a vote is necessary, most governing documents give the chair a second and casting vote in the event of equality of votes. At the conclusion of each agenda item, the chair should summarise the decisions, identify any actions arising from that decision, agree who will be responsible for that action and set a timescale for its conclusion.

In staffed organisations, the most senior employee (e.g. the Chief Executive) is usually managed by the chair.

To the outside world, the chair often represents the board and the charity.

Vice or deputy chair. The vice or deputy chair's role is to deputise for the chair in his or her absence. The role often involves other functions, such as working closely with the chair on business to be conducted between meetings, chairing sub-committees etc.

Secretary. The secretary sometimes has the most difficult position on the board. Their primary responsibility is to help the board ensure the probity of the organisation and its adherence to the governing document and legal environment, rather than allegiance to the board. Whilst a significant element of this role involves supporting the trustees in working effectively and legally, the cautions given by the secretary can sometimes be at odds with the wishes of the board, making the function something of a thankless task. The functions include working with the chair and senior staff to plan meetings and produce minutes, maintaining necessary documentation, executing the constitutional requirements (e.g. planning members' meetings and board elections) and reporting to regulators as necessary.

Treasurer. All the trustees share a collective responsibility for the financial health of the organisation, but it is the treasurer who carries out the board's finance function, often in partnership with senior staff and other board members, sometimes within a finance sub-committee. The treasurer's role includes budget setting, controlling and monitoring expenditure, producing management and annual accounts and presenting financial reports to the board and membership.

The proportion of this work that is actually done by the treasurer will depend on the charity. Much of the work will be done by paid staff or professional advisers, but it is the treasurer who must supervise the work and support the board in interpreting financial information and making finance decisions.

Other trustees may also have designated roles, such as staff liaison, volunteer recruitment or quality standards. Whatever the roles of individual trustees, boards must continue to act collectively, as the case study below illustrates.

CASE EXAMPLE

The treasurer of a charitable company limited by guarantee failed to coordinate the production of annual accounts for two years in succession. The treasurer had ignored letters sent by Companies House requesting the accounts and later enquiring if the company was still operating. The company was eventually struck off the Register of Companies. The organisation incurred considerable expense in restoring the company to the Register and engaging accountants to produce financial reports for the organisation. The treasurer admitted responsibility and resigned his position; however the responsibilities of the trustees are collective and the remaining trustees had taken no action regarding the failure to produce accounts. The charity's funders grew concerned about the remaining trustees' grasp of their responsibilities and their ability to manage the finances of the charity. They threatened to withdraw funding unless appropriate action was taken to remedy the deficiencies in financial management. As a result, several other trustees, including the chair, acknowledged their responsibility and resigned from the board.

Group dynamic roles

In addition to the formal roles determined by the structure of the board, trustees are likely to adopt different roles within the group depending on their own personalities and the inter-relationships between them. There is a host of literature on group/team dynamics and their impact on organisational performance. It is not a subject that will be discussed here in any great detail; however it is an issue which should be kept in mind when considering the board, whether reviewing its success or failure to function, its composition, leadership or tendency to dispute.

There are various models of team roles, but one of the most widely used models was developed by Dr Meredith Belbin in the early 1980s. Dr Belbin's model identifies nine roles set out below.

Clearly, some of these team roles naturally lend themselves to formal board roles. The coordinator is often the chair of trustees and the specialist may be the independent professional adviser. In small boards, trustees may fulfil more than one role and many boards will function effectively without giving any conscious thought to group dynamics.

However, the model can be extremely useful and can be a valuable tool for board appraisal.

Board appraisal is discussed at the end of this chapter.

BELBIN'S MODEL FOR EFFECTIVE TEAM WORKING

1 *Coordinator.* The coordinator will define roles and set goals within the team or group. As the person who coordinates the work and talents of others, the coordinator needs to be respected by the team.

2 *Plant.* The plant is the creative team member who comes up with new ideas.

3 *Shaper.* This is the dynamic, energetic and challenging member of the team.

4 *Resource investigator.* Extrovert, develops ideas and makes outside contacts, including securing necessary resources.

5 *Monitor evaluator.* This team member is the realist. Shrewd, prudent and analytical, the monitor evaluator will keep the team grounded by careful consideration of options.

6 *Implementer.* This team worker is also realistic and will make things happen through a practical and task-orientated approach.

7 *Completer finisher.* The completer finisher has great attention to detail, ensuring accurate and timely work.

8 *Teamworker.* This team member is caring, person orientated and prepared to work to other people's ideas.

9 *Specialist.* The specialist brings technical skill and professionalism to the team, rather than organisational loyalty.

Minutes

One of the biggest criticisms of meetings is that they involve a lot of talking, but then nothing ever happens. This should not happen with well-run meetings where decisions are made and actions identified. Minutes of meetings provide one of the key means of ensuring that action follows meetings. Minutes are important on a number of levels. In recording the principal discussion points and decisions of a meeting, they provide evidence that issues have been properly debated. They also serve as an *aide-mémoire* to the board and supply essential background information by acting as a historical record of the charity. By recording action points, minutes also serve as a workplan for the board. Some charities present their minutes with an 'action' column on the right hand side of the page, showing what action is to be taken in respect of each agenda item, the person responsible for that action, and the timescale required.

The fact that planned actions are recorded in the minutes is, of course, no guarantee that the action will be carried out. Board members must take individual responsibility for any tasks that are attributed to them and the board must collectively ensure that the actions proposed are implemented.

SAMPLE MINUTES OF A MEETING OF THE TRUSTEES OF [XCHARITY] HELD ON [DATE] AT [TIME] AT [LOCATION]

Present:

Mary Allen (Chair)	Alicia Jackson
Brenda Starr (Treasurer)	Indira Khan
Xavier Michel (Secretary)	George McIntyre
Sanjeev Bashir	Hannah Williams

In attendance: Maggie Harris, Anycounty Social Services

1 Welcome	**XM**
2 Apologies for absence: Tom O'Leary, Sam Weller	
3 Minutes of last meeting (15.3.20XX): Item 4 – amend third sentence of second paragraph to read 'The consultation period will run for three months'.	
4 Matters arising: No matters arising not appearing elsewhere on the agenda.	
5 Local authority plans for charging policy: The trustees opposed the implementation of a charging policy but recognised that its introduction was inevitable and agreed to consult with the wider membership on proposals to mitigate the effects of charging. Particular concerns were raised regarding parents of disabled children and the possibility that they would not access services because of the charges.	**MA, SB and AJ to draft proposals paper by 14.6.20XX**
6 Gaps in childcare provision: The trustees agreed with the analysis of unmet need in terms of childcare provision and added to the list the need for services for newly arrived asylum seekers. It was agreed to present the revised report to the members' meeting in June.	

SAMPLE MINUTES continued

7 Development of new family support service: MH reported that an application has been made to the Charity Commission for registration; office accommodation has been provided in the Social Services family centre in Anytown; and the posts of organiser and admin assistant were advertised two weeks ago. Response was good, with interviews due to take place early in June. MA will be a member of the interview panel.

8 Finance report: BS reported a slight overspend on travel expenses due to additional, unexpected work undertaken this year in attending meetings relating to the charging policy and the new family support scheme. However there was underspend on office costs and a small donation from the local children's clothes shop has led to a small surplus against target budgets for the first month of the financial year. Accounts for the previous financial year are currently being prepared by BS and the accountant and will be presented to the next meeting.

BS to prepare accounts by 15.7.20XX

9 Sub-committee reports: Reports were accepted as presented. Mandy Baker has resigned from the youth action sub-committee due to pressure of exam revision. It was agreed to write to Mandy thanking her for her contribution to the sub-committee. It was also agreed to seek a replacement youth representative.

MA to thank MB. GM to recruit new member.

10 Any other business: No other business.

11 Date of next meeting: 17.7.20XX

Meeting closed at 8.30pm.

CHECKLIST – RUNNING MEETINGS

 Date and time: Does the date clash with any major events, school holidays or religious celebrations? Is the timing of the meeting convenient for the majority of trustees?

Venue: Is the venue accessible to all trustees? Is there adequate space to run the meeting comfortably? Is the layout of the room suitable for a board meeting?

✓ Papers: Have all trustees had an opportunity to contribute to the agenda? Have the agenda, minutes of last meeting, financial reports and any further papers been circulated to the trustees in adequate time for them to prepare for the meeting?

✓ During the meeting: Have all distractions been dealt with (e.g. mobile phones switched off)? Is any necessary equipment in place (e.g. for presentations)? Are refreshments available? Is the meeting room at a comfortable temperature? Is discussion being kept to the agenda?

✓ Is everyone able to contribute to the debate? Is the meeting keeping to time?

✓ After the meeting: Are clear decisions being made? Has follow-up action been clearly defined and allocated and a timescale agreed? Has a date and venue for the next meeting been agreed? Have draft minutes been agreed by the chair and circulated to the board within a reasonable time following the end of the meeting? Have trustees followed up on agreed action points as appropriate?

Board appraisal

As the body with overall responsibility for the organisation, it is essential that a board functions effectively. Voluntary sector boards are increasingly recognising just how much the quality of their work impacts on the organisation and are considering their own performance, as well as the external work of the charity.

Board appraisal may have a number of purposes and take on a range of forms. At one extreme, it may be that the board no longer serves the needs of the charity and that the appraisal is part of an entire review of the governance structure; at the other, it may be a regular review of the contribution of individual board members and their function as a unit, used as a means of further developing individuals and improving board performance.

Whatever the format, board appraisal inevitably involves a high level of critical inspection of individual board members, their fellow trustees and the board as a whole. Understandably, this can be a difficult process and the whole concept of board appraisal can be challenging for many board members. It is therefore essential that all trustees are committed to the process and that the purpose of the exercise is clearly defined. It can take many months, if not years, of persuasion before the board as a whole feels ready to undertake such an exercise. Given the potential delicacy of the appraisal, it is essential that it is properly planned and executed.

Timing and purpose

The timing and purpose of a board appraisal are closely linked, as the stage of the charity's development is likely to determine the purpose of the appraisal. However, it is not advisable to undertake an appraisal during periods of crisis or conflict within the charity as the trustees are unlikely to agree a common purpose for the appraisal and the process risks deepening, rather than resolving, any conflict. In addition, the appraisal would distract the trustees from the primary purpose of addressing the crisis or conflict. More appropriate options are to conduct the appraisal following the appointment of a new chief executive, election of a new chair, in response to new funding (particularly if this will bring about large growth), a new business plan or some other external or internal factor. The purpose of the appraisal may be to ensure that the board is equipped to govern the charity following change or to plan or implement future developments. Equally, it may be for a more internal aim (e.g. to agree the boundaries between the roles of the board and chief executive or to clarify trustee roles and functions following the election of a new chair). The Belbin model of team roles, described at p. 99 would be helpful in this context.

Whatever the outcome of the decision, the purpose of the exercise should be clear and should determine the content of the appraisal.

Method

There are a number of methods of board appraisal. The most appropriate in each case will depend on the purpose of the appraisal and, perhaps most importantly, the culture of the board. For example, a board questionnaire would be best suited to a regular review of board function, whereas a detailed examination of the performance of a board laden with strong personalities and complex histories may be better conducted by an independent external facilitator. A thorough board appraisal exercise may involve a combination of different methods.

Do-it-yourself or independent consultant?

Perhaps the first question to address once the purpose of the appraisal has been agreed is whether to conduct the appraisal internally or to draw on the resources of an external facilitator or consultant. The table on p.104 summarises the advantages and disadvantages of both approaches.

The key question to ask may well be: would the board tolerate an outsider's intervention and accept the conclusions expressed or would they disregard any unpopular or difficult opinions? Much will depend on the quality of the independent consultant.

For boards that seek objectivity in the appraisal exercise but cannot afford the expense of an external facilitator, a compromise solution may be available in the form of a trustee from another organisation undertaking the appraisal. In this way charities can enter into reciprocal appraisal arrangements with like-minded organisations.

Internally managed board appraisals are often led by a sub-group of the trustee board. Although staff may input into the appraisal, they should not lead it.

DIY VS INDEPENDENT CONSULTANT

Advantages	Disadvantages
Knowing the issues, the history, the personalities and the desired outcome (rather than the conclusion) so the process can be sensitive to these	Lacks objectivity
	Lacks a fresh approach
	It may not be possible for people to be completely honest
	Labour intensive
Maintaining ownership	
Maintaining continuity	
Low out-of-pocket expenses	

Independent, external consultant

Advantages	Disadvantages
Objective	No knowledge of the history of the charity and the personalities involved
Fresh approach	
New ideas	Board may lose ownership
Experience of similar exercises with similar groups	May not be able to ensure implementation
Facilitates honesty and openness	Can be expensive

CHECKLIST – CHOOSING AN INDEPENDENT CONSULTANT

The correct choice of independent consultant is essential if an appraisal is to be successful. In selecting a consultant, charities should make their selection from a number of individuals or organisations, with particular attention to the following:

☑ Does the individual have appropriate experience of board appraisal within your type of organisation and circumstances?

☑ Can the consultant give references or recommendations from other voluntary groups?

☑ Does the consultant understand the issues affecting your charity and is he or she sympathetic to them?

☑ Does he or she listen to you?

☑ Do your board members respect the consultant?

☑ Is the method of appraisal proposed appropriate to your board?

☑ Will the proposed content of the process deliver the desired purposes?

☑ Will the consultant present his or her conclusions and recommendations in a manner which is useful to your board?

☑ Will the consultant undertake any follow up work?

Questionnaires

Questionnaires may be the first point of any appraisal process. These can provide information on areas of concern for trustees that will later form the focus for discussion. Trustees should be given adequate time to complete the questionnaires and arrangements should be made for trustees to complete them, anonymously if necessary.

Group discussions

These stimulate debate as different ideas can be raised and discussed. Group discussions may involve the whole board or small groups. Although some flexibility may be desirable, discussion should be based on an agenda. Such discussions should be conducted separately from regular trustee meetings. Many charities have 'away days' or retreats to discuss these issues away from daily distractions.

Individual interviews

These can be a constructive way of identifying the feelings of individual trustees towards the board as a whole and in respect of their own role on the board.

Conclusion and implementation

Whatever the method of appraisal, the process should end with the preparation of a conclusion. This should include a summary of the findings, an interpretation of what these findings mean and proposals for moving forward. Whether the appraisal is conducted internally or externally, the conclusion should be in written form and distributed to the whole board. In many cases, those responsible for the appraisal will also give a presentation of their conclusions. The document and presentation then serve as a starting point for the board to discuss the next course of action. Again, it may be best to have this debate at a retreat or an 'away day', as this allows time for options to be discussed fully, free from the distractions of other board business.

The board may decide to implement any proposals in their entirety or to take a more selective approach. Whatever the outcome, an implementation and review plan should be developed in order to ensure that the proposals are carried through and the work is not lost. As with all plans, this should look at actions, identify those responsible for each action and set timescales. Where significant changes are being made, due consideration should be given to the impact on all those involved and reviews built into the plan to monitor the progress of implementation and the efficacy of any new systems.

6 Trustee–staff relations: roles and responsibilities

INTRODUCTION

Establishing a healthy working relationship between trustees and staff is one of the hardest elements of charity management to get right and there are no absolute answers. This chapter looks at some of the problem issues, from recruitment and selection through to dealing with conflict issues and legal requirements. The legal framework relating to employment is discussed in this chapter, but the application of the law can be complex and specialist advice should be sought on any areas of concern. Personnel management and staff development are beyond the scope of this guide, but the Directory includes suggested reading on these issues.

Employing staff

The majority of charities start their lives by being run on an entirely voluntary basis, so trustees' roles extend beyond the governance function into day-to-day administrative and operational activities. Often this work is supported by a wider body of volunteers. This method of administration is entirely appropriate for voluntary organisations and many will never move beyond this model. However, for many charities there may come a point when, in order to ensure the survival of the organisation, to uphold the quality of its work or to expand its activities, it will be necessary to employ paid staff.

When to employ

The decision to employ a paid member of staff should not be based solely on the availability of funds; rather it should be a strategic choice founded in the wider context of the organisation's maturity, current practice and plans for development. In many cases, charities can function extremely effectively and for long periods of time supported solely by the effort of volunteers. This can be a secure and stable method of operation when work is evenly spread over a large body of volunteers and does not require huge commitments of time or resources, but there is an inherent vulnerability in organisations that are heavily dependent on a small group of volunteers. Such volunteers are difficult to replace and the departure of any one of them can have catastrophic effects on the operation of the organisation. Here the appointment of a member of staff, for example to undertake administrative duties and coordinate voluntary effort, can bring stability and continuity to the service. Although individual employees can become just as invaluable to the organisation as committed volunteers, the paid nature of their role makes staff much easier to replace.

Even where workloads are evenly spread amongst a large number of volunteers, many organisations find that there is a limit to what can be achieved by voluntary work alone and that it is necessary to employ staff to support any expansion of the service.

Whether staff are to be appointed to maintain or expand the service, the decision to employ them should be made not just in the context of a development plan for the service, but also with regard to the maturity of the board. The appointment of staff has major legal and governance implications as the charity/trustees will become employers. A board should not embark upon employing people unless the trustees understand the scope and nature of their legal responsibilities and are able to handle the softer (and often very tricky) elements of staff management, such as defining boundaries between board and staff and reviewing performance. It is important for trustees to have access to appropriate advice and support, whether this be through paid legal services or through a voluntary sector umbrella body.

In the voluntary sector, the biggest barrier to the employment of staff is the ability to pay wages. With the exception of endowed charities, most voluntary organisations will need to fundraise to finance staff salaries. Although large, well established, charities may raise significant sums through public donations and legacies, many voluntary sector employers will be dependent on grant income to cover salary costs. Given the intense competition for funds, whether from statutory bodies, lottery distributors, corporate foundations or charitable trusts, the charity will need to demonstrate that the appointment is necessary and that it has the capacity to recruit and manage staff properly. As a result, charities are often required to undertake much preparatory work in terms of agreeing job descriptions, setting salary levels and initiating appropriate infrastructure changes before funding can be secured.

Perhaps the most important element, whether employing a lone worker or the tenth member of the team, is to determine the exact function of that employee. It is tempting for trustees appointing their first member of staff to identify those aspects of the organisational workload that they like least and delegate this to the worker, retaining their own direct involvement in the more enjoyable elements of operation. This rarely results in an attractive or cohesive post and can lead to difficulties in determining boundaries between staff and trustees. It is far better to identify an element, or an appropriate collection of elements, of work that can be delegated to a member of staff without undermining the trustees' governance control.

Recruiting staff

The first step in any employment process is determining what that member of staff will do. Charities should not appoint just because they need another pair of hands. There should be clear guidelines as to the function of each worker. This may be very obvious in some cases, for example where elements of the charity's work are not being carried out, or where there is a need that is not being met by existing services. On many occasions it is more complex, and it may be necessary to review the operation of the organisation as a whole to identify those elements that would be best delivered by a paid member of staff. Issues to consider include whether the employee will:

- have operational responsibility;
- be involved in the direct delivery of services;
- undertake administrative tasks;
- manage other workers or volunteers;
- have a strategic or policy role;
- have any financial responsibility; and/or
- represent the organisation to external bodies and the wider public.

When determining the functions to be carried out by the employee, first consider the skills and experience that will be needed to undertake the role, paying particular attention to whether any one person is likely to possess the full range of skills and experience required. Trustees should be particularly wary of any requirements that are mutually exclusive or otherwise incompatible. It is quite common and reasonable to expect a project manager or lone worker within a small organisation to undertake managerial, administrative, financial and operational functions, but if someone with nursing skills is required, do not expect that individual to be an accountant, or vice versa. Once these issues have been decided, they should be recorded in the two documents that are critical to the recruitment process (i.e. the job description and the person specification).

CASE EXAMPLE

Problem: A small community charity had been running a range of services for several years, including a holiday play scheme and a lunch club for older people. The activities were run by the trustees and a group of volunteers. The trustees were struggling with the workload and finding it increasingly difficult to sustain the service. This pressure led to the resignation of a number of trustees, further increasing the burden on the remaining board members. They felt that the appointment of a member of staff would relieve the operational responsibilities of trustees. The service was highly valued by the local authority which indicated that it would provide a grant to finance a worker's salary. The trustees were keen to appoint a worker, but remained undecided about his or her exact role.

Solution: The trustees reviewed the services offered by the charity and its internal management activities, identifying those areas that were currently causing problems. They then considered which elements could be packaged together to form the job description of the worker. The trustees decided to delegate operational tasks such as the recruitment and coordination of volunteers, acceptance of referrals and service delivery to the worker. They also delegated day-to-day administrative duties. However, the trustees understood that the recruitment of new board members and compliance with legislation and good practice in relation to the services offered were governance roles and they should retain direct control over these areas.

Job description

The term is self-explanatory. The job description describes the job. It should give a clear indication to trustees, funders and (most importantly) applicants about the nature and scope of the job. It should include the following information:

- the name of the organisation;
- job title;
- purpose of the job;
- hours of work;
- rate of pay plus any other benefits (e.g. pension, car, health insurance etc.);
- who the post will be managed by;
- any management responsibilities;
- place of work;
- annual leave entitlement and any arrangements for overtime payments, time off in lieu of overtime payments, or flexible working arrangements;
- principal duties: these may give an outline of tasks to be undertaken or include more detail regarding the conduct of the duties (e.g. to work in partnership on particular aspects of the work); and
- any ancillary duties.

Job descriptions should be fairly succinct. A job description that extends beyond two sides of A4 gives a fairly clear indication that the job is either too much for one person, or that the trustees are being highly prescriptive in determining how the employee should carry out the work.

SAMPLE JOB DESCRIPTION

Anycounty Children and Families Forum

Job description

Title:	Coordinator
Responsible to:	Chair of the Board of Trustees
Responsible for:	Administrator
Salary:	£22,000–£26,000 per annum plus 5% pension contribution
Hours:	35 hours per week
Usual office hours:	9am–5pm with a lunch break of one hour. Occasional evening and weekend work required. Time off in lieu of overtime is available.
Annual leave:	25 days per annum, plus bank holidays
Place of work:	Anytown CVS, Anytown
Purpose:	Responsible for coordinating the work of Forum members and volunteers to achieve the organisation's aims of improving services for children and families in the county.

SAMPLE JOB DESCRIPTION continued

Principal duties:

1 To represent the Forum to other agencies.

2 To collate information on service provision and developments and present this information to Forum members and relevant third parties.

3 To canvas the opinion of Forum members on relevant issues, developments and documents and present these opinions to third parties as appropriate.

4 To support the development of new services for children and families in the county.

5 To coordinate the activities of Forum members through supporting special interest groups and other *ad hoc* bodies.

6 To assess the training needs of Forum members and arrange training as appropriate.

7 To organise and attend all meetings of the Forum and the board of trustees.

8 To manage the Forum administrator.

9 To report to the board of trustees on a quarterly basis.

Other tasks:

1 To prepare the annual report of the Forum, in partnership with the trustees.

2 To take part in fundraising events arranged by the trustees.

3 To compile monitoring information.

Person specification

The person specification should describe the skills, experience, knowledge and qualifications required of the employee. Applicants should be able to assess, from reading the person specification, whether they are suitable candidates for the job. Person specifications are normally presented as a table, stating whether the requirements are essential or desirable.

Some organisations also include personal qualities within the person specification. This should only be done where absolutely necessary, objective and relevant to the post. For example, it may be essential that an outreach worker be flexible but it is not necessary for a charity shop manager to have a 'good sense of humour', neither can such a quality be objectively defined.

tip

Adapt job descriptions and person specifications from those developed for similar jobs in other organisations. It may be possible to ask other organisations for copies of the relevant documents, or request job descriptions and person specifications for similar posts advertised in the press.

SAMPLE PERSON SPECIFICATION

**Anytown Children and Families Forum
Coordinator – Person Specification**

	Essential	**Desirable**
Skills	Good written and verbal communication skills. Good analytical skills.	
Experience	Minimum two years' experience of working in the voluntary sector. Experience of multi-agency work. Experience of working with children and families. Experience of organising meetings and conferences. Compilation of written reports.	Staff management. Arranging training. Monitoring and evaluation of individual pieces of work and/or projects.
Knowledge	Legal framework for children and families services.	Service provision in any county.
Qualifications		Recognised professional or academic qualification in relation to the voluntary sector, social care, management, teaching or youth work.
Other	Commitment to equal opportunities.	Clean driving licence and access to a car.

Setting salary levels and hours

It is important to get salary levels and the hours of work right. Salary is one of the key factors that applicants consider when looking for a job. As well as the fundamental question of whether the job pays enough to cover living expenses, salary also indicates the level of the job and whether it is a realistic prospect for the applicant. It is unlikely that someone on a current salary of £20,000 would apply for a £50,000 job, but it would not be overly ambitious to apply for a post paying £25,000. Salaries should be appropriate to the relative seniority of the post, the responsibility of the role and the required skills and experience of the postholder. Where there are existing staff within an organisation, there should be a proper pay structure which will include any new posts. The contracted hours should be realistic for the amount of work involved, and this should be checked by calculating the volume of work involved per week for each of the tasks within the job description. Poor pay and part-time posts are not uncommon in the voluntary sector, but there are myths regarding both (see box on p. 115 opposite). The setting of salaries should take account of the statutory rules regarding the payment of a minimum wage.

Charities adopt a variety of approaches to determine salaries.

1   Many local charities base staff salaries on local authority pay scales, for example setting the remuneration of a project worker at the same level as a social worker or a project manager at the same level as a senior social worker or social work manager.

2   Another option is to gather information about the salaries of comparable workers in other organisations. Look for posts with a similar level of responsibility that require similar skills and experience. This could be done either by contacting organisations directly or through reviewing job advertisements in the newspapers.

3   Where the organisation has a pay structure in place, consider the responsibilities of the post and the position within the organisational hierarchy when setting pay levels.

4   Consider regional variations – accommodation and transport costs are generally much higher in London and the South East and this is reflected in salaries and salary expectations.

Once job descriptions and person specifications are in place and salaries and hours of work have been set, it is time to start the recruitment process.

VOLUNTARY SECTOR MYTHS

Myth: 'People work in the sector because they are committed to the cause. We don't have to pay them much.'

Reality: It is true that voluntary sector pay is generally less than in comparable posts in the corporate sector. It is also true that voluntary sector staff largely accept this, perhaps because they are committed to the cause, because the work offers greater flexibility, or because organisational structures are less hierarchical. Whatever the reason, this does not justify deliberate underpayment. Although it may save money in the short term, this approach is counter-productive. It will discourage many suitable candidates from applying for the post and staff will feel exploited and undervalued, often resulting in high staff turnover. It also undermines equal opportunities, as only those staff who can afford to be poorly paid, usually because they have another source of income, will take the jobs. This is particularly a problem in areas of high employment and housing costs.

Myth: 'Part-time staff always put in extra hours, so why pay for a full-time worker?'

Reality: It is true that many part-time staff do work additional hours when necessary but this should not be a weekly occurrence due to the demands of the workload. People choose to work part-time because of their domestic commitments or other lifestyle choices and many will either not be prepared or able to work unpaid hours. To pay someone to work part-time and expect him or her to put in a 35-hour week is exploitative (and potentially in breach of national minimum wage legislation).

CAUTION

When considering the amount your charity can afford to pay in salary, remember to include the employer's national insurance contributions. This is the amount an employer is required to pay in national insurance for each member of staff. Contributions are calculated as a percentage of any salary above the earnings threshold. Rates and the threshold are subject to change every April, but as a rough guide contributions have recently been around 12–13% of salary above £5,200. HMRC publishes information on the current rates (www.hmrc.gov.uk/rates/nic.htm).

The recruitment process

Where to advertise?

Recruitment advertising is expensive but worthwhile as it is in the charity's interest for information about the post to be made available to as many people as possible. Many charities try to save resources by recruiting through word of mouth and advertising in a selection of newsletters or by e-mail. However, this method severely restricts the scope of the people who may hear about the vacancy. As a result, equal opportunities best practice is undermined and potential candidates may be overlooked. Instead, it is best practice to advertise in publicly available media, including general newspapers and specialist press. The internet provides another means of advertising.

The choice of advertising media will depend on the nature of the job and the person specification, with the location of the advertisement targeted at the most likely applicants. People looking for jobs will review the publications that best suit their requirements, so consider whether jobs should be advertised either nationally or locally, in the general press, in sector-specific media or in publications targeted at professionals. As a rule of thumb, national jobs should be nationally advertised. Within this, trustees may decide to target the voluntary sector itself, for example through special weekly supplements in national newspapers or sector publications such as *Third Sector*. Alternatively, trustees may decide to target a particular profession, for example through the IT pages of national newspapers or through professional journals such as *Community Care* (a publication on social work issues). This latter approach will be particularly relevant if the person specification requires an identified qualification (in this case in social work) as an essential requirement, but will be less suitable if this is only one of the acceptable qualifications specified alongside, say, a youth work or teaching qualification.

There may also be occasions when it is appropriate to advertise through lifestyle publications or those targeted at minority groups; for example, when recruiting staff to work within the lesbian, gay and transgender community or particular ethnic groups. Before going down this route, however, trustees should be aware of the statutory restrictions around positive discrimination (i.e. treating someone with a particular characteristic favourably, which in general terms is prohibited) and positive action (i.e. taking steps to assist groups which are underrepresented in a particular job).

Just because national jobs should be advertised nationally, this does not mean local jobs should only be advertised locally. Trustees should consider the nature of the job, the rate of pay, the skills required and whether people would be prepared to travel to work or relocate to take up the post. Local newspapers, even when part of a group of publications, tend to have limited geographic circulation and their recruitment advertising pages tend to focus on semi-skilled and unskilled jobs. Local advertising may, therefore, be entirely appropriate for the recruitment of care workers or administrative assistants, but not for managers or development workers.

Draw up a list of possible publications and websites for your recruitment advertisement. Review the recruitment pages to see if they include posts similar to the vacancy you will be advertising. Telephone some of the organisations that have placed advertisements and ask them what volume of response (and the quality of the responses) they have had to their advertisement.

Many voluntary sector funders will include recruitment costs for new workers within the amount of any grant. When replacing existing staff, there is often a delay between the departure of the previous employee and the start date of the new employee. This salary underspend can be used to finance recruitment advertisements. A rough guide would be to spend up to one month's salary on the advertising fee.

What to say?

Recruitment advertisements need to catch the eye of potential applicants, but they also need to communicate enough information to enable people to decide whether they want to request further details. As a minimum they should state:

- the name of the employer;
- the title of the post;
- the salary;
- the hours of work (including any evening or weekend work);
- the key elements of the job;
- the skills and experience required of applicants, including any definite restrictions or requirements (e.g. any professional qualification required);
- the place of work and any flexible working opportunities;

- the deadline for applications;
- the date of interviews (often expressed as a week, rather than a specific day); and
- how to obtain further information.

Many advertisements also contain a statement regarding the charity's commitment to equal opportunities.

Job advertisements may quote salary as a range (e.g. £22,000–£25,000 depending on the experience of the worker or as a starting salary with progression to the upper level). If the post is part-time, the advertisement should clearly state whether the salary quoted is for those hours or work (e.g. '£12,571 for 20 hours', or whether it is the full-time salary which will be reduced to take account of the part-time hours, e.g. '£22,000 pro rata'). In describing the main aspects of the role, organisations often include the challenges as well as the positive elements of the job.

Application packs or CVs?

It is good equal opportunities practice to use application packs and forms rather than to request CVs. This ensures that the same information is asked of all applicants and enables applicants to describe the specific relevance of their skills and experience to the advertised post. Applicants may, of course, attach their CVs if they wish.

Application packs should contain information about the organisation and the post. As a minimum they should contain the job description, person specification and application form. Many organisations also include documents such as the latest annual report, publicity literature and information about the background or context of the post. It is good practice to keep a record of the application packs distributed.

Application forms should request the following information:
- name and contact details;
- qualifications;
- work history (i.e. previous employers, job titles and responsibilities);
- other relevant experience (e.g. voluntary work and personal interests);
- supporting information: here applicants should be invited to explain how they meet the person specification;
- references; and
- equal opportunities monitoring form. The monitoring form should

be separate from, or detachable from, the main application form. The monitoring form should not include any data that identifies the applicant, but should ask for information on ethnicity, gender and disability. Once received, these forms should be separated from the application and used by the organisation to monitor the number of applications received from minority groups.

For many charities, the cost and time involved in sending acknowledgements to every applicant is prohibitive. If this is the case, include in the application pack a statement to the effect that only shortlisted applicants will be contacted, or ask applicants to enclose a stamped addressed envelope or a postcard that will be returned to them as receipt of their application.

Shortlisting, interviews and making your decision

Before shortlisting applicants for interview, the organisation should agree who will be on the interviewing panel. For senior positions, the panel should include at least one trustee. The interview panel should be involved in the shortlisting process, with additional input from other trustees or staff members as appropriate. It is important for the person who will be managing the new staff member to be involved at this stage.

Shortlisting should be based solely on the information submitted in the application and should focus on the extent to which each candidate meets the requirements of the person specification. Those who meet the requirements most closely should be invited for interview. The ideal number of candidates to interview is between four and six. This provides an adequate number for comparison, whilst remaining manageable.

The purpose of the interview is to gain additional information about the candidates and assess their suitability for the job and the organisation. The interviews should be planned in advance and all questions and tests should be relevant to the post. For example, a project manager may be required to give presentations in the course of the job, so it would be reasonable to ask candidates to give a presentation as part of the interview. However, the same would not be true of an administrative assistant, although applicants for that post could fairly be required to undertake a document production test. Under good equal opportunities practice, every candidate should have the same interview experience. This means that all candidates should be asked the same basic questions, although supplementary questions may be asked in relation to information given on the application form or responses during the interview. The interview panel should agree the questions in advance, the information they hope to receive in response ('model answers'), who will ask each questions, and how the responses will be scored.

Interview questions should address an applicant's previous experience and its relevance to the post, their skills in the context of the job (e.g. do they have the necessary analytical skills to summarise consultation papers and debate the key issues arising from them?) and their ability to deal with any challenges inherent to the job or the organisation. Scenario questions can be very useful (i.e. 'what would you do if...?'). Interview panels should not be wary of addressing any difficult issues relating to the post. If the role involves working with challenging individuals, ask applicants what experience they have had of similar situations and how they have managed them.

The scoring methods used in interviews vary in terms of the totals used (e.g. marks out of 3, 5 or 6) and whether the interview panel debates and agrees a score against each question or simply adds all the scores of individual panel members together. Similarly, some questions may be considered to be more important than others and scores should be weighted accordingly. The approach to scoring should be consistent across all candidates – the model answers agreed by the interview panel can be extremely helpful here. When scoring responses, interviewers should remember that few applicants will be able to answer every question perfectly, but it is important to find someone with the potential to do the job. In this context relevant skills and a willingness and ability to learn can be more valuable than knowledge.

Scoring is useful in bringing objectivity into the assessment of candidates, but is rarely adequate on its own. Although interview panels should not be unduly swayed by a candidate's personality, this can have a significant bearing on an individual's ability to work within the organisation. What impact would an introvert chief executive have on an extrovert staff team or vice versa? Would the candidate be accepted by the client group? Less formal selection procedures can be used to help make these decisions (e.g. all candidates could be invited to lunch with the staff team or a group of users). Staff and users could then be invited to give their feedback on the applicants to the interview panel. This 'trial by sandwich' interview is frequently used in the voluntary sector.

Second interviews, with a slightly different panel, may be appropriate for senior jobs or where the interview panel is having difficulty deciding between two or more candidates.

The favoured candidate should be offered the position subject to references. If he or she refuses the position, the interview panel will need to consider whether any of the other candidates interviewed were suitable, or whether the post should be re-advertised. Unsuccessful candidates should be offered feedback.

The time it takes to appoint new staff can be surprisingly lengthy, as illustrated in the table below.

TIMESCALE FOR RECRUITMENT AND SELECTION

Week 1: Place advertisement. Allow at least three weeks for applicants to request and receive application packs and then complete and return them.

Week 4: Shortlisting by interview panel and invitations to interview. Allow at least one week for shortlisting and sending out invitations and a minimum of one week's notice for shortlisted candidates.

Week 6: Interviews and offer. Allow a week for interview, decision, offer and acceptance. Many candidates will not resign from their current post until they have received a written offer. Further time will be required for taking up references. Although telephone references are quick, they should always be followed up in writing.

Once an offer has been accepted and satisfactory references provided, the new employee can start work, subject to the notice period of his or her existing job if currently employed. This could be up to three months or even longer for senior posts.

Total: 11 weeks +

The timescale shows the recruitment process from the placement of the advertisement, assuming that job descriptions etc. are already in place. In reality the process may take much longer. Where an existing member of staff is being replaced, it is good practice to review the job description and person specification before recruitment starts. This, together with agreeing the wording of the advertisement, can easily add another couple of weeks to the process.

Consider this timescale when determining the notice periods of your staff. If the charity really cannot function with a particular post being vacant, it may be useful to set a longer notice period than the standard one month, so that the length of vacancy is eliminated or at least minimised. Unfortunately this is of little benefit if the appointee also has a long notice period in his or her current role.

Once the successful candidate accepts the post, references should be taken up and start dates agreed. Other practical issues such as arranging desk space and IT systems log-ins and setting up payroll, etc will also need to be considered. Larger organisations may have internal structures in place for paying staff, deducting PAYE, tax and national insurance and paying employers' national insurance contributions. Smaller organisations may procure payroll services from other agencies. This service is often provided at low or no cost to local charities by local authorities (especially where the local authority is the funder), councils for voluntary services and community accountancy schemes.

When to use an agency

Rather than manage the whole recruitment and selection process themselves, some charities choose to use a recruitment agency. Agencies cater for every level of recruitment with some being sector or job specific, so whether recruiting for a care worker or a chief executive, there will be an appropriate agency.

The input of agencies into the process varies, with some drawing solely from their client base and others placing advertisements. The agency may shortlist a number of possible candidates from its existing clients and pass these forward for interview. Alternatively, it may actively solicit applications for the post, conduct initial interviews and pass a few candidates to the charity for final selection.

The charges made by agencies for these services vary, often taking the form of a percentage of salary for a successful placement. This can be an expensive form of recruitment, placing it beyond the reach of many charities, but it can be valuable to organisations that do not have the time, skills or contacts to manage the process themselves.

Defining boundaries

One of the most difficult problems within charities and one that frequently leads to friction, is drawing a line between the work of staff and that of trustees. As has been seen in the earlier chapters of this book, trustees have wide-ranging responsibilities and these cannot be delegated. The trustees are ultimately responsible for the charity and are potentially liable when things go wrong. Trustees can, however, delegate tasks that need to be conducted in the execution of their responsibilities. We have also seen that, in individual charities, trustees often take on roles that extend way beyond their legal responsibilities (e.g. by becoming involved in the operation of the charity). It is in the area of these delegated tasks and additional trustee activities that boundaries often become blurred.

The importance of agreeing the boundaries between trustee and staff activities can not be overemphasised. Where boundaries are ill-defined, there is a risk of staff and trustees tripping over each other in attempting to do the same work, leading at best to an unnecessary duplication of effort and at worst to resentment, mixed messages and the appearance of managerial incompetence. At the other extreme, whole aspects of activity risk being lost in a no man's land between trustee and staff roles.

So how can this be avoided? Unfortunately, there is no model solution. The distinctions between trustee and staff workloads will vary between organisations and within organisations over time. A useful starting point is for trustees to identify those areas of their responsibility over which they want to retain complete control and those which they are prepared to delegate. This was discussed earlier in the chapter when we looked at the function of staff and drafting job descriptions. In this context the value of the job description is apparent, as it provides documentary evidence of the boundaries. This can be further supported by including discussion of boundaries within the induction programme for new staff and trustees. Similarly, the business plan and other planning tools can be used to determine the work plans of both staff and trustees.

Circumstances will, however, inevitably arise which fall outside anybody's job description or work plan and both trustees and staff will often need to be flexible in determining responsibility for areas that are beyond the usual parameters. In order for such dilemmas to be negotiated appropriately, it is crucial that there is mutual respect between the trustees and the staff. This means that staff must acknowledge the overarching responsibilities of trustees and their need to retain control, whilst trustees must respect the fact that staff are paid to do a job and have been appointed, hopefully, because they have the skills and experience necessary to do the job properly. In this sense, you must allow your staff to get on with the job that they are paid to do.

CASE EXAMPLE

A charity providing home care services to people with disabilities had a staff team of 15 people. The majority of employees were care workers, with a senior employee responsible for management of the service and administrative duties. Trustees set policy in relation to quality standards for the service provided and health and safety issues. One of the care workers contacted the senior employee with concerns regarding the administration of medicines. The senior employee directed the worker as to the appropriate course of action and communicated the information to the other care workers so that they would know what to do in similar circumstances.

The trustees felt that the senior employee had acted outside her authority by instructing the worker on a health and safety issue. However, the employee believed that her actions were justified; it was a management issue and the advice she had given was consistent with organisational policy, as determined by the trustees. The incident was discussed in a regular line management meeting between the senior employee and the chair, with both sides presenting their arguments. The senior employee explained that the situation had required a swift response and she had acted within the terms of the health and safety policy and the organisation's insurance. She also highlighted her staff management role and her nursing background, believing that this qualified her to make such decisions. The chair accepted this argument.

Any problems that do arise should be discussed through appropriate procedures (i.e. line management, supervision and appraisal). The usual management structure in charities is for the most senior employee to report to the chair of the board of trustees, and for that employee to then manage any other staff. In large organisations there may be several layers of staff management. Some charities, particularly those with relatively flat internal management structures, operate a system where the various members of the senior staff are each managed by different trustees. Although there is a degree of common sense in this approach, in that workloads are shared, its success rests on strong communication between the trustees. Without good communication it is unlikely that the trustees will give consistent messages to the staff team.

Particular problems may arise where trustees also act as volunteers for the organisation and are then coordinated or managed by staff who are employed to run the service. This can be an awkward situation for staff and trustees alike and, again, there needs to be a mutual respect as to each other's roles. The trustees in question need to recognise that the employee has been appointed to manage the service and must be empowered to do so. The trustees should value the experience and opinions of the employee just as the employee should recognise that trustees with an understanding of operational practice and the issues faced by users are valuable board members. The situation may be helped by clear guidance to all volunteers of their role in operational issues and the responsibility of the employees to ensure the quality and safety of the service.

CASE EXAMPLE

A small charity had been running a day centre for older people for some years. The service had been run on an entirely voluntary basis, but this was becoming harder to sustain and the trustees sought and gained funding to appoint a manager. The post was advertised and the job description and person specification clearly stated that the role would include management responsibilities – this was also reflected in the salary. An appropriately skilled professional was appointed. When he started work, the trustees handed over administrative and operational tasks, but continued to act as volunteers, attending the centre on a daily basis and giving instructions to the other volunteers. The manager's role was regularly undermined by the trustees and he resigned within six months.

The chair/chief executive relationship

As has been mentioned earlier in this chapter, it is usually the chair of the board of trustees who manages the most senior employee. The term 'chief executive' is commonly used in the voluntary sector and is used here to describe the most senior staff role, whatever the actual title used.

It is not overstating the case to say that the success, or otherwise, of a charity frequently rests on the quality of this relationship. A positive, strong working relationship between chair and chief executive can lead a charity to great success. At the other extreme, a poor relationship can cripple the organisation. Poor relationships take a variety of forms:

- *Strong chair/strong chief executive.* This blend can be an asset to the charity, if the chair and chief executive work in harmony; however, if they do not, the resulting conflict will stifle any development and undermine the morale of the organisation as a whole.
- *Strong chair/weak chief executive.* In this circumstance, the chief executive may not be empowered to do his or her job and may end up working within a very small comfort zone. This is clearly unhealthy for organisational progress.
- *Weak chair/strong chief executive.* This relationship can undermine the authority of the governing body as there is a strong risk that the chief executive will manage the board, rather than the other way round. Although this may seem like an advantageous situation for chief executives, they will have little direction or constructive feedback from the board and will find themselves stranded when they most need support.
- *Weak chair/weak chief executive.* Charities that suffer from this governance/management relationship are likely to stagnate.

The ideal chair/chief executive relationship is an elusive balance between the two roles, where both are equipped to carry out their roles competently and with vision but without conflict. Chairs should lead the board in setting the direction of the charity and chief executives should act as the bridge between policy and operation, board and staff, and in their turn leading the staff team to achieve the charity's goals.

The relationship between chair and chief executive is crucial and charities should invest time and resources in cultivating it, starting at the recruitment stage. Chairs and chief executives should discuss their relative roles and working relationship. Where conflicts cannot be resolved by internal means, it may be worth calling on the help of an independent mediator.

The role of staff in supporting trustees

As the governing body of the organisation, one of the trustees' functions is to provide staff with the resources and support they need to achieve their job description. However, the relationship works both ways. Staff members also have a role in supporting the trustees in executing their responsibilities and some staff may be appointed expressly for this purpose.

By virtue of their daily involvement, the staff has an in-depth working knowledge of their organisation that is rarely experienced by voluntary trustees. They also have a range of professional skills and support networks that are not present or otherwise available to the trustee board. Similarly, staff may have time available and access to technology that may not be available to the trustees. As a result, staff members often play a key role in supporting the board.

This support may take a variety of forms, ranging from agenda planning and minute taking, induction of trustees (see chapter 3), arranging trustee training and providing speeches or briefings, through to providing the trustees with the information necessary for the board to make decisions regarding the charity. Such information or training may be general or specific to the charity. For example, the staff is often responsible for passing information to trustees on wider legal issues, but will also play a key role in informing trustees about the charity's services and finances and opportunities for development. It is not uncommon in well-staffed charities for senior staff to present complex reports to trustees, analysing wide-ranging information regarding the charity and the wider context of its operation and considering the different options for action and the implications of each. Whilst trustees should value this support (it is, after all, what the charity pays its staff for) they should not lose overall control, for no matter how competent the staff, it is the trustees who retain responsibility and liability for the charity.

Staff should also be wary of stepping outside the boundaries of their employment contracts. This is particularly true for staff of charitable companies as the concept of 'shadow directors' means that staff (or other non-board members) who have directed the board may share the responsibility and liability of the board for the decisions made.

Role of the company secretary

Charitable companies with a company secretary have the benefit of an appointment that is dedicated to supporting the governance of the organisation. Whether the company secretary is a post in its own right or whether the role is combined with that of the chief executive, finance director, other senior staff member, or a trustee, it is the company secretary's responsibility to ensure that the charity is run within the law and according to the terms of its governing document. A key element of this role is to support the trustees and help them to navigate their way through legal and constitutional requirements. This includes ensuring that trustees are correctly appointed and inducted and that board and members' meetings are properly run. In fulfilling this role, company secretaries work extremely closely with the board, particularly the chair.

When appointing a company secretary, due attention must be given to the demands of the role. Signing annual returns is only a minor element of the company secretarial function, but demonstrates the significant responsibility that the secretary has for the probity of the organisation. Company secretaries in charities should have a sound knowledge of both company and charity law and a basic knowledge of other legislation affecting the organisation and should use this knowledge to support and advise the trustees. In particular, they should identify danger zones and advise trustees to call on appropriate professional advice when necessary.

The interpretation of the company secretary's function will vary from one organisation to another, but company secretaries' activities often include responsibility for property and insurance issues, internal controls and audits and provision of information to regulators. They may also take responsibility for ensuring legal compliance in areas such as fundraising and employment.

Private companies such as charitable companies limited by guarantee are no longer compelled by company law to appoint a company secretary. Although the requirement to appoint has disappeared, trustees of charitable companies must ensure that the duties normally undertaken by the company secretary are fulfilled – whether or not the title is used; in practice, many charities have retained the role of company secretary.

Resolving conflicts

As soon as an organisation employs staff, it should develop appropriate procedures for resolving conflict within the staff team and between staff and trustees. It is also good practice to have policies in place relating to conflicts involving volunteers.

Conflicts come in many forms. An occasional difference of opinion between individuals is normal and is often swiftly resolved by those directly involved. Where such differences continue and have an impact on the operation of the organisation, for example because of deteriorating internal communications, it may still be possible to address the conflict through informal means, for example if a manager or other third party is able to mediate in the dispute.

If, however, the situation is or becomes more serious, recourse to grievance and disciplinary procedures is imperative. Please see further below.

Legal issues

Recent years have seen extensive legislative changes in relation to employment issues. The following section gives an overview of the requirements; however the law can be complex (and is regularly revised) and all organisations employing paid staff are advised to seek appropriate legal advice regarding their individual responsibilities.

Employment contracts

The contractual relationship between employer and employee is determined by a combination of written documents and conduct. However, in the interests of clarity, it is good practice to provide employees with a written contract describing their terms and conditions of service. As a legal minimum, employers must provide all staff who are employed for longer than one month with a written 'statement of particulars' describing the key terms and conditions of employment. This should be issued to staff within two months of starting work and should contain the following:

- identity of employer;
- identity of employee;
- job title;
- start date (if the employee has changed jobs within the organisation, the original employment date should also be included);
- normal place of work (for home-based or travelling workers, include the base to which they report or the head office);
- remuneration and any non-financial benefits;
- working hours;
- period of employment (if fixed or temporary);
- holiday and holiday pay entitlement;
- notice period;
- sick pay entitlement;
- pension provision and retirement age;

- disciplinary and grievance arrangements;
- trade union recognition and other arrangements for collective agreements; and
- signatures.

Issues such as maternity/paternity/adoption leave entitlements, pension provision and any disciplinary/grievance procedure are likely to be covered by detailed policy documents. It is acceptable for the statement of particulars to make reference to these documents and how they can be obtained (e.g. in the staff handbook or on the organisation's intranet site) rather than to include the full text within the statement.

It is worth including information on any probation period in the statement of particulars, especially if different terms and conditions apply during this time (e.g. shorter notice periods).

Grievance, dismissal and disciplinary procedures

Trustees should be aware of how to deal with disciplinary and grievance situations in the workplace. This area of law is periodically revised but, at the time of writing, trustees would be well advised to familiarise themselves with the Code of Practice on disciplinary and grievance procedures published by ACAS, the conciliation service. Organisations should also consider whether it would be appropriate to create their own policies, incorporating these principles.

Grievance procedure

When does it apply? If a complaint is being made by an employee (or an ex-employee) of the charity and if the issue cannot be resolved informally, a meeting should be convened to discuss the grievance. The employee should be allowed to be accompanied at that meeting, the purpose of which is to discuss the grievance in more detail. The employer may choose to supplement that discussion with additional investigatory steps. The employer should then decide what action (if any) should be taken in respect of the employee's grievance (and the employee should be allowed the right to appeal if they are not satisfied with the outcome). All organisations will hope only that grievances are a rare occurence: nonetheless, larger organisations would be well advised to consider training managers to handle grievances effectively.

Disciplinary procedure

When does it apply? If the charity trustees are contemplating taking disciplinary action against an employee (which in serious cases may include dismissal) this procedure will apply.

Again, the employer should try to take informal action where possible. If formal action is required, an employer should first establish the facts of a situation before notifying the employee of these in writing and convening a meeting to discuss them. The employee should be allowed to be accompanied at that meeting. The employer should then decide what action (if any) should be taken in respect of the employee's conduct (which might range from a first or final warning to dismissal, depending on the circumstances and conduct of performance history). The employee should be allowed the right to appeal if they are not satisfied with the outcome.

Why does the ACAS Code of Practice matter?

Failure to follow the code will not make a subsequent dismissal automatically unfair. However, an unreasonable failure to comply with it could lead to 25% uplift on any compensation award that is made. Professional advice should be taken to ensure that the charity complies with its requirements and minimises risks.

Equal pay and anti-discrimination

Employees have the right to equal pay for work of equal value. This applies to the overall package (not just salary) and includes other non-pay conditions such as working hours. In addition, all employees have a right not to be discriminated against on the grounds of sex (including marital status and gender reassignment), race, disability, sexual orientation, religion, belief or age. The law relates to both the selection and ongoing employment of staff and covers both direct and indirect discrimination, harassment and victimisation. Organisations may wish to consider formulating an Equal Opportunities policy reflecting these protections.

Sick pay and leave

The majority of employees are entitled to Statutory Sick Pay (SSP), provided they supply a self-certificate explaining the reasons for the first week of absence and doctors' certificates for any subsequent absence. For up-to-date and more detailed information, see www.direct.gov.uk.

Trustees may, and many do, provide for more generous terms as part of the contract of employment. Often this involves a set period of sickness absence on full pay followed by a similar period on half pay. In determining your policy on sick pay, consider what length of absence and rate of pay the charity can afford, both in terms of finances and operational impact, and balance this against the charity's values as a supportive employer.

Maternity leave

Maternity pay and leave provisions are complex, but the basic arrangements are as follows:

- pregnant women have the right to paid time off for ante-natal care;
- up to 52 weeks' maternity leave;
- during the leave period all rights including (e.g. seniority and holiday entitlements, but excluding remuneration, are preserved); and
- depending on when exactly they choose to return to work, women have the right to return to the same job or, if that is not possible, a suitable alternative.

Women who have been continuously employed for 26 weeks up to and including the fifteenth week before their due date and whose income is at or above the National Insurance lower earnings limit are entitled to Statutory Maternity Pay for nine months. Those who do not qualify may be able to claim Maternity Allowance, a DWP benefit.

Adoption leave

Parents are entitled to take adoption leave where a child is placed with them for adoption. The right is to 26 weeks' ordinary adoption leave, followed by up to 26 weeks' additional adoption leave, giving a maximum of up to 52 weeks' leave. If a couple is adopting jointly, only one parent can take adoption leave but the other parent may be entitled to paternity leave.

Paternity leave

The father of a child will have a right to a period of either one or two weeks' paid paternity leave within 56 days of the date of birth, if he has been continuously employed for 26 weeks up to and including the fifteenth week before the baby is due. He will qualify for Ordinary Paternity Pay for this period of leave. If the father's wife, civil partner or partner has returned to their work following a period of statutory leave, the father may take up to 26 weeks' leave, to be taken between 20 weeks and one year after the child is born or placed for adoption.

Family-friendly requirements

Domestic emergency. Employees have the right to reasonable time off in cases of domestic emergency. This includes caring for a spouse, child, parent or cohabitee, but does not cover lodgers or tenants. The right arises when:

- the dependant is ill, gives birth, is injured or assaulted;
- arrangements need to be made for the care of an ill or injured dependant;
- the dependant dies;
- there is an unexpected disruption of existing care arrangements; and
- there is an unexpected incident involving a child at school.

'Reasonable time off' means adequate time to make different arrangements. There is no obligation for the time off to be paid, nor can individuals be obliged to take it as annual leave or time off in lieu of overtime; instead, they may take the time as unpaid leave. Organisations can, of course, make more generous provision for employees, for example by providing for such time off to be paid or extending the availability to include siblings and close friends. Such additional provision should be described within an organisational compassionate leave policy and should be equally available to all staff.

Parental leave. The parental leave regulations give both parents the right to 13 weeks' unpaid leave in respect of children born or adopted. Parents must give 21 days' notice of the leave and leave can only be taken in blocks of one week, up to a maximum of four weeks' leave per year. The leave must be taken before the child is five. The provision is extended to the age of 18 in the case of children with disabilities.

Parents have an absolute right to return to the same post unless the leave extends beyond four weeks or is added to maternity leave, in which case employees have the right to return to an appropriate job.

Again, organisations can make more generous provision within their own staff policies.

E-mail and internet usage policy

Although not a legal requirement in itself, it is wise to have an e-mail policy in place to minimise the legal risks arising from employees' use of e-mails and the internet. Most e-mail policies include, for example, restrictions on the use of particular websites, expected behaviour when sending and receiving e-mails, and the likely repercussions for breach of the policy. Organisations may want to give particular thought to whether (and, if so, how) to address employees' use of social media – this may tie into a broader policy on the handling of confidential information.

Whistleblowing

The law protects employees who report concerns about misconduct or malpractice in their employer when to do so is in the public interest. The protection is limited to the right not to suffer any detriment because of the disclosure. This includes dismissal, dismissal in the guise of redundancy, victimisation and demotion. In order to enjoy legal protection, such disclosures must be made in good faith and the reasonable belief that the information reveals that one of the following has happened, is happening, or is likely to happen:

- a criminal offence;
- failure to comply with a legal obligation (statutory or contractual);
- endangerment of health and safety;
- environmental damage; or
- concealment of information.

In addition, the disclosure must be made to one of the following: the employer (or a person nominated by the employer in internal procedures); the person whose actions are in question; a legal adviser in the course of obtaining advice; or a person or body prescribed by the Secretary of State.

Employees who bypass internal disclosure and go straight to an external body will be protected provided that, in addition to the above, the disclosure has not been made for personal gain, it is reasonable for the disclosure to be made and either:

- the employee reasonably believes that he or she will be victimised by disclosing to the employer;
- the employee has already made the disclosure internally; or

- there is no prescribed body for disclosure to be made to and the employee believes that disclosure to the employer will result in the destruction or concealment of evidence.

Normal channels may also be bypassed in exceptionally serious cases that may be more appropriately reported to a third party, such as the police.

It is advisable to include whistleblowing within any disciplinary/grievance procedure or other internal policies.

Working Time Regulations

The Working Time Regulations include rights to a working week of a maximum of 48 hours, to regular rest breaks and to paid leave. The paid leave due is calculated by multiplying the number of days in an employee's normal working week by the factor of 5.6). There is a requirement to keep records of working time and these can be inspected by the Health and Safety Executive.

The length of the working week is calculated as an average over a 17-week 'reference period'. This may be extended to 26 weeks and it is possible to agree with the workforce to extend the period to one year. This means that occasional working weeks in excess of 48 hours should not present a problem in law, although they are not good employment practice. Workers may opt out of the 48-hour maximum and autonomous workers who have discretion over their own working hours are not covered (e.g. chief executives).

Workers must have unpaid rest breaks of 20 minutes if they work more than six hours, a daily rest of at least 11 hours and a weekly rest of at least 24 hours. Workers may choose not to take these entitlements. Where it is not possible to take these breaks within the working day, 'compensatory rest breaks' should be incorporated into staff rotas.

The right to paid leave includes casual workers and there can be no cash substitute except on termination.

Interpreting the application of these regulations within organisations can be extremely complicated, particularly for organisations offering off-site or residential services. Trustees should consider the range of the organisation's work and current staffing arrangements. Trustees should also consider whether it would be acceptable to allow staff to opt out of any of the provisions. The subsequent application of the regulations within the charity should be subject to staff consultation and appropriate legal advice. Arrangements for recording working hours should be compatible with the culture of the charity.

Flexible working

Employees have the right to request flexible working only if they wish to care for a child or particular categories of adult. It should be stressed that this is a right to request, rather than a right to receive. The procedure to be followed is set out in Part VIIIA of the Employment Rights Act 1996.

Part-time workers regulations

Part-time workers have the right not to be treated less favourably than comparable full-time workers. This right applies both to contractual terms and any detriment that may arise due to part-time status and extends to job applicants as well as existing employees.

In relation to contractual terms, pay and annual leave should be calculated on a *pro rata* basis. Employers should also consider entitlement to employee benefits such as pensions and health insurance.

Part-time workers should not be discriminated against in areas such as reorganisation of workload, training and promotion opportunities or redundancy selection. Employers should be cautious in such areas in case they unwittingly discriminate against part-time workers.

Minimum wage requirements

By law, employers must pay workers at or above the minimum wage. There are two rates of minimum wage, a lower rate for workers aged 18 to 20 and an increased rate for those aged 21 and over. Rates are subject to review, so trustees should check the current rate (see www.hmrc.gov. uk). As a guide, from 1 October 2011, the lower rate for 18-to-20-year-olds was £4.98 and the rate for those aged 21 and over was £6.08.

Transfer of undertakings

There are complex provisions in place for protecting the terms and conditions of staff where employment is transferred from one organisation to another. In the voluntary sector this may happen, for example, where a charity closes and another charity takes over one of its projects. In such circumstances, staff bring with them the employment conditions (including salary and period of continuous service) that they had with their previous employer prior to the transfer. This can result in complicated arrangements whereby different staff within the organisation operate under different (and potentially incompatible) terms and conditions. Trustees are advised to seek professional guidance before entering such arrangements.

Trade union recognition

Trade unions have a legal right to gain recognition in the workplace through claiming recognition with an employer. Recognition may take the form of a voluntary agreement between union and employer. Where no such agreement is reached, the Central Arbitration Committee (CAC) has a legal right to become involved. If the CAC finds that 50% of the workforce are already trade union members, the CAC will automatically recognise the union. If the figure is less than 50%, there must be a ballot. For the union to be recognised following a ballot, there must be a majority vote in favour and this must amount to at least 40% of the 'bargaining unit'.

The legislation may have limited impact on smaller charities, but those with large staff teams will be affected. Trustees of larger charities should consider their approach to staff consultation and involvement. For example, consider arrangements for union representation on any staff council, recognition of more than one union within the organisation and how to ensure that the views of staff who are not union members are represented. By taking a proactive approach to canvassing staff opinion, trustees will be better prepared for any subsequent claim for union recognition.

Pensions: stakeholder and auto-enrolment

At the time of writing, organisations that employ five or more staff are required to make stake-holder pensions available to their employees. Organisations may be exempt from the requirement if they offer an occupational or personal pension scheme to all staff.

Charities must consult with their employees on the selection of the stakeholder provider, although the final decision rests with the charity as employer. A list of providers is available from the Pensions Regulator.

Employers must make stakeholder pensions available for all staff except:

- those with less than three months' service;
- those with earnings below the national insurance lower earnings limit;
- those who do not normally live in the UK; and
- those who could have joined an occupational pension scheme offered by the employer but who chose not to do so.

It is up to individual employees to decide whether to take up a stakeholder pension. Pension providers will supply detailed information to help staff make this choice. Employees must complete written applications to join the scheme and specify their level of contribution. Similarly, there is no obligation on employers to make a contribution towards employee pensions, although an employer may decide to do so as a matter of good practice.

However, starting in late 2012, an employer will have to enrol every worker who meets the eligibility criteria into a workplace pension. 'Auto-enrolment' is being introduced on a gradual basis, with very large employers being first and smaller employees following over the next several years. Auto-enrolment will require the employer to contribute to the worker's pension if the worker earns over a minimum threshold. The Government and the Pensions Regulator have published a number of articles giving further details of the practicalities and timing of pensions auto-enrolment.

Redundancy

Unfortunately circumstances do arise, often due to lack of funding, where a charity is forced to make some staff redundant. Understandably, the law surrounding redundancies can be complex, and issues such as consultation with staff, redundancy selection, time off for staff to seek new employment and redundancy payments must all be considered. As well as ensuring any redundancy process is technically correct, charity trustees will need to be alert to the potential impact on the charity's reputation and it is advisable to seek professional advice to ensure that the process is handled properly and sensitively.

7 Accounting, financial management and control

INTRODUCTION

No matter how worthwhile the work of the charity and no matter how consider-able the contribution of volunteers, no charity can survive in the long term without good financial management and reporting. It is essential for charities to know how much money they have, how much they need and how to manage it wisely, control-ling expenditure to ensure that funds are used to further the objects of the charity. Accurate financial information is crucial to the decisions made by the trustees. Trustees cannot sanction the continuation or expansion of the charity's activities without information about the finances available. Similarly, financial indicators may drive any decisions to cut back or cease operations. Financial information, together with the trustees' vision for the direction of the charity, will determine how much the charity needs to raise, spend and save.

As stated earlier, it is the trustees who are responsible for the charity's financial health and, if they fail in this responsibility, it is the trustees who may be personally liable. Trustees also have a responsibility to maximise the income available to further the objects of the charity. Therefore it is critical, both from a governance and personal perspective, for trustees to act in full knowledge of the charity's financial situation. This means that all trustees, not just the treasurer, must have or develop the skills to under-stand the charity's finances and should take an active role in managing those finances in the best interests of the charity. Whilst the treasurer and any staff will play the lead part in financial matters, it is the function of the board as a whole to determine the objectives of financial management and to actively monitor finances.

Charity finance can be split into two parts – external reporting and internal reporting. External reporting involves the preparation of

CASE EXAMPLE

Charity finance has been the subject of many books. It is intended that this chapter will give trustees of small and medium-sized charities a basic understanding of charity finance and demystify some of the terminology used so that trustees can pick up a set of accounts without fear. It is not intended or feasible to cover some of the more technical aspects of charity finance in this guide. Trustees wanting a deeper understanding of charity finance are advised to refer to specialist publications and/or seek professional advice.

Further sources of information are listed in the Directory.

annual accounts for the use of a wide variety of stakeholders, including the Charity Commission, funders and beneficiaries. Internal reporting involves the preparation of timely management information to help trustees and staff make strategic and operational decisions. Both types of reporting are equally important.

External reporting – charity accounts

Every charity must produce annual accounts, also known as financial statements. The Charity Commission currently publishes accounts for over 35,000 charities on its website – roughly all charities with annual incomes over £20,000 (see www.charity-commission.gov.uk). The annual accounts are therefore a public document and should be seen as a promotional tool, rather than an annual chore.

Accounts are presented in financial years. Each charity determines its own financial year. Many charities choose to reflect the national fiscal year by running from 1 April to 31 March, although the calendar year (1 January to 31 December) is also popular.

There are a number of ways to present charity accounts, depending on the size of the charity and whether it is a charitable company or an unincorporated charity. This is discussed in more detail later in this chapter.

All accounts have a number of common features:

- name of the charity and period covered by the accounts (the name should be included as a header on each page);
- trustees' annual report: an opportunity for the trustees to explain the areas that the numbers do not explain;

- income: all accounts must record the amount and sources of income received in the financial year;
- expenditure: accounts must report the expenditure in the financial year, with a breakdown of spending (e.g. staff salaries, accommodation costs, etc);
- fund accounting: all accounts must split income and expenditure between unrestricted, restricted and endowment funds;
- balance sheet: all accounts should include a statement of the charity's funds at the end of the financial year;
- notes to the accounts: these should describe the accounting methods used and give more detailed information on items in the accounts, for example a breakdown of any grants received;
- comparative figures for the previous financial year etc; and
- signature (with date) of the chair, secretary or treasurer to indicate that the accounts have been accepted and adopted by the board of trustees.

Most (but not all) charities are required by law or their governing documents to have their accounts examined by an independent person. The type of external scrutiny required will again depend on the size of the charity and whether it is a charitable company or an unincorporated charity. This is discussed in more detail later on. Where such an examination has taken place, a signed and dated copy of the subsequent report should be included in the accounts.

The more important features of accounts will now be discussed in more detail.

Trustees' annual report

All registered charities are required to produce a trustees' report as part of their annual accounts. This gives the trustees the opportunity to explain what the charity has achieved during the year and what impact this has had on its beneficiaries. The report need not be a lengthy, glossy document, but it should be clear and easy to read. No one appreciates having to plough through paragraph after paragraph of badly written small type. Remember that the accounts will be a matter of public record. Most people will not understand the numbers, so will turn to the trustees' report to find out whether the charity is worthwhile.

The contents of the report are dictated by charity accounting regulations and should cover the following:

Reference and administrative details
- the name of the charity and its charity registration number;
- the registered address;
- a list of trustees and the name of the chief executive (or other senior staff member);* and
- the names and addresses of professional advisers (including bankers and solicitors).*

Structure, governance and management
- details of the legal structure of the charity (i.e. is it an unincorporated association or a limited company) and the nature of the governing document;
- methods for recruiting and appointing new trustees;
- methods for training and inducting trustees;*
- the organisational structure of the charity and how decisions are made;* and
- a statement confirming that the major risks to which the charity is exposed have been identified and reviewed and that systems have been put in place to manage those risks.*

Objectives and activities
- a summary of the objects of the charity;
- the aims, objectives and strategies for achieving the objects;*
- the principal activities contributing to the achievement of the objects; and
- a public benefit statement.

Achievements and performance
- a review of the achievements and performance of the charity against the stated objects.

Financial review
- a review of the financial position of the charity;
- reserves policy and investment policy;

- details of any funds in deficit;
- details of principal funding sources;* and
- details of funds held on behalf of others (i.e. as custodian trustees).

Plans for future periods

- a summary of the charity' plans for the future.*

Items marked * are not required for charities with incomes of under £500,000 per annum.

The trustees' report should be adopted by the board and signed (and dated) on their behalf by one of the trustees, usually the chairperson or secretary.

Some of the areas in the trustees' report require more thought than is initially apparent. The disclosure of the methods for training trustees is a fairly new requirement and may cause problems to those charities who have never considered training their trustees. Similarly, the statement about risk management does require trustees to have performed some kind of risk assessment exercise.

The public benefit statement should state that trustees have had regard to Charity Commission guidance on public benefit. In addition, the trustees' report should specifically identify those activities undertaken to further a charity's purposes for the public benefit.

The review of achievements and performance is something that some small and medium-sized charities are poor at doing. They will happily describe the numerous activities that have taken place during the year, but not how successful these activities have been in achieving their stated objects. It may be useful to include details of performance indicators or milestones in this review.

The reserves policy is discussed in more detail later on in this chapter.

Statement of financial activities (SOFA)

This is the prescribed format for presenting income and expenditure for charities using accruals accounting (see later in the chapter for a definition, but basically this includes all charities apart from non-company charities with income under £250,000 per year). See the example on page 144. The SOFA presents incoming resources (income) and resources expended (expenditure) in a columnar format showing the split between different funds. There should be separate columns for unrestricted funds, restricted funds and endowment funds, and for the totals for the current and previous year. If the charity does not have a particular type of fund, then the appropriate column does not need to be included.

As well as having standard columns, the rows in the SOFA are standardised to show income and expenditure by its nature, followed by totals.

SAMPLE SOFA

Anytown Children and Families Forum
Statement of Financial Activities
For the year ending 31 March 2011

	Note	Unrestricted funds	Restricted funds	TOTAL 2011	TOTAL 2010
Incoming resources					
Incoming resources from generated funds					
Voluntary income	2	3,450	–	3,450	2,000
Activities for generating funds	3	4,000	–	4,000	2,000
Investment income	4	1,000	–	1,000	500
Incoming resources from charitable activities	5	1,500	6,500	8,000	6,000
Other incoming resources	6	500	–	500	–
Total incoming resources		10,450	6,500	16,950	10,500
Resources expended					
Costs of generating funds	7	1,500	–	1,500	1,250
Charitable activities	8	7,250	5,000	12,250	9,750
Governance costs	9	1,250	–	1,250	1,000
Total resources expended		10,000	5,000	15,000	12,000
Net incoming/outgoing resources before transfers		450	1,500	1,950	(1,500)
Transfers	10	500	(500)	–	–
Net incoming/outgoing resources after transfers		950	1,000	1,950	(1,500)
Funds brought forward		3,800	4,000	7,800	9,300
Funds carried forward		4,750	5,000	9,750	7,800

Incoming resources are split into:

- *Voluntary income.* This includes all income given without expectation of a return (e.g. donations, legacies, core grants, sponsorship and membership subscriptions).
- *Activities for generating funds.* This includes all income from fundraising and trading activities.
- *Investment income.* This includes bank interest, rental income, dividends and all income from any trading subsidiaries.
- *Income from charitable activities.* This includes all income given in exchange for goods and/or services provided for the benefit of the charity's beneficiaries (e.g. service level agreements, grants specifically for the provision of goods and/or services, fees for services).
- *Other incoming resources.*

Resources expended are split into:

- *Costs of generating funds.* The costs of raising all voluntary income, fundraising income and investment income.
- *Charitable activities.* This includes the costs of achieving the charitable objects.
- *Governance costs.* The costs of running the charity (e.g. accountancy, audit and legal fees, the costs of trustees' meetings).
- *Other resources expended.*

As with the columns for funds, rows for income or expenditure that are not relevant to the charity may be omitted.

Columns should be totalled to show the net movement in funds during the year, the funds brought forward from the previous financial year and those that will be carried forward. The SOFA should also show any movement between funds, such as transfers from the general fund into a designated fund, or to cover a deficit in restricted funds.

As can be seen from this example, the SOFA format provides a useful means for trustees and other readers of the accounts to monitor not just expenditure, but expenditure within different funds and between direct charitable activities and the governance of the charity.

Fund accounting

Charities hold their resources as unrestricted, restricted, endowment or designated funds. Accounts should clearly identify these funds. The distinction between them is as follows.

Unrestricted funds. These are funds that may be used for any purpose within the charity's objects. Often these funds are obtained from general donations and fundraising and income from investments. Some funders, such as local authorities, may give grants on an unrestricted basis.

Restricted funds. These are moneys that have been given to the charity for a specific purpose.

Where a charity has been given a grant for a particular project or donations to work with an identified client group, these funds can only be used for the purpose for which they were given and, as such, are restricted. Such money cannot be used for the general administration of the charity or to finance work in another project or with a different beneficiary group.

Endowment funds. These are funds where there is no power to convert the capital into income (e.g. a gift of money given to the charity for investment purposes on the proviso that the original capital sum cannot be treated as income).

Designated funds. This is money that was received on an unrestricted basis that has since been allocated by the trustees to a particular purpose (e.g. a building refurbishment or new project). Because the funds were allocated by trustee decision, not by the funder, the trustees can decide to 'unallocate' them and move the money back to unrestricted funds for general use or to re-designate it to another project.

Charities are not required to report designated funds as a separate column in the SOFA, although they should be separately recorded in the balance sheet.

Balance sheet

In addition to information on the income and expenditure of the charity over the year, all accounts must include a balance sheet, describing the assets and liabilities at the end of the financial year. The balance sheet acts like a photograph of the charity's financial position on the day that marks the end of the financial year. A sample balance sheet is presented in the box below, but first we will look at the key elements of the balance sheet.

The balance sheet should record the charity's assets split into fixed assets and current assets. Fixed assets are for the long-term use of the charity (e.g. buildings, vehicles, equipment and long-term investments). Current assets are 'liquid' assets that will be converted into cash during the charity's operations (e.g. stock, short-term investments, money owed to the charity, bank balances and actual cash).

The balance sheet should also show any liabilities (money owed by the charity). These should be divided into current liabilities payable in the next 12 months (e.g. payments owed to suppliers and other creditors) and liabilities due after one year or more, such as mortgages and other long-term loan arrangements.

A comparison of current assets to current liabilities will give some indication of the charity's ability to meet its debts as they fall due. The difference between current assets and current liabilities is shown on the

SAMPLE BALANCE SHEET

Anytown Children and Families Forum
Balance sheet as at 31 March 2011

	Note	2011 £	2010 £
Fixed assets			
Tangible assets	11	3,250	2,000
Investments	12	2,000	2,000
Total		5,250	4,000
Current assets			
Debtors	13	1,500	1,250
Cash at bank and in hand		4,000	3,500
Total		5,500	4,750
Creditors: amount falling due within one year	14	1,000	950
Net current assets		4,500	3,800
Total assets less current liabilities		9,750	7,800
Funds			
Unrestricted funds			
General	15	2,750	1,800
Designated	16	2,000	2,000
Restricted funds	17	5,000	4,000
Total		9,750	7,800

balance sheet as positive net current assets (current assets are greater than current liabilities) or negative net current liabilities (current assets are less than current liabilities). A net current liability figure is a clear danger sign regarding the financial health of the charity. However, a charity with a net current asset figure may still have financial problems if the current assets are represented by slow-moving stock and debtors with three-month payment terms rather than actual cash in the bank.

The balance sheet should also show the breakdown of funds into unrestricted, restricted, endowment and designated funds. This should agree with the 'Funds carried forward' in the SOFA.

Notes to the accounts

Accruals accounts include explanatory notes that give more details about the figures in the SOFA and balance sheet. The first note to the accounts normally explains the charity's accounting policies (e.g. what depreciation rates are used and at what point income is recognised in the accounts). The subsequent notes will include a breakdown of most of the figures in the SOFA and balance sheet. The following additional information should also be included in the notes to the accounts.

Related party transactions. Any arrangements between the charity and any individual or other organisation to which it is related must be reported in the notes to the accounts. Related parties include trustees, people connected with the trustees, and organisations that are related because, for example, they have power to appoint members of the board or share a significant proportion of common trustees. Such reporting encourages transparency in managing potential conflicts of interest.

Payments to trustees. Any payments to trustees from charity funds must be recorded in the accounts. Detailed disclosure is required, with payments separately recorded and the legal justification for such payments (e.g. provision within the governing document) explained.

Trustee expenses. Charities do not need to declare collective trustee expenses (e.g. room hire for meetings) or reimbursement of trustees for purchases, such as stationery, made on the charity's behalf. Charities do need to record in their accounts expenses reimbursed to trustees on an individual basis in respect of costs incurred as part of their trusteeship.

Staffing costs. Charities which employ staff should record in their accounts their total staffing costs, the average number of full-time equivalent staff employed during the year and the number of staff receiving individual remuneration above £60,000. This should be presented as the number of staff falling into each £10,000 band from £60,000pa upwards.

Legal requirements

The presentation, content and examination of charity and company accounts are determined by legislation and regulation including the Charities Acts 1993 and 2006, the Companies Acts 1985 and 2006 (for charitable companies) and the Statement of Recommended Practice for Accounting and Reporting by Charities (revised 2005) (SORP 2005). The SORP is revised every five years, the Charities Acts and Companies Acts less frequently. The legal requirements are determined by income thresholds, with a lighter touch for smaller charities.

They represent the minimum standard that must be applied by charities. A charity may decide to apply a higher standard than is required for its income band and may be required to apply a higher standard if it is specified in the governing document. Some registered charities may be subject to accounting requirements under different legislation or regulatory bodies. For example, there is a separate SORP for housing associations.

CAUTION!

The requirements of the SORP are detailed, wide-ranging and sometimes complex. The precise interpretation of the regulations into your accounts will depend on the circumstances of your charity. As this book is aimed at the trustees of small to medium charities we have focused on the key issues for those groups. More detailed guidance is available from the Charity Commission and specialist publications, some of which are listed in the Directory. Trustees should also seek professional support as necessary.

Presentation and content

Receipts and payments: Unincorporated charities with an annual income of £250,000 or less may use this simple form of presentation. The accounts comprise a summary of money paid out and received over the year and listing remaining cash and non-cash assets and any liabilities at the end of the year. A short trustees' annual report is also required. Such accounts do not give a detailed view of the charity's finances and so are not appropriate for large charities.

Accruals accounts: Charities with an income in excess of £250,000 and all charitable companies must compile accruals accounts. These are more detailed accounts showing a 'true and fair' record of charity finances over the year. Accruals accounts contain a full balance sheet, a statement of financial activities (described previously) and explanatory notes. The sample accounts below use the accruals presentation.

> **CAUTION!**
>
> Trustees of charities with an income of £250,000 or less may decide or be required by their governing document to adopt the accruals format. In such circumstances, trustees cannot take a 'pick and mix' approach to the format, rather they must fully comply with the SORP regulations.

External scrutiny

Most (but not all) charities are required by law or their governing documents to have their accounts examined by an independent person. The type of external scrutiny required depends on the size of the charity and whether it is a charitable company or an unincorporated charity. The following thresholds are currently in force.

Annual income	Type of scrutiny
Under £25,000	None
£25,000–£249,000	Independent examination by an 'appropriately experienced' examiner
£250,000–£500,000	Independent examination by an examiner belonging to a recognised accountancy body
Above £500,000	Audit

In addition, a charity requires an audit if it has annual income above £250,000 and assets exceeding £3.26 million.

The different categories of inspection are described below.

Audit. This is the most onerous form of inspection and must be carried out by a qualified auditor. The intention of this form of inspection is to verify whether the accounts present a true and fair view of the charity's financial status. The auditor will subject the financial statements to a thorough examination including a consideration of the sources of income and any restrictions on incoming resources; the allocation of expenditure and the matching of expenditure to income streams; evidence to support the financial statements; financial controls; legal compliance and analysis of risk, including fraud. The auditor will need to see a wide range of supporting documents in order to collate the information necessary to audit the accounts effectively.

Independent examination. A lighter touch than audit. An unblemished independent examiner's report will state that nothing has come to the examiner's attention that indicates that proper accounting records have not been kept, or that the accounts do not agree with the accounting records. That does not mean that no problems exist – just that the examiner hasn't identified any. For charities with annual income under £250,000 the examination may be carried out by someone independent of the charity who the trustees have reason to believe has appropriate skills to conduct the examination. Examples include bank managers, finance officers etc. For charities with income between £250,000 and £500,000, the examiner must be a qualified accountant.

Whatever the method of inspection, the person inspecting the accounts will produce a report on the basis of his or her examination which should be included within the final copy of the accounts. Where the inspection of accounts shows everything to be in order, the accounts are termed 'clean'. Where a discrepancy has been discovered, perhaps because the charity could not provide supporting evidence, the report will be 'qualified'. Qualified accounts are often interpreted as an indicator of poor financial management.

tip

Bear in mind that an independent examination is nowhere near as stringent a form of scrutiny as an audit, and consequently an examiner's report has less value than that of an auditor in terms of certifying the veracity of the accounts and the financial health of a charity. In contrast, auditors can play a valuable role in raising the standard of charities' financial reporting and controls. Trustees who are concerned about their charity's financial status and management may do well to subject their accounts to a full audit as a means of monitoring the situation and identifying solutions to difficult areas.

Choosing an accountant

Charity accounts are very much a specialist area of accountancy, and not every accountant will have this specialist knowledge. As with all professionals, a recommendation from another charity is probably the best approach, and bear in mind that the better professionals do not need to advertise. Other points to take into account when choosing an accountant include the number of other charity clients handled, any additional services provided (e.g. advice and support throughout the year, not just at the year end) and of course cost. However, do not let cost alone dictate your choice – a poor set of year end accounts can cost you more in terms of poor understanding of the charity's financial position, and poor promotion.

Branches

In chapter 4 we looked at group structures and the sometimes complex arrangements that can exist in terms of branches. The SORP defines branches as falling within two categories: those that are part of the administration of the parent charity; and those that have a separate legal status, but are administered by, or on behalf of, the parent body. In the latter case, branch funds will be held for the purposes of the parent charity which will in turn have significant influence over that branch.

Where branches are not autonomous entities, the SORP requires that all branch transactions, assets and liabilities should be included gross (rather than netted off) in the parent charity's accounts. Such branches may also produce their own accounts for the benefit of local supporters. Branch funds should be recorded as restricted or unrestricted funds as appropriate.

Autonomous charities which are known as branches but fall outside the above definition should prepare their own annual accounts and describe the relationship with their parent body in their trustees' report.

Other requirements

There are some further key requirements in relation to charity accounts.

Retention of accounts. Financial records, including invoices and receipts as well as the accounts themselves, must be kept for six years.

Submission of accounts. All registered charities which have an annual income in excess of £25,000 must submit their accounts to the Charity

Commission within ten months of their financial year end. All charitable companies must also submit their accounts to Companies House within nine months of the year end. Charities with an income of £25,000 or less must submit accounts to the Commission on request. In addition, charities must also complete and submit the Commission's annual return, giving summary information on income and expenditure, fundraising costs, trustees and trustee benefits and the use of property.

Supply of accounts. Registered charities are required to supply their accounts to those who request them. Any financial statements distributed must include the trustees' report and any external examiner's report.

Funders' requirements

Some funders may also place requirements on the recording of their grants in the accounts. For example, it may be a condition of the grant that income and expenditure under the agreement is separately identified, labelled in a certain way and recorded as a restricted fund.

Internal reporting – management accounts

So far we have looked at annual accounts. Whilst annual accounts are useful for trustees in reflecting the current financial position and long-term planning, their infrequency makes them less useful in ensuring financial viability on a day-to-day basis. Once the end of the financial year has arrived, it may be too late. This is where management accounts may prove valuable. Management accounts, usually produced monthly or quarterly, are an essential tool for trustees and senior staff in monitoring ongoing expenditure.

Establishing cost centres

Bald indicators of income and expenditure are of limited help as a day-to-day management tool. Instead, trustees need to know where income is being spent and whether this expenditure reflects their intentions. To do this, the trustees need to establish cost centres. Cost centres are areas of expenditure or items that are grouped together for the purpose of budget setting and monitoring expenditure. Small, single function charities are unlikely to have many separate cost centres, but charities running multiple projects or in receipt of restricted funds will need to have more complex arrangements in place. For example, there might be a cost centre for each project or a cost centre for each restricted fund. This allows the trustees to monitor income and expenditure in different areas of the charity, pinpointing issues of concern. Within each cost centre there are likely to be common elements (e.g. travel expenses, training costs, running expenses, salaries etc).

Trustees should look at the work of the charity as a whole and identify those areas that can be divided into cost centres and establish budget areas (e.g. salaries, travel expenses etc) within each cost centre.

Setting and controlling budgets

Once cost centres have been identified, trustees should set budgets for each one. Although staff often play a key role in budgeting, the final responsibility for budgets rests with the trustees so the board must scrutinise this area carefully to ensure that income targets are realistic and planned expenditure is appropriate and within the charity's objects, powers and resources.

Budget setting involves considering the activities undertaken within each cost centre, the likely cost of each activity, and the resources available. This is obviously easier where a cost centre is well established and trustees can use previous expenditure as a foundation for future budgets, considering item by item whether the next year's activities will cost more, less or a similar amount and whether any additional items should be included. It is also easier where a cost centre is fully funded, for example by a specific grant or contract, as trustees will know the exact amount available for that work. In all other cases, the trustees will have to strike a balance between the costs of the activities and realistic fundraising targets. It is dangerous to set a budget based on unattainable fundraising targets. In contrast, budgets based solely on secured income can be unduly restrictive, particularly in cases where the charity has a good track record of raising additional funds.

When setting budgets for a new activity or a new charity, look at the expenditure of similar projects and groups as well as researching the costs of individual items, such as any necessary capital equipment, rental charges for premises, salary levels etc.

The collective total of the different cost centres represents the budget for the charity as a whole. Budgets are commonly set on an annual basis, but within this figure, the budgets for each funding item for each cost centre should be broken down on a monthly basis. This information allows trustees to use management accounts as a monitoring tool. Some budget items may be easily split into one-twelfth to represent each month's planned expenditure. For example, static costs such as salaries and rent will stay the same each month. There may be other items that are seasonal, annual, bi-monthly or quarterly, such as training fees, insurance premiums and special events. Costs for these items should be included within the breakdown under the appropriate month or months.

tip

> Month-by-month budgeting can help in managing cash flow and investments as it will illustrate how much money is needed at any given point in the year.

Management accounts may then show, by cost centre, and within cost centre by item:

- budget for the month;
- expenditure for the month;
- budget to date;
- expenditure to date; and
- annual budget.

Trustees can then measure overspend and underspend against each item. This gives a much better understanding of charity finances and allows greater control over expenditure to be exercised. As part of the budget setting exercise, trustees may identify performance indicators or other forms of measurement that will clearly signal to the board whether the finances are healthy or in danger. Such performance indicators will be linked to charity objectives and may include, for example, spending to target, reducing expenditure in some areas (e.g. office costs) and/or increasing expenditure in others (e.g. grants to beneficiaries or staff training). The combination of detailed budgeting and performance measures helps trustees to ask the right questions regarding variations from budget. Does an underspend represent a lack of activity? Why has an over-spend occurred in a certain area? Can budgets be revised to move funds from areas with an underspending to new development? Is income genera-tion on target and on time? Why are some cost centres spending more than others on common budget items, such as telephone and office costs?

Cost centres such as these obviously require fairly sophisticated daily financial management, as each item of income or expenditure needs to be recorded against a cost centre and budget heading within that centre. The benefits do justify the effort. As has been seen above, the trustees gain useful information and it also allows them to delegate an appropriate degree of financial control to staff. For example, a project manager may be given spending authority within the cost centre for the project, without being able to sign off expenditure in other areas of the charity.

Financial controls

Documented and implemented financial controls are crucial to the proper governance of any organisation, regardless of its size or sector. For charity trustees, financial controls are the means by which they retain a meaningful responsibility for charity finances. Such controls support accurate financial reporting, provide a means by which trustees can demonstrate financial probity and, critically, are a key weapon in preventing fraud. As such, financial controls should be developed in every charity, including those run entirely by the trustees.

Financial controls determine the way in which all funds of the charity are handled, governing both the process of receiving and spending money and the authorities within the charity to make financial decisions. Basic principles include:

- spreading responsibility across a range of individuals, for example through arrangements for checking or countersigning transactions (on the premise that vesting too much responsibility in one person heightens the risk of abuse);
- detailed recording of all transactions; and
- escalating spending authorities within the charity, so that all expenditure over a certain level has to be signed off by trustees.

Trustees should develop a written financial control policy. Trustees and any staff or volunteers who have financial responsibilities should be aware of the contents of the policy and apply its requirements consistently. The procedure should cover the following areas.

Spending authority

Who will have authority to make payments from the charity's funds? The following are common scenarios.

1   In small charities the trustees may decide not to delegate any authority to staff or volunteers for spending charitable funds. It is still necessary to consider whether, for example, two trustees can authorise expenditure up to a certain threshold but expenditure above the threshold must be endorsed by the full board.

2   In charities with a small staff team, staff can often authorise expenditure up to the first threshold, a member of staff together with a trustee can authorise expenditure up to the second threshold, but any expenditure above that level must be approved by two trustees and, ultimately, the whole trustee board.

3   In larger charities, different staff may have spending authority within their own cost centres, with senior employees such as the chief executive or finance manager having overall authority. In such circumstances, staff with cost centre spending authority will usually be subject to an upper threshold before the expenditure has to be approved by one of the senior employees. Some funders do not like these arrangements, and may require that expenditure over a certain amount has to have trustee authorisation.

Whatever the model adopted, some basic principles apply:

- only the trustees should have authority to endorse expenditure that is outside the budget or above a certain level;
- no payment should be released on the approval of one person alone, instead every expenditure should be countersigned by another person with appropriate spending authority;
- nobody should have authority to approve payments to themselves or to some other individual or organisation in which they have an interest (e.g. staff and trustees should not be able to sign off their own expenses); and
- two people from the same family or household should not have authority to authorise the same expenditure (e.g. they should not be able to sign the same cheque).

Setting spending authorities

We have not suggested threshold levels for spending authorities because these are very individual to the charity. Issues to consider include the level of spending authority relative to the charity's budget, the need (if any) to access money quickly, the level and frequency of expenditure and the role of individual staff members. For example, a small charity with a lone worker carrying out administrative functions may limit that worker's spending authority to, for example, £25 to cover the cost of stationery. A multi-million pound charity with a professionally qualified and highly experienced senior management team may give senior management a spending authority of £100,000, provided that the expenditure has been budgeted for. If employees' job descriptions include an element of management, especially financial management, and they have been recruited for these skills, then it is likely to be appropriate that such posts should carry a degree of spending authority.

If the nature of the charity's work means that spending is limited to regular and predictable items such as salaries, rent and utilities, there may be no need for the trustees to delegate any control. In contrast, other charities may have frequent calls on their finances that, although within budget, are unpredictable and urgent. For example, a charity providing crisis grants or loans to its clients will need to delegate spending authority to those working with the beneficiaries.

Documentation

Record keeping. Records should be kept of all money received and spent. These should include basic information such as: the amount; from whom the money was received or to whom it was paid; and the date and purpose of the transaction. Any documentation such as receipts and invoices should be retained. Each transaction should be recorded against the appropriate cost centre and budget heading within that cost centre. Records should be reconciled against balances, with no single person responsible for record keeping. Instead, all records should be checked by one other person. In small charities the responsibility is often split between the senior member of staff and the treasurer.

Cheques. All charities should require two signatures on each cheque as a means of verifying the genuine purpose of the payment. Cheque signatories should be authorised in line with the charity's spending authorities. Some charities have difficulties with cheque payments because of problems in bringing cheque signatories together; they attempt to address this by asking one of the signatories to pre-sign blank cheques. This completely undermines the value of the joint signing arrangements and lays the charity wide open to cheque fraud. If arranging joint signatures is a problem, review spending authorities and see if the availability of signatories can be approved by, for example, adding an additional signatory to the list.

Internet banking. More and more charities are using internet banking to make payments. However, few banks offer a 'dual authority' internet banking system. Therefore, there is a danger that payments are being made by one trustee or even one member of staff. Trustees need to ensure that there is sufficient backup documentation that shows that the payment has been appropriately authorised.

Handling cash. Cash transactions represent an area of charity finance that is extremely vulnerable to abuse. Charities are advised to avoid cash transactions as far as possible. Where they are unavoidable, for example in relation to voluntary donations, charities should make sure that a stringent process is in place for the documentation of cash transactions and witnessed recording. For example, opening of post or opening collecting tins should be witnessed by a second person and any cash recorded. Receipts should be given to all those paying cash to the charity and copies of receipts should be kept. Any cash payments in respect of expenses should be provided only upon receipt of appropriate evidence (e.g. bus tickets, mileage forms etc.) and should be properly recorded. If it is necessary to keep petty cash, again any expenditure must be documented and trustees should specify a maximum float. Safe arrangements should be made for the storage of cash, with access details known only to a limited number of people.

ESSENTIALS

NEVER release funds without appropriate documentation.
ALWAYS issue receipts for funds received.
ALWAYS record all financial transactions.

Accounting systems

There are three main types of accounting systems:

Manual. Derided by many in favour of computer-based systems, the old-fashioned paper-based approach can nevertheless produce as good results as either of the other options, if you are patient and accurate.

Spreadsheets. Probably the best compromise for smaller charities with no in-house accountancy expertise. A simple record of receipts and payments analysed into cost centres will usually suffice.

Accounting software. Recommended for all charities with income of over £100,000 (although there are charities with income of over £1 million that are successfully using a spreadsheet-based system). There are a number of software providers supplying accounting software, but bear in mind that most accounting software at the bottom end of the scale is designed primarily for businesses and so may not be adequate for fund accounting. Whatever software providers claim, some bookkeeping knowledge is essential if you are to make the most out of any accounting software. If you are thinking of purchasing accounting software, ask for recommendations from your accountant and other charities before spending any money.

Reserves

Many charities struggle to raise cash, with wealthy voluntary groups being in the lucky minority, but whether cash-strapped or cash rich, charities should consider the level of funds they will require as a safety net in case normal funding sources dry up or expenses unexpectedly rise. These safety net or rainy day funds are the charity's reserves (i.e. the income funds that are freely available to the charity for its general purposes, once it has met its financial commitments and provided for other planned expenditure). Although for many charities, talk of high levels of reserves will be a pipe dream, trustees should consider the function of the funds they hold, which can result in a delicate balancing act between organisational prudence and furthering charitable objectives. Funds given for charitable purposes must be spent on charitable purposes rather than hoarded for some future, unidentified eventuality; consequently, the holding of funds in reserve without justification may amount to a breach of trust. At the same time trustees have an obligation to act in the best interests of the charity as an organisation. This will inevitably involve maintaining a healthy cashflow and adequate funds to meet future liabilities. The Charity Commission recognises the need to maintain such a balance and so expects trustees to develop a reserves policy that identifies the purpose and amount of reserves held or desirable to justify the retention of charitable funds. The SORP requires that this policy is discussed in the trustees' report within charities' annual accounts.

tip

> If your reserves sit at a level higher than that needed to fulfil your organisation's charitable purposes and meet any future financial commitments, you should contact the Charity Commission. A possible solution is a Commission Scheme to extend the objects of your charity (e.g. by increasing the area of benefit). Trustees have a legal duty to apply for a Scheme where this is an appropriate course of action.

Developing your reserves policy

Reserves policies will differ between charities depending on the nature of their activities, financial commitments, potential liabilities and future plans, including any plans to develop services, forecasts of income and expenditure and reliability of income sources.

If a charity plans future expansion, for example through the purchase of a new property or development of a new project, the trustees may include within the reserves policy the allocation of a proportion of current assets to a designated fund for this purpose. This acts very much like a personal savings account and the trustees may set a target figure to be attained by a certain date through an annual allocation to the designated fund. Designated funds are not always included in the total figure for reserves.

If the charity already owns a building, it may allocate a proportion of funds from its assets, in addition to its annual maintenance budget, to expenditure on unexpected maintenance tasks that will not be covered by insurance. It may also know of forthcoming maintenance tasks, such as repainting, that do not form part of the annual budget, but can be provided for through a reserves policy.

Trustees will also need to look at the balance between financial security and commitments. Have the trustees entered into any contractual arrangements that extend beyond the period of secured funding? These may include property and equipment leases and staff employment contracts. The reserves policy should include provision for meeting liabilities under these contracts should funding cease, for example by including sums to cover break clause penalties and redundancy payments. In contrast, if a charity has secure funding for a three-year project, risks will be much lower and the approach to reserves should reflect this.

Many reserves policies include provision for rescue or run-down time in the event of funding ceasing. This may be anything between three to 12 months' running costs and allows time for the charity to continue operating whilst seeking alternative funding. If unsuccessful, it allows the charity to be wound up in a way that minimises disruption and meets liabilities.

Taking these different elements together, you will be able to identify both why you need reserves and a target figure for reserves. These factors should form the basis of the policy, even if the target figure is currently unattainable. You should then look at how these funds will be made up. For charities without fixed assets, this is simple. Reserves can only be cash and investments. For charities with property the issue is slightly different. For example, it may be possible to realise cash through mortgages (although the charity must be in a position to repay them). Where the property is not used for the delivery of the charity's services (e.g. it is rented to a third party) it may be possible to use the value of that property within the reserves sum as its sale would not affect the functioning of the organisation. Where the property is key to organisational activities, such as a day care centre, the value of the property could be included in that part of the reserves policy which considers liabilities on closure of the charity.

Organisations with inadequate funds to achieve their ideal reserves policy may operate a two-tier approach, keeping the overall policy as a target to aim for and to which any operating surplus is committed, whilst running a more modest achievable policy. These modest policies usually relate to cash flow and immediate liabilities. For example, a charity may have a policy of not taking on liabilities that cannot be met from current cash resources (rather than next month's grant cheque) and maintaining adequate current assets to meet running costs for the next three months.

The charity's activities and financial obligations will inevitably change over time, so the reserves policy should include details of how the policy itself will be monitored and reviewed.

Calculating the level of reserves

There are different methods of calculating reserves and the method chosen should be determined within your reserves policy and applied consistently. The definition used in the SORP is 'that part of the charity's income funds that is freely available'. This normally excludes endowment funds, restricted funds and any part of unrestricted funds not readily available for spending (e.g. income funds that could only be realised by disposing of fixed assets). The SORP also recognises that individual charities may have unrestricted funds earmarked or designated for essential future spending which further reduce the amount readily available. However, trustees should be aware that funders may adopt a different approach to that of the Charity Commission (e.g. by including designated funds within the reserves figure).

CALCULATING RESERVES

Based on the SORP's definition, reserves can, therefore, be calculated as follows:

Net assets (i.e. all assets minus all liabilities)

Minus tangible fixed assets

Minus endowments

Minus restricted funds

Minus designated funds

= Free reserves

When calculating your level of reserves, be careful not to 'double minus' any of the figures. We can illustrate this problem by using the sample balance sheet considered earlier in this chapter. Using this formula, free reserves would be calculated as follows:

£9,750 net assets
£3,250 fixed assets
£2,000 designated fund
£5,000 restricted fund

= £500 free reserves

This calculation has resulted in a negative free reserves figure; however, if the fixed assets represent part of the restricted funds, their value will have been double counted in the calculation. The true reserves figure would look more like this:

£9,750 net assets
£2,000 designated fund
£5,000 restricted fund (including £3,250 fixed assets)

= £2,750 free reserves

The period, in weeks, of running costs that this figure represents can be calculated using the following equation:

Reserves divided by unrestricted expenditure for the year multiplied by 52 = number of weeks running costs.

From our sample balance sheet and SOFA:

$$\frac{£2,750}{£10,000} \times 52$$

= 14 weeks' running costs

Reserves and funding applications

Funding bodies, and some canny individual donors, will look at charities' reserve levels. After all, why should they give money for a project or expense that the charity could afford to cover itself? On the other hand, would they want to give money to a charity that could fold at any moment? For these reasons, in addition to the SORP requirements, charities need to have a reserves policy in place and to be able to communicate this to potential funders. High levels of reserves may be completely justifiable if the charity is committing significant amounts of its own money to a project or would have heavy financial commitments in the event of closure, just as non-existent reserves may be acceptable if the charity is tightly funded but maintains a good cashflow.

CAUTION!

Never include restricted funds in your reserves figure. Restricted funds may only be used for the purpose for which they were given. Charities cannot use these funds for any other purpose, even in order to bail them out of a difficult situation. If they do, they may be required to return the funds to the original intended purpose or repay the misspent amount to the funder.

Cashflow forecasts

In the last section we talked about cashflow in the context of reserves. Good cashflow would ensure that the charity is always able to pay its bills and meet immediate liabilities. Poor cashflow would result in overdrafts and other forms of debt and late payments of bills, incurring interest and other penalty charges. As well as being financially damaging, poor cashflow may harm the charity's reputation and its relationships with creditors, be they external suppliers or internal creditors (e.g. staff).

Cashflow can be managed through a cashflow forecast. This plans 'money in' and 'money out', allowing organisations to assess their financial viability on an ongoing basis, planning the best timing for expenditure, avoiding the need for overdrafts or short-term loans and maximising the benefits of available funds by investing spare cash wherever possible. A tool that should be used by all organisations, cash flow forecasts are particularly valuable for charities on tight budgets with limited reserves and new charities and projects that have yet to develop an established spending cycle or back-up funds.

Producing a cashflow forecast

As a planning tool for voluntary organisations, cashflow forecasts should cover a 12-month period with a month-by-month breakdown of resources coming into and out of the charity or project account. It should consider the balance (and thus the availability of cash) on a monthly and cumulative basis. The forecast should start with any balances available at the beginning of the year, with the figures for the forthcoming year heavily based on the budget. Any fixed income and expenditure, such as grant payments and salaries, should be included, before adding any variables. Through this method, trustees may be able to identify payments that should be rescheduled to another time of year when more resources are available, or the best time to run a large fundraising event in terms of maintaining positive cash balances. They may also be able to identify periods of surplus that present short-term investment opportunities.

A sample cashflow for the Anytown Children and Families Forum is given on the following page.

Managing funds

Trustees have an obligation to maximise the funds available to be applied to charitable causes. This is not limited to raising money, but includes management of the funds that the charity already has. In the previous section we looked at using cashflow forecasts to minimise debts incurred across the year and referred to the opportunities that may be presented for trustees to increase resources by investing spare cash on a month-by-month basis. Structures can be established to enable trustees to manage resources even more effectively. The obvious example is the selection of appropriate bank or building society accounts to gain the most interest on funds held. Within each month, income and expenditure can be managed to exploit such arrangements. For example, many grants are paid quarterly, but payments against that grant will be made at various stages throughout the quarter, so funds should be placed appropriately during that period. The same is true of income that is received at the beginning of the month but not paid out until the end. For example, trustees may

Sample Cashflow – Anytown Children and Families Forum

	Apr	May	June	July	Aug	Sept	Oct	Nov	Dec	Jan	Feb	Mar
Income												
Local Authority grant	6,000			6,000			6,000			6,000		
Lottery grant		5,000			5,000			5,000			5,000	
Donations	20	20	40	40	10	30	50	40	100	50		10
Fundraising events			500	600			250		600		500	
Fees	200	300	300	200		200	300	300	200	250	300	300
Total income	6,220	5,320	840	6,840	5,010	230	6,600	5,340	900	6,300	5,800	310
Expenditure												
Salaries	3,000	3,000	3,000	3,000	3,000	3,000	3,000	3,000	3,000	3,000	3,000	3,000
Rent & Running costs	800	800	800	800	2,000	800	800	800	800	800	800	800
Subscriptions	20			100			2,000	100	100			
Events		150	50			50	25					
Total expenditure	3,820	3,950	3,850	3,900	5,000	3,850	5,825	3,900	3,900	3,800	3,800	3,800
Monthly balance	2,400	1,370	–3,010	2,940	10	–3,620	775	1,440	–3,000	2,500	2,000	–3,490
Cumulative balance (open £2000)	4,400	5,770	2,760	5,700	5,710	2,090	2,865	4,305	1,305	3,805	5,805	2,315

collect fee or rental income at the beginning of the month and hold those sums for four weeks before using them to part-fund salary payments at the end of the month. Investment of charitable funds is discussed in more detail in chapter 8.

Other opportunities should also be considered, such as the availability of direct debit payments and their impact in terms of bottom line expenditure and cash flow planning.

Risk management

Given trustees' legal responsibilities towards their charities, it has long been a matter of good governance practice for trustees to assess and manage any risks to the charity. As discussed earlier in this chapter, the SORP now requires a statement on the management of major risks to be included in the trustees' report. We looked at the broader concepts of risk management in chapter 2. Throughout this chapter we have discussed measures to control risk directly in relation to financial stability.

Obviously, when considering financial risk, the worst case scenario for a charity is insolvency. However there are many other, less devastating, but more frequent, financial risks that need to be managed by the trustees. These include:

- budget deficits;
- a drop in income;
- inability to pay liabilities in time (this does not necessarily make an organisation insolvent);
- theft of charitable funds;
- breach of trust through incorrect use of charitable funds;
- loss of a grant due to incorrect expenditure of restricted funds or some other failure to meet grant terms and conditions; and
- legal action against the charity due to negligence or breach of contract.

As we discussed in chapter 2, trustees need to consider the likelihood of the risk and the impact on the charity, should it occur, to decide whether managing the risk is a priority. Obviously, a charity facing imminent insolvency needs to address that risk immediately. Except in extreme circumstances, charities that have been effectively 'risk managed' by trustees should not face such a situation, because trustees will already have tackled the root problems, such as budget deficits and declining income.

The financial management practices discussed in this chapter are a crucial element of any financial risk management strategy. Effective financial reporting will act as an early warning system of financial troubles ahead. As such, they can help trustees analyse and prioritise different risks. Similarly, budget setting allows trustees to tackle problems of falling resources and budget deficits whilst proper financial controls will reduce risks in relation to misspent funds and theft.

Other risks, such as conflicts of interest, failures of health and safety and employment disputes can also have a financial impact on charities, especially if compensation is sought. Trustees must manage such risks to reduce the likelihood of them occurring, but should also consider mitigating the financial ill-effects if they do occur, for example by arranging appropriate insurance cover. Insurance is discussed in more detail in chapter 2.

8 Taxation and other financial issues

INTRODUCTION

It is a common misconception that charities do not pay tax. Whilst charities do enjoy a range of tax concessions, it is simply not true to state that charities do not pay tax at all. In this section we will look at some of the key issues trustees need to consider in terms of taxation.

There is no distinction for tax or VAT purposes between registered charities and charitable bodies that are not registered with the Charity Commission. Unregistered charities who wish to claim tax or VAT relief will need to demonstrate their charitable status to HM Revenue & Customs, based on the charity's objects, as described in the governing document.

CAUTION!

Trustees should be aware that taxation is a complex issue and the nature of each charity's activities will greatly influence the application of the law and its effect on the charity's tax burden. For this reason, trustees are advised to seek professional advice on tax issues.

In addition, tax and VAT provisions are subject to regular review, particularly in terms of changes to thresholds so always check the most up-to-date requirements with HM Revenue & Customs.

Tax

Exemptions

The following sources of income and gains are usually exempt from tax:

1 Rental income, bank interest and other investment income (but not dividends from UK companies).
2 Capital gains from disposal of assets.

3 Grant income.

4 Donations and legacies.

5 Income from primary purpose trading (see the section on trading later in this chapter).

In addition, charities do not pay stamp duty land tax when buying a property or a lease. They are also entitled to rates relief, paying no more than 20% on any non-domestic property used for charitable purposes.

Note that the amount of tax that a charity is exempted may be restricted if the charity has not spent all of its income or gains on charitable activities.

Charities can usually reclaim any UK tax that has been deducted at source from their income (e.g. tax deducted from bank interest). Note that tax credits on dividend income are non-refundable.

Donations

One of the tax concessions available to charities is the ability to receive tax-efficient donations, either through donations made before tax has been deducted (payroll giving) or through reclaiming tax on donations under the gift aid system.

Payroll giving. Payroll giving is a system whereby individuals make donations to charity that are deducted directly from their pay or occupational pension. The donations are taken by the employer from the employee's gross pay, before tax deductions are made, thus no income tax is paid on the donation element of the salary. Donations are passed to an agency charity which distributes the funds to the charities nominated by the employees. There is no limit on the value of an individual employee's donations.

Trustees of charities receiving donations under payroll giving should be wary of offering benefits to donors as this may disqualify the donation from relief under the scheme. Benefits of negligible financial value, such as stickers or newsletters, are normally acceptable within the scheme.

Gift aid. The gift aid scheme provides for flexible tax-efficient donations to charities. Gift aid is available for monetary donations (rather than gifts in kind) from tax-paying individuals and from companies.

In the case of individuals, the charity can claim back the basic rate tax paid for the donation, whilst the donor can claim back the difference between the basic rate tax paid and any higher rate of tax that was paid in relation to the donation. The reduction in the basic rate of tax from 22% to 20% from 6 April 2008 was set to cost charities many millions of pounds in gift aid. A transitional relief was, however, announced, such that charities have been able to reclaim a 'gift-aid tax repayment supplement' of 3p for every £1 donation for three years from 6 April 2008 until 5 April 2011. This meant that charities have been able to continue to reclaim tax at 22/78 of the original donation (rather than 20/80) up to 5 April 2011. Since 6 April 2011, charities have been able to reclaim tax at only 20/80 of the original donation.

Gift aid donations from companies are paid without deduction of income tax which means that the company gets the tax relief rather than the charity. Unlike the requirements for individual donors, no declaration is required and the charity only needs to keep the accounting records necessary to record donations. Company donors should retain any correspondence as evidence of the donation.

Gift aid declaration. In order to reclaim tax on a donation, charities must obtain a gift aid declaration from the donor. Although HM Revenue & Customs has produced a model form, there is no prescribed format for the declaration. Declarations may be made before, at the time of, or after the donation and may cover single or multiple donations. The declaration may be given in writing (including fax and e-mail) or orally and should contain the following information:

- name and home address of the donor;
- the name of the charity;
- a description of the donations covered by the declaration (e.g. a single donation or all donations from a certain date onwards); and
- a declaration that donations are to be treated as gift aid donations. Written declarations should also contain a note explaining that the donor must pay income tax and/or capital gains tax equivalent to the tax deducted from donations.

Although there is no requirement for the declaration to be signed and dated it is good practice to do so and a date will be essential if it defines the donations made under the scheme.

If the charity receives an oral gift aid declaration it should follow this up in writing by sending the donor a record of the declaration. This should include the details provided by the donor in the declaration, the date of the donation and of the charity's written confirmation, together with notes relating to the tax requirements and the donor's right to cancel the declaration within 30 days. Oral declarations are not effective until the written record has been sent.

For sponsored events, forms can be designed that serve as a gift aid declaration for each sponsor. The declaration can be placed at the top of each sheet, with an opt-in box for sponsors to tick if they want their donation to be treated as gift aid. The form should include each sponsor's full name and home address, the amount pledged and paid, the date each donation was made and the total handed over to the charity. A model form is available from HM Revenue & Customs.

Donors may cancel their declarations through any means. Cancellations will be effective from the date of notification or some future date identified by the donor. Retrospective cancellations are only effective during the 30-day 'cooling off' period after written confirmation has been sent in respect of an oral declaration.

Charities need to keep documentary evidence to support their tax claims. In particular, they must be able to show how much has been received from each donor. There is no set format for storing this information and charities will need to develop procedures that are compatible with their other administrative systems.

Funds given to charities for the provision of services or some other form of significant benefit will not qualify under the gift aid scheme although limited benefits to gift aid donors are acceptable.

The charity must claim gift aid within four years of the end of the accounting period in which the donation was made. Transitional relief must be claimed within two years of the end of the accounting period in which the donation was made.

Charities must maintain records that provide an audit trail linking each donation to an identifiable donor who has given a valid Gift Aid declaration, and must also maintain a clear auditable record of declarations. These records must be maintained for the later of four years after the end of the accounting period in which the donation was made or one year after the gift aid repayment claim has been made.

From 2013, the government is hoping to have in place a new online filing system for gift aid claims. Also proposed from 2013 is a scheme where charities will be able to claim gift aid on donations under £10 without the need for written declarations up to a maximum of £5,000 per charity per year.

There is a substantial amount of information about gift aid available on the website of HM Revenue & Customs.

Shares. There is provision for those who donate certain shares to charities to reclaim some tax in relation to those shares.

VAT

Value added tax (VAT) is a tax on the supply of goods and services in the UK and the Isle of Man. VAT is charged at either:
- standard rate (this applies to most goods and services);
- reduced rate (e.g. on fuel and power); or
- zero rate (e.g. food and books).

The standard rate of VAT was temporarily reduced to 15% on 1 December 2008 and returned to 17.5% on 1 January 2010. On 4 January 2011, the standard rate increased to 20%.

Business supplies in the UK are generally taxed at the standard rate unless a specific relief or exemption applies. 'Non-business income' is outside the scope of VAT.

Some supplies of goods and services are exempt from VAT. You do not charge VAT to your customers on exempt business supplies and you cannot reclaim the VAT that you are charged on purchases relating to those supplies.

The VAT treatment of a charity's income is therefore dependent on identifying business and non-business activities and then for business activities, identifying taxable and exempt activities. This is discussed in more detail later in this chapter.

Those business supplies that are subject to VAT at any of the three rates are the organisation's taxable supplies and it is the measurement of the turnover of the taxable supplies against the registration threshold that determines whether the organisation should register for VAT. The registration threshold increases each year and for the tax year 6 April 2011 to 5 April 2012 is £73,000.

The amount of VAT paid to HM Revenue & Customs by a VAT-registered organisation is determined by the difference between input tax and output tax.
- **Output tax.** This is the VAT charged on standard and reduced rate supplies.

- **_Input tax._** This is the VAT paid on purchases in relation to the taxable supplies.

If the output tax is greater than the input tax, the charity must pay the difference to HM Revenue & Customs. If the charity has paid more input tax than it has charged as output tax, then it may claim the difference back. The amounts are submitted to HM Revenue & Customs on a VAT return.

Input tax paid by charities in relation to goods and services connected to the charity's non-business and exempt activities cannot be offset against output tax or reclaimed.

Clearly, extensive documentation is required to account for input and output tax and to support the VAT return. The VAT paid on input supplies can only be claimed back if the charity is VAT registered. It is possible for organisations falling below the threshold to register voluntarily, but trustees will need to consider whether the charity will be able to reclaim any tax and balance the financial benefit against the corresponding administrative burden.

Business or non-business?

As can be seen from the discussion above, it is essential for trustees to assess the services offered by their charity and to consider which elements represent business activities and whether the value of these activities crosses the registration threshold, requiring the charity to register. Unfortunately, some of the distinctions between business and non-business activities are very fine. In addition, although some charitable activity is considered business, the supplies in question may be either zero-rated or exempt from VAT. The table on pp. 175–177 gives an overview of the provisions. Trustees who believe that their charity should be VAT registered should seek further advice, for example by contacting their local HM Revenue & Customs office.

Zero-rated supplies to charities

A number of supplies made to charities are zero-rated, meaning the charity does not have to pay any VAT on the goods and services in question. In these circumstances, the onus is on the charity to provide the supplier with a written declaration of its eligibility for zero-rating on the supplies in question.

Activity	Business	Non-Business
Donations, bequests and grants	A funding agreement where the funder directly receives a benefit from the service provided will be subject to VAT. This is a very grey area and professional advice is usually required.	Voluntary contributions and grants which are freely given and which are not a purchase of services are non-business and outside the scope of VAT. Grants subsidising a service which would be provided by the charity anyway are also non-business.
Voluntary services provided without charge		Free services are non-business activities (e.g. first aid, sea rescue and worship). Any genuine donations freely given by the recipients of these services are outside the scope of VAT.
Sale of goods (including charity shops)	The sale of goods is a business activity. The sale of donated goods is zero-rated, whether the sale is through a shop or not. The sale of bought-in goods is standard-rated unless they are covered by another zero-rating (e.g. books).	
Hire of charity-run buildings (e.g. village halls)	The hire of a charity-run building for a fee is business. This includes village halls and other community buildings. The fee is normally exempt from VAT unless the charity chooses to waive the exemption, allowing it to register and recover input tax. The exemption cannot be waived or let to another charity for non-business use.	

Activity	Business	Non-Business
Welfare services (incuding spiritual welfare)	Welfare services supplied by charities, together with any related goods, are business but are exempt, provided the supplies are not made for profit (i.e. any surplus made is reinvested in the same service). If the surplus was used for a different charitable activity, the supply of welfare would be standard rated.	The same services are non-business when they are consistently supplied below cost (i.e. subsidised by at least 15% from the charity's funds) to relieve the distress of beneficiaries.
Education	The provision of education in exchange for consideration (i.e. a fee) is a business activity, but it is exempt from VAT provided any surplus made is reinvested in the same service. If the surplus was used for a different charitable activity, the provision of education would be standard rated.	The same provision is non-business if it is provided for free (e.g. in a state school).
Cultural services (e.g. admission to museums, galleries, zoos and theatres)	Admission charges are exempt from VAT provided any surplus made is reinvested in the same activity and the organisation is managed and administered on a voluntary basis.	Admission is non-business if provided for free.
Membership subscriptions	If members receive benefits in return for their subscriptions (e.g. publications, advice services or events) then the subscriptions will be considered to be business and subject to VAT.	Subscriptions are non-business if the members are entitled to nothing more than copies of statutory documents (i.e. annual reports and accounts) and voting rights at general meetings.

Activity	Business	Non-Business
Corporate sponsorship	Sponsorship from companies and other bodies is subject the the standard rate of VAT if the funds are conditional on some benefit, such as the publication of the organisation's logo. The fundraising exemption (see opposite) will apply to sponsorship in relation to one-off events.	Corporate donations are outside the scope of VAT if there is no reciprocal benefit. A small acknowledgement in an annual report will not change a donation into a sponsorship.
Sales of advertising in charity publications	If less than 50% of the advertisements in the publication are from private individuals, the income from all the adverts will be subject to standard rate VAT. The supply of advertising to a charity may be zero rated and the publication may be exempt if it is part of a one-off fundraising event.	If 50% or more of the advertisements in the publication are clearly from private individuals, the income may be treated as donations and outside the scope of VAT.
Interest payments		Interest earned on funds kept in bank and building society accounts is non-business.

Zero-rating is available on the following:

- advertising in all types of media and all preparation work (e.g. design and artwork);
- recording and playback equipment for the production of talking books and newspapers for people with visual impairments (cassette tapes are standard rated);
- supply, repair, maintenance and importation of sea rescue equipment;
- construction of new self-contained buildings and annexes, excluding professional services, which are standard rated; and
- the purchase of a freehold or leasehold (exceeding 21 years) where the property will be used for a relevant charitable or residential purpose.

Fundraising events

As has been mentioned in the table on pp. 175–177, fundraising events may be exempt from VAT. The exemption applies to events that meet the following criteria:

1 The event must be organised and promoted primarily to raise money for the benefit of the charity.

2 The people attending the event must be aware of the fundraising purpose.

3 The event must not be part of continuous or semi-regular activities (frequent events would represent trading and would not qualify for the exemption). In effect, this means that charities are limited to holding 15 events of the same kind in the same location in each financial year, although more frequent small-scale events (where gross weekly income does not exceed £1,000) are acceptable. Trustees should be aware that small-scale events taking place, for example, once or twice weekly, may be considered as trading.

The exemption applies to a wide range of events, including quizzes, dances, concerts, fêtes and jumble sales.

The VAT exemption is mandatory for events that fulfil all the conditions and all the charity's income in connection with the event will be exempt, although the sale of commemorative goods for a period after the event will not enjoy a VAT exemption. Goods and services purchased for the event are subject to the normal VAT treatment. However, charities can make zero-rated supplies at an event, for example through the sale of programmes and donated goods, and can claim back their input tax in relation to those supplies.

CAUTION!

If charities exceed the 15-event limit, none of the fundraising events will qualify for the VAT exemption.

Charities can hold joint fundraising events with other charities, but be careful when holding joint events in partnership with non-charities as the exemption may not apply.

VAT and branches

Where branches are part of the parent charity, the obligation to register for VAT is determined by the total taxable supplies of the branches and main charity combined. Where the branch is independent and legally separate from the parent, the requirement for the branch to register will be dependent on its own turnover of taxable supplies. In this situation, any donation made by the branch to the parent body which is a genuine donation (i.e. not a subscription for services) will be treated as non-business.

Employment

As has been stated in chapter 6, when we discussed employment issues, charities must pay employers' national insurance contributions for all employees with an income above a certain level. Thresholds are reviewed annually so trustees are advised to check the current level, but for the tax year 6 April 20011 to 5 April 2012, employer's national insurance contributions are payable on salaries above £7,072 at a rate of 13.8%.

Charity staff members are, of course, required to pay income tax on their income and to pay national insurance contributions. A charity which operates its own payroll will be responsible for collecting these sums and passing payment to the government.

Trading

There is a general presumption against commercial trading by charities. Charities are established to promote a particular charitable purpose and to act in the public interest and this is not always compatible with commercial trading. Depending on the wording of an individual charity's governing document, trading may be beyond the organisation's constitutional remit, so trustees who sanction such activities will be acting in breach of trust. In addition, commercial trading is financially risky and it is not appropriate for organisations to subject charitable funds to business risk. Finally, charities enjoy tax exemptions that are not available to commercial organisations so it would be inequitable for charities to compete with companies within the same arena. However, the law is pragmatic: it recognises that there are occasions when charitable organisations will be perfectly justified in selling goods and services to meet charitable objectives and to raise funds, so some trading is permissible and exempt from tax, provided it falls within one of the following categories.

Primary purpose trading. This involves the sale of goods or services that contributes directly to the primary objects of the charity. Such trading is permissible as it will further the objects of the charity. Ancillary trading, which contributes to the main charitable purpose, is also acceptable.

CASE EXAMPLE

A charity whose object is to promote the welfare of older people may charge for the provision of day centres, residential or domiciliary care. It is under this provision that many local charities are able to have service level agreements or other forms of contracts with statutory agencies for the provision of care services. Ancillary trading may include the sale of refreshments or emergency groceries in the day centre.

Trading that is not wholly focused on the charity's primary purpose will be acceptable, provided the non-primary purpose element is small both in financial value and as a proportion of the trade as a whole.

A charity with objects that include increasing the independence of people with disabilities may sell aids and adaptations.

Primary purpose and ancillary trading can be carried out within the charity and are exempt from direct tax providing the profits are applied for charitable purposes

Small trading. Charities can trade on a small scale outside their primary purpose. Small trading is restricted to a limited annual turnover of £5,000 or, if greater than £5,000, 25% of the charity's annual income, subject to a maximum of £50,000. It may be acceptable for charities to exceed these limits if they had a reasonable expectation that their turnover would be within the restrictions. The profits from small-scale trading are exempt from tax only if applied for charitable purposes.

Trade carried out by the beneficiaries. Charities can trade in goods that have been manufactured by their beneficiaries and in services provided by the beneficiaries. The involvement in non-beneficiaries in the trade (e.g. in a management or advisory capacity) will not present problems as long as the majority of the work is carried out by beneficiaries. Once again, the profits are only exempt from tax if they are applied for charitable purposes.

CASE EXAMPLE

Charities may sell books or provide training not related to their primary purpose.

Charity shops selling craft and art work produced by beneficiaries within a charity's sheltered workshop or a catering service staffed by people with learning disabilities.

Lotteries: Lotteries are classed as trading, but charities are allowed to hold them and the profits are exempt from tax provided that they are either (a) Small Lotteries or (b) Society Lotteries and the profits are again applied for charitable purposes. Small lotteries are typically held at an event (e.g. a raffle at a fete) with the prizes being under £250 in total and there being no cash prizes.

Further tax exemptions are available for:

- the sale of donated goods, provided the goods have not been significantly modified; and
- profits from lettings where the income is used for charitable purposes (this exemption may be waived if additional services are provided).

Business sponsorship and payment for the use of a charity's logo may or may not be considered to be a trade and subject to tax, depending on the exact circumstances of the agreement between the parties. In addition, VAT may be payable.

Even tax exempt trading may be subject to VAT. See the VAT section above for further information.

Charities which trade outside these permitted areas may find that they have acted outside the terms of their governing document and, consequently, the trustees have acted either *ultra vires* and/or in breach of trust. They may also find that they are required to pay tax on any profits from trading. It may be held to be inappropriate to claim these liabilities from charitable funds and that the trustees should pay.

Any profits from trading activities that are not covered by the tax exemptions will be subject to tax. When calculating profits, trustees should pay attention to any indirect overheads, such as accommodation of the trading activity within the charity's premises. Where goods or services have been supplied to the trading activity free of charge or at a reduced rate, trustees should consider the commercial value of such items when determining profits.

Trading companies

There is a way for charities to trade outside of the permitted areas that does not expose charitable funds to business risk and does not result in a breach of trust. Charities wishing to trade on a larger scale may set up a separate trading company. This device may be used by charities wanting to trade outside of their primary objects and the tax concessions (e.g. for larger fundraising purposes) and by those who intend to trade within their objects, but who wish to protect the charity itself from the inherent business risks.

Trading companies operate as normal commercial companies, unrestricted by the limitations on charity trading. They may seek investment from a number of sources but are often established by charities as a wholly owned subsidiary (i.e. the charity is the sole shareholder, although this is not essential). Trading subsidiaries are subject to the same taxes as regular commercial companies. However, under the gift aid scheme, they may donate their profits to the charity prior to the deduction of taxes. The charity does not need to reclaim any tax and the company will receive a deduction in corporation tax for the gift aid payment. The scheme allows for gift aid payments relating to a particular accounting period to be made up to nine months after the end of that accounting period.

The company will probably need to keep a proportion of its profits to maintain adequate cash balances to continue trading. Alternatively the charity can establish the company with sufficient capital to allow it to gift all of its profits to the charity. However, to qualify for the tax benefits, the charity's financial investment in setting up and maintaining the company must be made for charitable purposes only and for the benefit of the charity. It should also be secure and offer a fair rate of return, with provision for the recovery of any loans to the company. In addition, trustees should be aware that whilst trading losses on primary purpose trading may be classed as charitable expenditure, trading losses on non-primary purpose trading will be non-charitable expenditure and potentially *ultra vires*.

On a practical level, a number of the trustees of the charity should serve as directors of the subsidiary trading company to ensure that the company is operating in the interests of the charity, including consistency between the charity and the company in areas such as public image, employment practices etc. It is also advisable to bring in directors from the commercial sector who possess the appropriate business skills.

WHEN TO SET UP A TRADING COMPANY

1 Do you want to trade on a regular, significant basis (i.e. not small trading)?
   No – trading company not necessary
   Yes – go to 2
2 Do you want to trade outside the primary objects of the charity or enter into trading that is not carried out by your beneficiaries?
   No – trading company not necessary, go to 3
   Yes – trading company necessary
3 Is the level of trading or the capital investment required such that it is necessary to protect the charity from business risks?
   No – trading company not required
   Yes – trading company necessary

Investments

The law and the governing document

Trustees have a general power of investment. This was introduced by the Trustee Act 2000 and supersedes the limited powers that existed under previous legislation, even where these are specifically mentioned in a charity's governing document. Within this general power, existing restrictions or exclusions on specific types of investment that may be included in the governing document (e.g. a restriction on the purchase of shares in tobacco companies) are still valid. If trustees wish to remove these restrictions, they should consult the Charity Commission.

The general power of investment allows for trustees to place charity funds in any kind of investment (except land) as if they were the absolute owner of those funds. However, trustees are required to seek appropriate advice and to consider the suitability of investments and the need to diversify the range of investments held. They are also required to review their investments on a regular basis, which should be at least once a year.

Trustees must use their skills and knowledge in a way that is reasonable in the circumstances. This means that a trustee with investment experience is expected to show a higher level of skills and knowledge than a trustee with no such experience.

Trustees can delegate investment functions, but any delegated asset management must be under a written agreement and must be reviewed periodically.

Different types of investments

There is a large range of investments available for charities to choose from and the terminology can be bewildering for the uninitiated.

Shares are sold by companies to raise revenue. There is no obligation for companies to repay or buy back shares. The owners of the shares (the shareholders) share in the ownership and profits of the company. Profits are distributed through dividends. There are different types of shares and this affects the dividend received:

1 Owners of ordinary shares (also known as equities) may not receive a dividend if the company is in financial trouble, but will receive higher dividends in successful years. Ordinary shareholders also have voting rights at general meetings.
2 Preference shares pay a predetermined dividend, unconnected to the company's profit level. Although preference shareholders take priority over ordinary shareholders in the payment of dividends, they have limited voting rights.
3 Debentures pay a specified dividend at specified intervals.
4 Convertible shares pay a fixed rate of interest, rather than a dividend, but may be converted into ordinary shares at some point in the future.

Bonds can also be sold to raise revenue, but do not confer any ownership or pay out profits. Instead, bonds pay a fixed rate of interest (the coupon) to the bond holder up to the set date when the issuer of the bond will repay the holder. This is called the redemption or maturity date. They may be issued by companies (corporate bonds) and by statutory bodies, including overseas governments. UK government bonds are known as gilts. Interest rates tend to be lower on the more secure bonds (e.g. gilts) and higher on the riskier investments (e.g. corporate bonds). Bonds are also known as fixed interest stocks or fixed interest securities.

Stock is the overall term for shares, bonds and gilts. Stock may be bought and sold freely, hence the term 'stock market'.

Deposits are funds kept with financial institutions such as banks and building societies. The rate of interest paid on deposits is variable.

Accounts that offer access to funds with little or no notice often have low interest rates, whereas those with long notice periods offer higher interest, with penalties on early withdrawal.

Property can also be an investment. Property is dealt with separately, later in this chapter.

Yield is the annual return received from an investment (e.g. in dividends or interest).

Collective investments provide opportunities to invest relatively small sums of money in the stock market whilst spreading those funds across a wide range of stock. The basic premise is that the resources of a group of investors are collectively invested and managed for the common benefit, with the yield from the investments distributed amongst the different investors. There are a number of different forms of collective investments.

1 Unit trusts – here, the total investment is divided into units. The individual units represent a proportion of the value of all the investments held and income received from the investment is distributed to unit holders in accordance with the number of units held. Alternatively income may be accumulated for the benefit of the unit holders. Investments are selected according to the objectives of the particular scheme (i.e. capital or income). Management fees are charged and some unit trusts charge exit fees. Returns are not guaranteed.

2 Investment trusts are companies which invest in shares. Investors buy shares in the investment trust company itself, with the company issuing a fixed number of shares. Share price is determined by a number of factors, including the value of the investments in the fund and supply and demand. Charges include the dealing price of buying and selling the shares.

3 Open-ended investment companies (OEICs) manage investment funds and you invest in them by purchasing shares. Unlike investment trusts, OEICs can continue to issue shares in response to demand. There may be an initial charge for share purchase or an exit charge for leaving the OEIC.

4 A common investment fund is a form of collective investment that is only available to registered charities. These are themselves registered charities and work on a similar model to unit trusts; however, charges are lower with a smaller minimum investment.

Those who invest in these collective vehicles are not the owners of the shares; instead shares are owned by the fund, company or trust.

When reviewing the investment opportunities available, in partnership with their professional advisers, trustees should consider the requirements of their investment policy. For example, cash and bonds are low-risk investments, but may not offer sufficient returns to protect against inflation. In contrast, equities tend to offer long-term protection against inflation, but charities will need to balance their selection of shares against their accepted risk level and any ethical concerns. Other issues to consider will be the need to access funds (as has already been said, some high-interest-bearing deposits have lengthy notice periods) and whether the charges made in relation to certain investments are justified by the level of return. The likely response will be a diversified approach, with investments spread across cash deposits, shares and bonds. This offers a trade off between risk and return. However, the balance of this spread will depend on the policy of the charity.

Developing an investment policy

Trustees have an obligation to maximise the funds available for furthering the objects of the charity. For many charities this means fundraising to support a hand-to-mouth existence, but for those organisations holding reserves or endowments, the obligation extends to the investment of those funds.

Whether the charity is holding the next quarter's grant cheque or a permanent endowment, decisions need to be made about where best to place the funds to maximise the resources available to develop the charity's work. For this, charities need an investment policy and trustees need, as a starting point, to have agreed the direction of the charity and determined the resources necessary to reach that destination. There are two key questions on which an investment policy rests:

1 Capital or income?
2 Long term or short term?

Does the charity need to accrue capital (e.g. for the purchase or refurbishment of a building or to update equipment) or does it need its investments to bring in a regular income to fund the charity's work? Does it need the money in the short term (e.g. to fund an individual piece of work) or is it a medium- or long-term requirement, perhaps to fund expansion or to make up the shortfall of a predicted loss of income, such as the end of a fixed-term grant? Few cases will be black and white, with many investment policies involving a mixed approach of capital and income returns and long- and short-term investments. The function of the trustees is to determine the balance between the different demands.

Is quick access to the funds likely to be needed? How much of your balance can be committed to investments on a long-term basis and how much should be kept in more open investments that will allow funds to be withdrawn swiftly in the event of an emergency? For example, trustees may decide to keep the equivalent of one month's running costs or an adequate sum for emergency building repairs in a more flexible investment.

Balance of risk

Trustees also need to consider the level of risk into which they are prepared to enter and this should be included within the policy.

Unfortunately, the nature of the investment market means that the investments with the highest returns carry the highest risks and those that are lowest risk offer fewer returns. There are limits on the investment opportunities available to charities precisely because it would be inappropriate for trustees to place charitable funds in highly risky investments. Restrictions on charity investment are considered in more detail in the next few sections. Within the investments that are available, trustees must decide how they wish to balance risk against returns.

Funds invested for the short and medium term should be relatively risk free, as charities will want to avoid sudden drops in capital values which could reduce their available funding. A drop in capital value for funds invested for the longer term is less critical because such investments can be held until their value has recovered.

Ethical investment

Investment decisions can be difficult for those with a social conscience. Many charity trustees may be understandably reluctant to invest charitable funds in companies or governments if they consider their activities to be morally questionable. However, trustees need to balance any qualms against their obligation to act in the best interests of the charity and to maximise the resources available. This is not a straightforward equation. Even a high returning investment can damage a charity's funding base if the investment in question directly contradicts the organisation's objectives, or is so unpopular with donors that it loses fundraising income. As a result, some basic principles have evolved.

1 Charities should not make investments that contradict the objects of the charity as these would not further the charity's objects and as such may result in a breach of trust (because the trustees have acted outside the objects).

EXAMPLE

Charities involved in cancer research and treatment should not invest in tobacco companies and charities supporting landmine victims should not invest in arms companies.

Similarly, charities supporting refugees who are seeking asylum from particular regimes should not buy the government bonds of those regimes.

2 Charities may decide not to make investments that they reasonably believe would adversely affect fundraising income or would lose them supporters or beneficiaries.

EXAMPLE

A charity working with older people might decide not to invest in cosmetic companies that test products on animals, provided that it could establish that it would deter

donors from making further gifts (e.g. because of the weight of public opinion against such testing or because of the expressed opinions of the charity's regular donors).

3 Trustees cannot, however, decide not to purchase a particular investment simply because it would be against their personal conscience. Some potential adverse affect on the charity must be demonstrated.

EXAMPLE

Trustees of a disability charity could not make a decision not to invest in a company simply because they

personally advocated healthy eating and were consequently opposed to fast food.

Ethical investment questions focus very much on screening out inappropriate investments and, as such, this is sometimes seen as a negative approach. The alternative, known as socially responsible investment, aims to proactively invest in those companies with good track records in chosen areas, such as employment practice, environmental responsibility and corporate social involvement.

The investment policy is an important tool for trustees to instruct and monitor their advisers. As well as shaping the requirements of the investments in terms of the nature of the return, balance of risk and any ethical restrictions, the policy should also consider the charity's investment powers and any restrictions on investments, as determined by the charity's governing document and by law.

Professional advisers

Trustees must take and consider advice from someone experienced in investment matters before making investments and when reviewing them, unless they have good reasons for not doing so. They may decide not to take external advice if they have sufficient experience within the charity.

However, the investment market is complex and subject to frequent fluctuations and few trustees will be truly qualified to manage charities' investments in a detailed way. Most charities will need to place funds in a variety of different investments to meet the requirements of their investment policy by achieving the desired balance of income and capital generation, long- and short-term investments and also catering for risk and ethical considerations. This range of investments is known as an investment portfolio and the management of this portfolio is the responsibility of a fund or investment manager. The fund manager will normally be employed by an investment company and is a professional appointed by the trustees to make detailed decisions about when to switch funds between different investments, perhaps to reduce risk or increase returns, whilst maintaining the balance and generating the returns required by the charity's investment policy. Alternatively, an investment broker may serve as an intermediary between the board and the fund manager.

Appointing a fund manager

Some investment companies do specialise in working with medium-sized charities, but trustees may have to shop around for these services. It is worth considering the service provided by a number of different companies, paying particular attention to the points listed below.

Authorisation. Check that the fund manager is authorised to carry out investment business by the Financial Services Authority (see further p. 191).

Charges. Fund managers' fees will depend on the service offered and the size of your investments. Charges may be expressed as a percentage of the portfolio value based on a sliding scale (the larger the investment, the smaller the percentage fee) or on the number of transactions. Look out for any hidden fees (e.g. for producing reports).

Services. The different services available include discretionary management (where the fund manager makes the decisions) and advisory services (where the manager always consults the client before making transactions). Consider whether investments are made in tracker funds (i.e. money is invested in a set group of companies) or actively managed; whether cash management services are available (if required); and whether any ethical concerns can be accommodated.

Past performance. Although not always an indicator of future success, trustees should look for a consistent track record in terms of investment performance and also question the company's stability, particularly in terms of retaining key staff.

Personality. Trustees need to be comfortable that their fund manager is someone whom they respect and feel confident working with.

Voting. You may want to consider the investment company's approach to shareholder voting. Does it exercise its right to vote and, if so, does it consult its clients (who are the beneficial shareholders) on the direction of the voting?

Other issues. Trustees may also want to consider a range of other issues, such as the company's risk management strategy, internal controls, arrangements for reporting to clients and charity experience.

Once appropriate firms have been identified, ask them to submit written proposals in response to the charity's investment policy and shortlist a number of firms to meet with before making the final decision.

Monitoring the fund manager's performance

Trustees should monitor the fund manager's performance against an agreed standard or benchmark. This may be negotiated with the fund manager, based on the expectations of the investment policy, it may be linked to a particular stock market index or it may be a published common benchmark (known as a 'universe'), based on the opinions of a range of industry specialists.

Charities should keep all correspondence and documentation regarding the relationship with the fund manager.

The appointment of the fund manager should also be subject to regular review (e.g. every three years) to ensure that the chosen fund manager remains the most appropriate for the charity. If at any point the trustees have serious concerns about the appointment, it should be reviewed immediately.

Protection for investors

All investment managers must be authorised under the Financial Services and Markets Act 2000 and regulated by the Financial Services Authority (FSA). The FSA is the investment industry regulator and keeps a register of the firms that are authorised to conduct investment business. In order to be placed on the FSA's register, firms must meet certain requirements in relation to competence, financial stability and treatment of customers. The register includes the details of the services that each firm is authorised to deliver and details of any disciplinary action that has been taken against the firm. Investors can access the FSA's register through the FSA's Firm Check Service.

In the event of a complaint regarding an investment professional, trustees should first contact the firm in question (contact details are available on the FSA's register). If their response is not satisfactory, the issue may be raised with the FSA. If an authorised firm has been used, access to complaints procedures and compensation is provided by the Financial Ombudsman Service and the Financial Services Compensation Scheme. (See the Directory for contact details.)

Programme Related Investments

The investments discussed above are all financial investments. The purpose of a financial investment is to yield the best financial return within the level of risk considered to be acceptable – this return can then be spent to further the charity's aims.

Programme Related Investments (PRIs) aim to use a charity's assets directly to further its aims in a way that may also produce some financial return for the charity. PRI is different from financial investment in that the justification for making a PRI is to further the charity's aims rather than to yield the best financial return. An example of a PRI would be making low-interest loans to beneficiaries.

In order to fulfil their duties and act within the law, trustees:

- must be able to show that the PRI is wholly in furtherance of the charity's aims;
- should make sure that any benefit to private individuals is necessary, reasonable and in the interests of the charity; and
- should consider reasonable and practical ways to exit from a PRI if it is no longer furthering the charity's aims.

Appointing nominees and custodians

Charitable companies have a legal identity and can hold investments in their own name. Unincorporated charities (e.g. trusts and associations) do not have their own legal identity, so charity trustees will have to hold investments in their own names. It is usually more convenient to use a nominee and/or custodian.

Nominee. A nominee is appointed by the trustees to hold the charity's property. The property (e.g. shares) is held in the name of the nominee but on behalf of the charity.

Custodian. Custodians have custody of a charity's assets, or documents relating to those assets, for safe-keeping.

Nominee and custodial services can be particularly useful if the charity has extensive documentation in relation to its assets, or has a frequent turnover of trustees as these services eliminate the need for repeated legal transfers of property or handing over of documentation.

Charities have a statutory power to appoint nominees and custodians, unless this is specifically excluded by the governing document. The power does not apply to assets which are vested in the Official Custodian for Charities (see the section on property and land below) or where the charity has its own custodian trustee, as is often the case with older, land-owning charities. There must be written evidence of the appointment and the individual or organisation appointed must be appropriate.

Trustees may determine the conditions of appointment, including remuneration, bearing in mind the requirements of the governing document and the need to avoid conflicts of interest. The appointment should be reviewed periodically. Trustees must ensure that the charity's ownership of the assets in question remains legally provable and should receive reports from the nominee or custodian regarding the arrangements to ensure safe-keeping of the charity's property.

Property and land

GENERAL PRINCIPLES

Charities must always engage appropriate professional support, including solicitors and surveyors, when considering land transactions. Provisions are complex and the discussion below can only give an overview of some of the key requirements.

Land transactions must be in the best interests of the charity, which means securing the best price, best mortgage deals etc.

Trustees must use their skills and knowledge in a way that is reasonable in the circumstances. This means that a trustee with property experience is expected to show a higher level of skill and knowledge than a trustee with no such experience.

Land transactions between the charity and a connected party (e.g. a trustee) represent a conflict of interest and should be discussed with the Charity Commission.

Trustees should seek advice on proposed land transactions involving permanent endowments.

Authority to own land

There is a general statutory power for charities to acquire land in the UK for charitable or investment purposes. Charities with governing documents that expressly contradict this power should check with the Charity Commission before purchasing land. Trustees should engage professional advice as necessary and ensure that the purchase is in the best interests of the charity (e.g. the property should be appropriate for its intended use, with any necessary planning permission in place, the price (and mortgage terms) should be fair, and the charity should be able to afford the purchase and any corresponding mortgage).

If purchasing the property for investment purposes, the general investment provisions apply (i.e. the trustees must seek appropriate professional advice and the investment must be suitable and part of a diversified range of investments). As with other investments, the investment in property should be subject to review. Trustees should pay particular attention to the need to actively manage property investments and the difficulty in withdrawing funds from such investments.

Mortgages and charities are not a natural partnership and restrictions do apply. A charity wishing to take out a mortgage on new or existing property should have appropriate powers within its governing document (if not, it should contact the Charity Commission). The trustees should also seek appropriate advice on the need for the loan, the suitability of the terms of the loan and their ability to repay it.

Disposal of charity land

Many governing documents give trustees the power to dispose of charity land and this is supported by a general statutory power. Constitutional powers may be subject to certain conditions, such as public notice of disposal of property that is central to the charity's objects (e.g. a playground or village hall). Any such conditions should be followed.

Before trustees may sell, lease or otherwise dispose of land or buildings, they will normally have to follow a statutory procedure. In certain circumstances, this will require trustees to obtain an Order from the Charity Commission giving prior consent. Trustees considering the sale of charity property should read the Charity Commission's publication 'Disposing of Charity Land' (CC28).

There are specific requirements when disposing of land. Briefly, trustees must instruct a qualified surveyor and must consider the advice given. Trustees must not sell land for less than the best price reasonably obtainable. To lease land for more than seven years, trustees must follow the statutory procedure for sales, but there is a simpler procedure for some leases for seven years or less. If, in either case, trustees are unable to follow the statutory procedure, or they wish to sell land to a person connected with themselves, they must obtain an order from the Charity Commission.

When the property being sold or leased is subject to trusts requiring it to be used for a charity's specific purposes, the trustees must normally give public notice of the disposal. They may also need to apply to the Charity Commission for a scheme to give them power to sell the property; this should be done before the property is marketed.

Different considerations may apply to a sale by one charity to another charity. The trusts of the first charity may authorise the disposal of the land to the other charity for less than the best price reasonably obtainable.

In order to reduce the risk of conflicts of interest and fraud, any decisions or actions in relation to the disposal or mortgaging of charity land must be taken by the trustees acting together and should not be delegated to a single trustee, employee or adviser.

Documentation

As discussed above, trustees may decide to pass property documentation (title deeds, land registry certificates etc.) to a custodian. Any custodian trustee (including the Official Custodian of Charities) must be party to the transfer of charity property.

Although trustees must act collectively when disposing of land, only two trustees need to sign the deeds.

Trustees who dispose of charity land are required to include certain statements and certificates in the contract with the purchaser and in the conveyance, lease, transfer and any other deed or document affecting the disposal. Similar requirements are in place for mortgage deeds. There are prescribed forms of these statements and certificates in relation to registered land. In other cases, the solicitor will determine the wording. The purpose of this requirement is to ensure that the purchaser is aware that the land has been bought from a charity and to enable trustees to certify that they have followed the relevant requirements.

Official Custodian for Charities

The Official Custodian for Charities holds land and, very occasionally, investments on behalf of charities. The Official Custodian is an employee of the Charity Commission. As with other custodian services, this means that there is no need to make new deeds in relation to the property when the trustees change. It eliminates the risk of charity property being vested in individuals who have since moved on and are no longer connected with the organisation. If this does happen, vesting the land in the Official Custodian is a way of demonstrating the charity's ownership.

Property is vested in the Official Custodian by an order of the court or of the Charity Commissioners. Charities can apply for an order of the Commissioners and appropriate forms are available from the Commission. The services of the Official Custodian are free of charge.

The Official Custodian does not become involved in managing the property: this responsibility remains with the trustees. The trustees normally retain the title deeds and related documentation.

Maintenance and health and safety requirements

Charities who own land will be responsible for the maintenance of that land, insurance arrangements and compliance with any related health and safety requirements, unless the land is leased to a third party, in which case responsibility will be determined by the tenancy agreement. Trustees should pay full attention to their obligations in this respect (see chapter 2).

9 Fundraising

INTRODUCTION

Some organisations, such as grant-making charitable trusts with extensive endowments, are in the fortunate position of not having to raise funds from the public to continue their work, but for most charities fundraising is crucial to their ongoing viability. As trustees are responsible for the financial health of their charity, they must ensure that it has adequate resources to deliver its objectives. However, trustees' responsibility for fundraising extends beyond the bottom line, they must also ensure that the charity complies with the law and must consider the effect of the fundraising activity on the reputation of the charity.

In this chapter, we will look at trustees' responsibilities in relation to fundraising, including developing the charity's strategy and ensuring that its fundraising activities stay within the law. However, this chapter will not include advice on how to raise money or on different fundraising approaches. There are many books on the practical aspects of fundraising and a selection is listed in the Directory.

Developing the fundraising strategy

Fundraising should be an integral part of the trustees' planning process. In earlier chapters we have looked at trustees' roles in relation to business planning, budget setting and investment. As part of these processes, trustees must determine how much money they need to run existing activities and to establish new ones. Within this global figure, the different sources of income should be identified and this information will form the foundation of the fundraising strategy. In this section, we will consider the areas to cover when developing a fundraising strategy. An action plan that can be used to draft your strategy is included at the end of this section.

Where is the money coming from?

Relying on a single source of income may make an organisation vulnerable and could compromise its independence. Historically, many local charities have been largely or entirely financed by local authority grants and so have been highly vulnerable to funding cuts. In recent years many charities suffered following cuts in EU funding and as a result of the comprehensive spending review implemented by the Coalition Government following the 2010 General Election. Diversifying income sources offers charities a degree of protection, or at least some breathing space, should a particular income stream run dry.

Different areas of work may lend themselves naturally to certain sources of income and some income streams may already be secure. For example, charities may already have a number of contracts or grants in place. Ongoing projects, such as the employment of a worker dedicated to a particular aspect of the charity's work (e.g. supporting a particular element of its client group) require continuing funding and are frequently funded by renewable grants or contracts. In contrast, activities that require expenditure over a relatively short period, such as extending a building or commissioning a piece of research can be funded by one-off or short-term funding such as a specific grant or money from the proceeds of an appeal. Fundraising events and street collections can be useful ways of raising unrestricted funds; these can be used for any purpose within the organisation.

Ethical issues relating to fundraising should be considered. This may be covered by the charity's ethical investment policy. If a charity would not invest in tobacco companies, should it accept donations from them? Trustees may agree on wider restrictions, for example not to raise money through gambling or not to encourage events involving dangerous sports. As always with ethical issues, trustees should ensure that any self-imposed restrictions on sources of fundraising income are in the best interests of the charity, either because of the risk of direct conflict with charitable objects or because of a likely negative impact on other funding streams. Trustees may want to divide their fundraising strategy into raising money for specific purposes and raising money for the general purposes of the charity. Many charities find it easier to raise funds for specific purposes, as corporate sponsors, grant makers and the public like to feel that they are supporting a specific project. As discussed below, such appeals should include a statement that funds raised from the appeal that cannot be spent on the subject of the appeal will be used for the general purposes of the charity. Where an appeal is held for a specific activity, trustees should consider opening a separate bank account to hold funds raised by that appeal.

Funds to finance the general activities and overheads of the charity may be raised through a variety of approaches, including general appeals, sponsorship, fundraising events, trading activities and legacy appeals.

Timescale

As well as identifying the amount of income required and potential sources of income, the fundraising strategy should include details of when funding is required as it is no good raising money in two years' time for a project that is currently only funded for the next six months. By identifying what money is needed and when, trustees can prioritise the different elements of the fundraising strategy and create an action plan. In this way, the charity's fundraising strategy will be closely linked to its business plan.

Timescales should also be set for individual appeals, indicating when the appeal will end. This makes for better appeal planning and facilitates clearer accounting of appeal funds.

'Joined up thinking'

As well as linking into business planning, budgeting and the investment policy, the fundraising strategy should be consistent with any public relations approach agreed by the organisation, be complementary to operational work, and be sympathetic with the organisation's objectives. For example, it may be considered inappropriate for a charity working to alleviate family poverty to raise funds through events involving gambling, such as race nights. Similarly, the message of a charity promoting the independence of its beneficiaries would be undermined by a fundraising campaign that sought to evoke pity for its beneficiaries from the public.

Studies have indicated that some members of the public resent street collections carried out by fundraisers known as 'chuggers'; trustees should balance the potential for triggering resentment among the public against the funds that might be raised through such methods. Trustees should also ensure that any advertising campaign carried out by the charity complies with the relevant advertising regulations.

Is it worth it?

The strategy should also consider the 'effort: reward' ratio. Will the anticipated benefit of the fundraising activity including the income raised and the publicity generated justify the resources, including time and money invested in carrying out the activity? Using innovative or particularly well-targeted fundraising methods, a relatively small investment of resources can reap great rewards. In contrast if a charity's fundraising strategy is not well planned or executed, the amount spent on major fundraising campaigns, employing specialist fundraising staff or consultants may not be reflected in the benefits to the charity (e.g. the amount of money raised or publicity generated). Fundraising events can be labour intensive for local charities, but they may only generate small financial rewards (although the collateral benefits of increased profile or user involvement may make such events worthwhile).

It is for the trustees to decide in each case whether the reward is sufficient to make the effort worthwhile. For example, is expenditure of £1,000 generating a total income of £1,500 and a net gain of £500 justifiable, or would the activity have to generate a net gain of £1,000 to be worthwhile?

The trustees should also question whether the anticipated outcome is a realistic prediction. Are estimated returns for a street collection, legacy appeal or other fundraising event based on guesswork, previous experience or other factors? Are grant applications likely to be successful – have the applications been targeted at those grant makers most likely to fund your type of organisation or project?

Reporting the costs

The amount of money spent on fundraising should be reported in the charity's annual accounts. Charities with an annual income exceeding £1 million are required to submit a Summary Information Return to the Charity Commission each year. Some fundraising activities also serve as a means of promoting charitable objectives (e.g. by raising awareness of the charity's work and message).

Who is responsible?

The respective roles of trustees, staff and supporters should be considered as part of the fundraising strategy and reflected in the job descriptions of staff and trustees. Fundraising is one of those areas of charity work that can easily fall through the gaps in the clearly defined responsibilities of staff and trustees, particularly in small charities.

Trustees should be clear about who will take responsibility for the day-to-day tasks involved in fundraising, from project managing 'charity of the year' bids to business to negotiating with grant-making bodies. If these tasks are to be delegated to a member of staff, the scope of the role should be explicitly described in the employee's job description and the skills and experience required should be an integral part of the person specification. As always, trustees should be conscious of the blend of skills that they are looking for and the balance between fundraising and other activities. For instance, it might be unrealistic for trustees to expect that a worker who had been employed for their social care and counselling skills will also be an experienced fundraiser. It might also be unrealistic to expect the same worker to take a lead role in securing ongoing funding, without compromising an already full workload for providing client services. In such circumstances, the trustees have a clear responsibility to seek ongoing funding to sustain the charity and they should take the lead in any relevant negotiations.

In charities that employ a reasonable number of staff, it will usually be appropriate for trustees to delegate fundraising activities to the relevant members of staff, particularly if the team includes employees dedicated to the internal functioning and development of the organisation rather than operational roles. For example, a chief executive, office manager or finance manager may all play active roles in fundraising, from drafting funding applications through to arranging street collections or fundraising events.

Even where fundraising is delegated to employees of the charity, the trustees are ultimately responsibility for the financial viability of the organisation. The appointment of professional fundraising staff does not absolve them of this responsibility; it merely allows them to delegate the fundraising task to people with the appropriate skills and experience.

The fundraising of many local charities is led by volunteers. Whilst such volunteers are often extremely successful and hugely valuable to the

FUNDRAISING STRATEGY – ACTION PLAN

Task	Who is responsible
Identify the most appropriate sources of funding.	Trustees and senior staff, including any fundraising staff.
Check that the proposed fundraising approach is consistent with the organisation's public image and operational concerns.	Trustees and senior staff, in consultation with operational staff and any PR personnel.
Agree a baseline in terms of the ratio of fundraising costs to fundraising income.	Trustees (particularly the treasurer), senior officer and senior finance officer.
Consider any legal restrictions or best practice issues relating to your preferred methods of fundraising.	Trustees with the advice and support of senior staff.

charity, the trustees have the overall responsibility for fundraising and must exercise authority over the actions of volunteers. This is frequently achieved through a fundraising sub-committee involving trustees and volunteers.

The use of fundraising consultants is discussed at pp. 209–211.

Rules and good practice

Trustees also need to be aware of the regulatory framework that surrounds fundraising activities. In addition to the information given below, the application of other legal requirements should also be considered. For example, information held on donors is subject to the provisions of the Data Protection Act 1998 and health and safety requirements should be complied with in relation to any fundraising events. Both of these subjects are discussed in chapter 2.

The focus of this section is on those fundraising activities that are most commonly used by small to medium-sized charities. Sources of information on other activities such as overseas challenge events and internet and social media fundraising are listed in the Directory.

The regulation of charitable fundraising activities has been reviewed many times and is the subject of yet another review as part of the wider review of the Charities Act referred to in chapter 1. It is expected that future changes in this area of law may be made in the next few years. This section will set out the current rules and outline likely future changes.

Street collections

A permit or licence is normally required for charity collections or sales taking place in the street or other public places. Under the current scheme, licences and permits can be obtained from the relevant local authority or, for collections in London, from the Police or the City of London authorities.

Permits and licences are granted under local regulations. Issues that will be considered include obstructions to both human and vehicular traffic, financial controls and accounting arrangements for any funds raised through the collection and the frequency of collections (some high streets have street collections booked throughout the year, whilst other local authorities prefer to keep the number of collections down). Charities should contact your local authority for information about the regulations in your area.

Pay particular attention to arrangements for public places that are privately owned (e.g. shopping centres and railway stations). Under provisions of the Charities Act 2011 that *may* come into force in the next few years, charities wishing to carry out collections in public places, including street collections, would, unless an exemption applied, require a public collections certificate issued by the Charity Commission and a permit granted by the relevant local authority. This is an area that the ongoing review of the Charities Act is focusing upon, so there may be further change here.

Door-to-door collections

Door-to-door collections are also subject to licensing arrangements, again controlled by the local authority or, in London, the Police or the City of London. The arrangements apply to charity sales and collections of money and goods from residential and business premises (including public houses). Exemptions from licensing requirements are available from the Home Secretary for collections covering a wide area (i.e. a substantial part of the country). Exemptions are available from the police for local collections taking place over a short period of time.

It is good practice to collect cash donations from street and door-to-door collections in sealed collecting tins. This not only helps reduce the risk of theft from the collection, but also reassures donors that the risk of theft has been reduced.

Those collecting public donations should always wear visible identity cards establishing their connection with the charity and the legality of the collection.

Under provisions of the Charities Act 2011 that *may* come into force in the next few years, charities wishing to carry out door-to-door collections will, unless an exemption applies, require a public collections certificate and must notify the local authority before the collection. Again, this is an area that the ongoing review of the Charities Act is focusing upon and there may be further change here.

Events

Charities raise funds through a wide variety of events, from jumble sales and raffles through to high-profile auctions and expensive balls. Trustees need to research carefully any legal requirements relating to the events planned. The tax exemptions available for fundraising and trading are discussed in chapter 8. Other issues include health and safety requirements (e.g. maximum capacity for venues used), insurance and specific regulations relating to the nature of the event, such as any licences required for gambling or the sale of alcohol.

Lotteries (including raffles)

Charities and their subsidiary companies may run lotteries to raise money for their charitable purposes. These are regulated by the Gambling Commission under the Gambling Act 2005. Charity lotteries fall into two categories:

1 *Incidental lotteries.* There is no requirement to register a lottery that is incidental to an exempt entertainment that is not held for private gain, for example a charity fête or concert. The classic example of a small lottery is a raffle. Such lotteries must comply with certain requirements, for example, tickets must be sold and issued and the results announced during the event and on the premises where it is held and no more than £500 of the takings may be spent on prizes and no more than £100 of the takings may be spent on expenses.

2 *Society lotteries.* Other charity lotteries must be registered with the local authority or the Gambling Commission. Gambling Commission registration is required where ticket sales exceed £20,000 for a single lottery or £250,000 for lotteries organised by a charity in a one-year period. Trustees undertaking society lotteries should contact their local authority or (if necessary) the Gambling Commission for information on the detailed requirements relating to issues such as the price of tickets, prize money, deduction of costs, age restrictions and accounting requirements.

Further information about the regulation of lotteries may be found on the Gambling Commission website: www.gamblingcommission.gov.uk.

Lottery profits are tax exempt as long as they are used solely for the charity's objects and all regulatory requirements are complied with. The tax exemption does not apply to lotteries run by subsidiary companies, although the company can donate all pre-tax profits to the charity under the gift aid scheme (see chapter 8).

Telephone and broadcast media

Codes of conduct are available for both telephone fundraising and broadcast appeals. Even trustees of small charities may find opportunities for broadcast appeals (e.g. on local radio and television).

Trustees have a duty to ensure clarity in terms of identifying the charity (not just the cause) that will receive the funds and the proportion of the donation that will be spent on the charity's objects. Funds raised must be transferred directly to the charity.

Legacies

Legacy fundraising is a sensitive and complex area of fundraising and trustees looking to raise resources through legacies should plan their approach carefully. It is particularly important to develop a code for fundraisers, be they volunteers, employees or external fundraisers, that covers legal requirements and best practice. Such a code should also consider wider issues, such as the marketing of a legacy campaign. An insensitive campaign runs the risk of offending people and alienating potential donors. The Institute of Fundraising has produced a code of practice for legacy fundraising: see the Directory. Trustees should also bear in mind the length of time that is likely to pass between the appeal being made and the funds coming to the charity when considering the resources used on legacy fundraising and the reliance placed on legacies.

When seeking legacies, it is important to follow the basic principles of fundraising, including communicating clear information on the organisation's charitable status and the way in which the donation will be used. Given the sensitivity of legacy fundraising, it is critical that donors are not pressurised into making a donation. Particular care should be taken when dealing with vulnerable people (e.g. those who are terminally ill, elderly or recently bereaved). If it can be proved that the legacy was made under undue influence, the will could be held to be invalid and the gift will fail. Fundraisers should recommend to donors that they take the appropriate legal advice, although they should not recommend individual solicitors or comment on their competence. In addition, wills must not be witnessed by a representative of the charity. When a donor decides to make a donation to a charity, they should be encouraged to include the charity's registered number as well as its name to avoid confusion with other organisations: the name of the charity may change before the supporter dies, or the supporter may confuse the charity with a similarly named organisation.

It is not unusual for donors to want their legacy to be used for a particular purpose. If a charity decides to make an appeal encouraging donors to make legacies to be used for a particular purpose, the charity should make it clear that if the legacy cannot be used for that purpose it will be used for the general purposes of the charity.

Declaration of charitable status

Registered charities with a gross annual income of £10,000 or more are required to declare their charitable status on all media that solicits funds. It is good practice for all charities to do so. Similarly, although charities are not required to state their Charity Commission registration number, it is good practice to do so. Further information may be found on the Charity Commission website. Details of the requirements for charities registered in Scotland may be found on the website of the Office of the Scottish Charity Regulator (OSCR). In Northern Ireland, the Charity Commission for Northern Ireland has not yet begun to register charities, but its website contains information on the latest developments for the regulation of charities operating there.

Restricted funds

If funds have been raised for a particular purpose, they may only be spent on that purpose. This principle of restricted funds applies to public appeals, as well as to grant applications and can create difficulties if a specific fundraising appeal is more, or less, successful than anticipated. In such circumstances, any unspent funds cannot be applied to other causes within the charity without the express permission of the donor.

Many charities prefer to base fundraising campaigns and street collections on a specific issue, partly because they need money for that particular cause but also because, as has already been said, people like to give on this basis rather than just contributing to the general funds of the charity. If, as in the first example in the box below, more funds are raised than required, the charity will have to seek advice from the Charity Commission on whether a Commission Scheme will be necessary to enable the funds to be used for other purposes within the charity's objects. If the funds raised are insufficient, trustees must try to return any funds given by identifiable donors. If donors do not wish to take their money back, they must sign a disclaimer to this effect. Funds raised through collecting tins, competitions and lotteries are presumed to be from unidentifiable donors. The Charity Commission can make a Scheme to apply any remaining funds to other similar purposes within the charity. These funds must be kept in reserve for six months in order to meet any outstanding claims from donors.

Trustees facing either situation should contact the Charity Commission for advice.

Charities may avoid this problem by ensuring that every request for funds for a specified purpose is accompanied by a statement that funds that cannot be used for that purpose will be used for the general purposes of the charity.

Audit trail

Organisations that receive cash donations or undertake any form of public collection must have clear and effective cash-handling procedures. Procedures should cover issues such as the use of sealed collecting tins and envelopes, joint counting of donated cash and careful recording of donations.

Funds given for a specific appeal should be treated as restricted, subject to the points made above, and should be recorded as such on receipt.

Institute of Fundraising: Code of Conduct and codes of fundraising practice

In response to public concerns about charity fundraising techniques, the Institute of Fundraising has developed a Code of Conduct for Fundraisers and codes of conduct with which all members of the Institute are expected to comply. Copies of the code of conduct and the codes of practice are available on the Institute's website (details can be found in the Directory).

The Institute encourages charities to sign up to the scheme established by the Fundraising Standards Board, an independent body established to promote the self-regulation of fundraising by charities. Member charities are entitled to display the FRSB logo on their fundraising materials and are required to comply with the FRSB Fundraising Promise (formerly known as the 'Donors' Charter') which is a commitment made to the public to comply with key principles, including:

- honesty, transparency and legal compliance by the charity;
- respect for the donor, including consideration of the donor's wishes, privacy, confidentiality and data protection concerns; and
- responsible handling of the donation, covering the use of the donation for the purposes given and for the greatest advantage of the beneficiaries, whilst preserving the dignity of beneficiaries.

The charter also covers arrangements for handling complaints made by donors.

Members of the public who believe that a charity has not complied with the promise can make a complaint to FRSB if the charity concerned is a member.

Unauthorised fundraising

Unfortunately, some charities encounter problems with over-zealous supporters who raise funds on behalf of the charity without the organisation's consent and unscrupulous people who raise money fraudulently by claiming that it will be given to charity. This may lead to regulatory problems, clashes with the charity's fundraising policy and alienation of the organisation's existing or potential supporters. Problems may also occur if a professional fundraiser with whom the charity has an agreement acts outside that agreement. Of course, the first approach is for charities to seek to persuade the fundraiser to stop the unauthorised activity. However, a legal remedy is also available in the form of an injunction to prevent unauthorised fundraising. Trustees wishing to take this course of action will need to obtain appropriate legal advice.

Instructing professional fundraisers

Many charities choose to engage professional fundraisers instead of, or in addition to, employing fundraising staff. As with all fundraising approaches, trustees need to ensure that the reward justifies the resources used, so if professional fundraisers are to be used, the trustees must be confident that this will represent good value for money.

Selecting consultants

We have looked at the appointment of external professionals in earlier chapters of this book in relation to board appraisal (chapter 4) and investment fund managers (chapter 8) and many of the same principles apply to professional fundraisers. Trustees should first determine the role of the professional fundraiser, for example, whether the fundraiser will be developing or implementing strategy or both and whether the consultant will be responsible for a complete campaign or elements within the campaign (e.g. events, donor development or grant applications). The trustees will then need to identify a number of appropriate individuals, perhaps through names provided by an umbrella body such as NCVO (the National Council for Voluntary Organisations) or the Institute of Fundraising. They should consider the following issues in relation to each professional fundraiser:

- relevant qualifications;
- experience, including experience of similar campaigns in comparable organisations;
- success record;
- sympathy with the charity and its culture;
- arrangements for monitoring activities and reporting to the trustees; and
- costs.

Fundraisers' fees may be determined in a number of ways, including flat fees and commission based on a percentage of the total amount of money raised.

Fundraising with businesses

Long-term relationships with corporate sponsors can offer charities a degree of financial stability.

When working with businesses on fundraising promotions and activities, the trustees will need to consider additional wider issues, such as whether the charity wishes to be associated with the company or product sold and whether the perceived business practices of the company and the product sold are compatible with the charity's objectives. Is the company seeking to use the relationship to promote sales or to target a specific market and, if so, is the charity comfortable with this?

Where a company or individual represents that part of the price paid for goods or services provided in the course of their business will be donated to charity they are known as a 'commercial participator'.

Charity law requires commercial participators to comply with certain requirements. For example, where a commercial participator represents that a donation will be made to charity, they must state the amount that will be donated to the charity and they must enter into an agreement with the charity, as set out below.

Trustees should also consider the VAT implications of any sponsorship arrangements (see chapter 8).

Agreements with Professional Fundraisers and Commercial Participators

The requirements for agreements between charities and professional fundraisers and commercial participators are laid down by law. All such agreements must be made in writing and be signed by both parties.

The agreement, whether with a professional fundraiser or commercial participator, must contain the following information:
- the name and address of each party;
- the date and period of the agreement;
- terms regarding the variation or early termination of the agreement;

- the objectives of the agreement and the methods to be used in achieving those objectives;
- if more than one charity is involved in the agreement, the proportion of benefit to each charity (e.g. will the funds raised be equally divided or will there be a weighted split?); and
- provision for the amount of remuneration or expenses to be paid to the fundraiser or participator under the agreement and the method for calculating the amount (e.g. a percentage of funds raised or a flat amount).

In addition, for commercial participators, the agreement should cover the following:

- the proportion of the sale price that will be given to the charity or the donations that will be made; and
- a description of the type of contributions which will be made and of the circumstances in which they will be made.

Fundraisers and commercial participators' documents and other records relating to the agreement should be available to the charity. Funds raised under the agreement should be paid to the charity within an agreed period, often within 28 days of receipt.

The Institute of Fundraising has developed model agreements for relationships between charities and commercial participators and between charities and professional fundraisers.

10 Monitoring, evaluation and quality

INTRODUCTION

The pressures of delivering and developing a charity's services can lead to the trustees and senior staff having little time to reflect and the charity becoming stuck on its particular treadmill and growing stale or out of date. Monitoring and evaluation of the charity's work and structures can easily be overlooked, but are crucial to ensuring the charity's continued relevance and helping the trustees to plan for the survival and growth of the charity. They are also key tools in the delivery of quality services. As such, monitoring and evaluation represent a key element of the trustee's role.

This is reflected in the Code of Good Governance for the Voluntary and Community Sector which provides as a second principle of good governance that an effective board will provide good governance and leadership by ensuring delivery of organisational purpose. The board should ensure that a charity delivers its stated purposes or aims by: ensuring organisational purposes remain relevant and valid; developing a long-term strategy; agreeing operational plans and budgets; monitoring progress and spending against plan and budget; evaluating results, assessing outcomes and impact; and reviewing and/or amending the plan and budget as appropriate.

In this chapter, we will consider the value of monitoring and evaluation and look at some of the tools available, including 'off the shelf' models and quality standards. We will also look at some of the pitfalls to avoid when monitoring and evaluating the charity's work.

As statutory funding moves increasingly towards a 'payment by results' model – measuring and demonstrating outcomes and impact has never been more important.

DEFINITIONS

Monitoring. Monitoring is the ongoing measurement and interpretation of information. It is the process of collecting the data that will be used to measure current activities and their impact and to inform any review of the work.

Evaluation. Evaluation is a 'stop and look' periodic assessment of an organisation and/or its work. It involves considering outcomes against the wider context, objectives and targets and analysing the reasons behind successes and failures, identifying alternative approaches and future developments.

Monitoring and evaluation are considered together because they are co-dependent. Monitoring can stand on its own and is an extremely useful governance and management information tool if properly used. However, it is not possible to carry out a proper evaluation without having the necessary information on which to base your assessment.

Why?

It used to be relatively easy for charities to tick along, day after day, year after year, believing that they were doing good work. If beneficiaries kept coming back to use the service and never, or only occasionally, complained, then the charities assumed that the beneficiaries were happy. This overlooks the fact that beneficiaries may recognise that a poor service is better than no service and disregards the reasons why they may not complain, for example for fear of losing the service or receiving prejudicial treatment as a result. This places the charity at risk of failing to meet its objects properly and of losing funds, beneficiaries, staff and volunteers to more effective providers.

A certain amount of *ad hoc* monitoring may give the organisation some useful feedback on its service, but will never truly be adequate for planning purposes. A structured programme of monitoring and evaluation is needed to ensure that the service is meeting objectives, identify any unmet needs, and target areas for improvement. As well as measuring the success or otherwise of individual projects or services, monitoring and evaluation tools should be used to assess the performance of the organisation as a whole and to focus on individual elements of the charity's internal functioning. This may include consideration of the impact of a change to the governance structure or the introduction of revised policies.

Increased competition for funds, higher expectations from funders and greater public scrutiny of charities have forced many organisations to take monitoring, evaluation and quality measures seriously, but trustees should not view this as a chore imposed by external pressures. The use of evaluation and quality standards as a means of demonstrating the organisation's validity to external stakeholders should be seen very much as a secondary benefit. Monitoring and evaluation are essential tools if an organisation is to develop and this is their primary purpose. Together with quality measures, monitoring and evaluation can raise the standards and performance of an organisation. If properly carried out, these can be a valuable tool which trustees can use to identify problems faced by the charity and to highlight and celebrate good practice and successes. The information gathered will also help trustees to manage staff effectively, to value their contributions and to plan for the future.

What to measure

Before any monitoring and evaluation process can begin, trustees should identify what needs to be measured and assessed. To do this they need to know the aims of both the 'thing' being measured – be that a structural change within the organisation, a new policy or a service – and the standards that they expect to be achieved. This will determine the focus of the monitoring or evaluation exercise. It may be helpful at this stage to look at outputs and outcomes and their bearing on efficiency and effectiveness.

Boards of trustees need to set their expectations in terms of organisational achievement in relation to outputs (i.e. the amount of work done), outcomes (i.e. the impact of that work) and organisational process (e.g. customer care). Some expectations may be purely quantitative: 'how many?', 'how long?' type questions. This can be extremely useful information, helping identify, for example, areas of poor take up and levels of need. This form of monitoring is commonly used by charities, particularly to collect referral information such as gender, age, ethnicity, postcode and presenting problems.

However, this type of output-driven, number-crunching approach is rarely adequate on its own. A qualitative element may be required for the monitoring to have any real meaning. The fact that a particular client has

OUTPUTS AND OUTCOMES

Output is the product of an activity, (e.g. the number of presentations given or the number of clients seen). There is limited opportunity for quality measurement within output, but it is useful in demonstrating efficiency (e.g. by considering the number of clients seen against the cost of the service or the resources available).

Outcome is the result of the activity. Ideally, this should relate to the original aims and reflect what you were hoping to achieve. For example, a welfare benefits advice service would hope to see an increase in benefit take up amongst its clients, and a drug rehabilitation project would hope to see a reduction in drug use. Monitoring outcomes measures the effectiveness of the project. Outcomes are usually quality related and can be very difficult to monitor. This may be because a voluntary organisation is aiming for preventative or long-term benefits (at what point do you say a project to reduce youth offending is successful?) or because it can be hard to establish causality between the work of the organisation and the outcome. Outcome measurement can also be problematic because although the desired outcome may not be achieved, there may still be other positive results.

used your information service five times is not necessarily a good sign: it may mean that the client did not get what he or she wanted on the first four occasions. The trustees should set quality standards which describe the level which an activity, service or product must attain. Once these standards have been agreed, the charity will need to monitor performance against them and performance indicators may be used as a numerical measure of the degree to which the standard, outcome, or any other objective, is being achieved.

Quality standards and key performance indicators may be used across the range of an organisation's work. It may be that trustees decide that every donation should be acknowledged within five working days, or that clients receiving domiciliary care should not receive care services from more than three separate care workers in any six-week period. The standards should be monitored regularly so that trends can be identified, whether these are improvements in a service provided or declining performance. In this way, a set of performance indicators that cuts across the different areas of work can serve as a valuable tool for trustees in pre-empting and tracking problems and prioritising areas of concern.

In recognition of the fact that you will not get it right all of the time, you may also want to set targets for your key performance indicators. These targets could be set to increase over time as improvements in service are anticipated. The case study below illustrates how trustees can use the aims of the service to develop quality standards and performance indicators that then determine the information to be collected for monitoring and evaluation.

As can be seen from the case study, setting quality standards and key performance indicators that are related to the aims automatically leads to certain information being collected. The same approach can be used for intended outcomes. The table opposite illustrates how organisations can work through their aims and intended outcomes and/or quality standards to identify what they are measuring and the information they need to collect in order to monitor it.

CASE EXAMPLE

A charity running a respite care service for carers of people suffering with dementia has the reliability of the service as one of its aims. The trustees appreciate the stresses placed on the carers and recognise that missed appointments and lateness cause additional stress. Consequently they have developed a quality standard that says that appointments will not be cancelled with less than 24 hours' notice and that care assistants will arrive for appointments within ten minutes of the agreed time. The service was temporarily short staffed and staff sickness and holidays made it difficult to provide a totally reliable service. In response, the trustees set a target that the reliability standard would be met in relation to 75% of appointments for the first month, rising to 90% for the following month when new staff would be in post. The achievement against these targets would represent the organisation's performance indicators, and 80% reliability in the first month would indicate that the organisation had performed above its target.

In order to monitor performance against these standards and targets the charity kept details of all appointments attended (including the time of arrival) and all appointments cancelled, including the time of cancellation.

Example	New equal opportunities policy	Customer service standards
Aim of service or policy	To promote the take up of services by minority ethnic groups	Provide a timely response to queries
Quality standard or intended outcome	Intended outcome of policy: number of people from minority ethnic groups using the service to be proportional to the local demographic	Quality standard: respond to telephone and e-mail queries within four hours and to letters within two working days
Performance Indicator	Increase take up from current level (5%) to 10% in year 1 and 17% in year 2	Respond to 80% of telephone and e-mail queries within four hours and 95% of letters within two working days
What information to collect	Ethnicity of service users	Date and time of incoming queries, method of query and date and time of response

tip

Do not forget that qualitative monitoring can include user satisfaction and the views of other stakeholders. This is discussed in the next section.

If you do not meet your performance indicator targets – ask why. There could be a valid reason, or it could indicate a flaw in your services or systems.

Do not reinvent the wheel – there are a number of widely available quality models that your charity could use or adapt. Some of these are discussed towards the end of this chapter.

How?

Some charities see monitoring and evaluation as an inconvenience, but they need not be. As has been demonstrated in this chapter, monitoring and evaluation are fundamental to the delivery of charitable objectives. If applied as an 'add on' to the charity's workload, any monitoring system can be awkward to administer. Instead, monitoring arrangements should be integral to the work of the organisation and the planning of new services and projects. The examples used above showed how monitoring and evaluation are founded in the objectives of the work, so the actual process of monitoring should be based within the administration system. For example, referral procedures should collect all the information required for monitoring purposes and client reviews should include provision for recording the views of beneficiaries. Systems should be integrated into the charity's regular administration for the purposes of capturing statistical data whilst the 'soft' or qualitative monitoring can take place through other means, such as regular surveys and user groups. Integrating monitoring into regular activities in this way should add value to the charity's work, rather than get in the way of services.

Different services or activities lend themselves to different approaches. It may not be possible to keep client records for confidential helplines, but this would be appropriate for care or training projects. Group discussion may be the best approach for those who have difficulty with written language, but surveys would be better suited for services that are spread over a wide geographical area.

Analysing all this data may seem daunting and should be done a bit at a time. Data collection should be designed in a way that makes information easy to retrieve. Similarly, monitoring information should be presented to trustees in a way that is readily understandable. Tables and graphs can often illustrate findings more effectively than text (e.g. cross tables can be used to show a number of factors together, such as a breakdown of clients by location and presenting problem).

Methods of evaluation will be based on the foundation of data collection and canvassing views. Evaluations should, however, be more thorough than monitoring, covering a wider range of issues and stakeholders. They may, for example, look at whether the service is innovative, whether it should be more outcome-focused and should take in the opinions of staff, volunteers, trustees, users and partner agencies. An evaluation will also pay greater attention to the wider context (e.g. professional standards, academic opinion and accepted best practice). Findings and opinions may be presented to stakeholders for discussion at various points throughout the evaluation in order to refine understanding, culminating in a written report.

Given that monitoring and evaluation should be included in a project from the outset, arrangements and budgeting will be integral to project planning and should be considered within funding applications.

APPROACHES TO MONITORING

Hard monitoring (quantitative measures, statistics etc.)
- Diary records (i.e. what happened each day)
- Client records
- Records by staff member or volunteer who delivers service

Soft monitoring (qualitative measures, views and impact)
- Surveys and questionnaires
- Group discussion
- Individual discussion

Sampling – where it is not possible or practicable to collect monitoring information on every user, sample a cross section of the activity (e.g. every tenth user or every user for a week each month).

Piloting – rather than introducing a new monitoring system across the board and permanently, try piloting it. This could involve, for example, testing a new data collection form with one team of staff or for a limited period before reviewing and editing it to make it more user friendly and useful. Alternatively, ask a group of users to complete a pilot survey before rolling the form out across the user sample.

Consistency – for monitoring information to have any value it must be consistent, otherwise it will not be comparing like with like. This means client records should contain the same classes of information for each client and group discussions should cover the same topics each time. Forms and agendas can be designed to facilitate this. This does not prevent additional information being recorded or discussed, and space should be made in any monitoring system for a wider range of information to be recorded as necessary (e.g. a space for notes on a client's records or for additional comments on a questionnaire).

Review – monitoring arrangements should be reviewed on a periodic basis. Are the arrangements providing you with the information you need?

Internal or external evaluation?

Although many organisations conduct their own monitoring and evaluation processes, external evaluation may offer a fresh approach and objectivity. This can be particularly useful for demonstrating the value of a service within the wider external context. Charities may implement a degree of external evaluation themselves by measuring outputs against regional or national figures, but an evaluation conducted by an independent and external organisation or individual offers a completely objective account of the charity's work.

Similar arrangements exist in relation to quality standards. We have already discussed the need for charities to develop their own quality standards, but 'off the shelf' standards can provide an objective check and opportunities for comparison with other organisations. Some of the widely available quality measures are discussed later in this chapter.

We have considered the use of external consultants before, and the discussion in chapter 5 in relation to externally conducted board appraisal will be equally relevant here. Evaluation can be a sensitive issue and it is easy for those involved in the charity to complain about the evaluator if they do not like what has been said. In selecting an external evaluator, it is important to be particularly alert to the individual's experience with your type of organisation and his or her empathy with the concerns of all involved. Consider how the evaluator will involve staff and volunteers in the process and, crucially, how the trustees will retain ownership of the evaluation. Ownership is not just about the final publication of the evaluation report, it is also concerned with ensuring that evaluation remains relevant, is accepted by the charity, and that it is controlled by the trustees, in partnership with the external evaluator.

Any externally conducted evaluation should be subject to written terms of reference, describing the purpose, process and timescale of the evaluation as well as other crucial issues such as ownership, interim reporting and publication.

Process

As has been discussed above, monitoring should be an ongoing process of collecting data that is to be presented to the board or senior staff to allow them to measure progress and make adjustments as necessary. In this sense, monitoring forms part of management and governance information in much the same way as management accounts (see chapter 7).

In terms of quality standards, internal standards are often developed and implemented by a subcommittee of trustees, supported by senior and operational staff. External standards, as discussed later in this chapter, may well define the process to be followed.

Evaluations can be complex and lengthy and it is useful to set a timescale for any evaluation exercise before it starts. Working backwards (i.e. from the date on which it is expected that the evaluation will be completed) gives a strong indication of the workload and viability of the exercise. The process will involve reading background information, collecting and analysing all relevant statistical data and canvassing the views of a variety of stakeholders. Once the analysis and opinion forming is underway, it will be necessary to test preliminary findings with the relevant parties to ensure the accuracy of views and gather any wider contextual information. There may be valid justifications for practices that initially appear to be questionable. Draft reports will need to be presented to trustees and others and amended as necessary. Throughout the process, trustees should be kept informed and involved. The process normally concludes with a final written report, which may be supported by presentations to relevant internal and external stakeholders. It is critical to any monitoring and evaluation exercise that findings are communicated to the organisation as a whole.

Potential problems

'You get what you measure'

In developing monitoring and evaluation procedures, trustees should be aware that there is a risk that 'you get what you measure' (i.e. staff will focus on the areas that they know are being monitored (e.g. increased recruitment of black and minority ethnic volunteers) at the expense of areas of work that are not under review). Alternatively, whilst the targets may be achieved, the anticipated improvements may not happen (e.g. the charity may be successful in recruiting more volunteers from black and minority ethnic groups, but may not retain them). Consequently trustees will need to develop a more sophisticated approach, such as specifying not only targets for recruitment of volunteers, but also retention.

Monitoring the outcomes of services enables trustees to identify the impact of the charity's work, but the 'you get what you measure' approach can be particularly dangerous here, as the pressure to perform to targets may unduly influence the direction of the service.

The case study opposite not only illustrates the risk that 'you get what you measure', but also the concern that funders may drive monitoring and evaluation requirements and consequently influence the nature of the service. It is entirely appropriate that funders should require organisations to monitor and evaluate the work that they fund. They need to know that their money is being spent on the purposes for which it was given and is achieving the desired results. However, trustees must ensure that these monitoring requirements do not pollute the charity's activities or divert it from its objects. In the example above, the change in emphasis was introduced by the funder of the scheme and resulted in the charity working with a group of users that fell outside its beneficiary area. In accepting the funding on these terms and consequently being unduly influenced by these requirements, the trustees may well have acted in breach of trust.

CASE EXAMPLE

A charity ran a supported employment scheme for the long-term unemployed. The scheme involved securing temporary work placements for clients, with the aim of improving self-esteem and confidence, developing new skills and adapting back into employment. In accordance with its objects, the charity focused on unemployed people from high-need groups, including people with disabilities and those with a history of homelessness, substance misuse or mental ill-health. It originally evaluated its success based on the number of people matched in temporary placements and achieving positive outcomes following the completion of the placement. Given the nature of the client group, these outcomes could be quite modest, for example clients moving onto voluntary work, or maintaining the social support networks developed during the placement. A change in the requirements imposed by the funder, which redefined a positive outcome as gaining permanent employment, completely changed the nature of the scheme. The charity was influenced by the evaluation requirements to move away from providing for the high-need group of long-term unemployed people to those more likely to find work at the conclusion of the placement.

Resistance

Many people within charities, from the board to the volunteers, see monitoring, evaluation and quality measures as challenging and even threatening. They may consider that their own work is being inspected or questioned or that the service or project is being evaluated to identify potential funding cuts. Equally, they may simply resent any extra work involved. For these reasons any programme should be introduced sensitively and its objectives and any subsequent findings clearly communicated to all participants. An exercise that is committed to celebrating successes, acknowledging difficulties and giving opportunities for learning and improving, is likely to find a warmer reception than a 'justify yourself' approach.

Bad news

Trustees, given their leadership role, should consider how they would respond to any negative findings of a monitoring, evaluation or quality programme. Whilst the whole point of the work is to pinpoint problems and identify remedial action, what would happen if the results were worse than expected? How would operational staff and volunteers be supported in addressing such findings? Trustees should receive interim progress reports on any evaluation exercise in order to prepare for any difficult issues that might arise.

CHECKLIST

Have you...

- [✓] Identified the aims of the activity?
- [✓] Set the standards you hope to achieve and any targets within those standards?
- [✓] Identified what needs to be measured in order to check performance against the standards?
- [✓] Developed a system for collecting information (both qualitative and quantitative)?
- [✓] Checked that the monitoring approach is not undermining original aims or adversely affecting other areas of work?
- [✓] Identified who will be responsible for monitoring?
- [✓] Identified the aims of your evaluation?
- [✓] Identified who will be responsible for evaluation?
- [✓] Agreed the plan and terms of reference for the evaluation, including scope, timescale, interim reporting, stakeholder involvement and budget?
- [✓] Achieved stakeholder buy in?
- [✓] Considered how to move forward from the completed evaluation, including handling bad news?

Quality models

There are a number of different ready-made models for quality management and validation. Each model is based on a documented system designed to measure practices against standards and to promote improvement. Organisations may choose to adopt one of these rather than develop their own systems. As the models consider different elements of organisational function, it is important to identify the model which is most appropriate for the charity in question.

The advantage of these models is that they demonstrate a charity's commitment to quality and ongoing organisational improvement. In the case of those that are externally evaluated, the models also show that the charity has attained a nationally (or in some cases internationally) recognised standard. Although the process of attaining and maintaining these standards can be both hard work and time consuming, it should also serve to improve the governance and management of the organisation, the quality of the service and the morale and involvement of staff and volunteers. Trustees should, therefore, view these models as a means of achieving continuous improvement, rather than as badge to be worn for the benefit of funders or other stakeholders.

PQASSO

The Practical Quality Assurance System for Small Organisations (PQASSO) was designed by the Charities Evaluation Services specifically for small to medium-sized voluntary organisations. It can also be used to measure the quality of projects or branches within larger charities. The system promotes continuous improvement and is comprehensive, covering all aspects of an organisations' work with the focus on the following areas:

- planning;
- governance;
- leadership and management;
- user-centred service;
- managing people;
- learning and development;
- managing money;
- managing resources;
- communications and promotion;

- working with others;
- monitoring and evaluation; and
- results.

PQASSO breaks down each topic into three levels. This enables organisations to assess how they are doing and to plan a clear path for development in each area.

PQASSO may be used in a variety of ways, including as an organisational health check or to help guide organisational development and growth. Organisations implement PQASSO by assessing themselves against standards and indicators using evidence to support judgements made. PQASSO also offers an external accreditation: the PQASSO Quality Mark.

Business Excellence Model

Like PQASSO, the Business Excellence Model considers all elements of organisational activity. Unlike PQASSO (and as the name implies) the Business Excellence Model was originally designed for the corporate sector; however it has been implemented by public sector organisations and voluntary groups. This is a Europe-wide tool and is also known as the EFQM Excellence Model. EFQM is the European Foundation for Quality Management. The model is administered in the UK by the British Quality Foundation, itself a not-for-profit organisation.

The Business Excellence Model focuses on the key elements that sustain business excellence, five of which are enablers (what the organisation does) and four of which are results (what an organisation achieves). The model gives equal emphasis to enablers and results.

The five enablers are: leadership; people; policy and strategy; partnership and resources; and processes. The four areas focusing on results are: people; customers; society and key performance.

The cost of implementing the model varies greatly, depending on the degree of implementation. Although a basic self-assessment can be done fairly cheaply, more rigorous appraisals can become very expensive, particularly if external consultants are asked to support the assessment process.

Registered charities can join the British Quality Foundation for a reduced fee. Membership gives access to networking groups and a range of information.

Customer Service Excellence

The Customer Service Excellence standard is a government initiative that has been in existence for over three years. It is a practical tool to support and drive public services that are more responsive to people's needs.

The aim of Customer Service Excellence is to encourage, enable and reward organisations that are delivering services based on a genuine understanding of the needs and preferences of their customers and communities. The standard will test in great depth those areas that research has indicated are a priority for customers with particular focus on delivery, timeliness, information, professionalism and staff attitude.

The Customer Service Excellence standard replaced the Charter Mark Award.

ISO 9000

ISO 9000 is the collective name for a group of international standards for quality management systems. Issues considered under the standard include the organisation's quality management system, management responsibility, the management of resources, the end product or service, and monitoring and improvement. The standard considers not only whether appropriate quality management systems are in place, but also whether the standards are being consistently applied.

Those wishing to register for the standard have to prepare a quality manual and supporting procedures to ensure implementation. The award is subject to external assessment by a registering body. Once registered, the quality management systems of organisations holding the standard are reviewed periodically.

ISO 9000 is not cheap, being subject to initial assessment fees and an annual fee; it is more appropriate for larger voluntary groups.

Investors in People

Investors in People (IIP) is a national cross-sector standard concerned with the training and development of people within an organisation or project. The standard is focused on training and development as a means of achieving organisational objectives and is based on the four principles of:

- commitment to invest in people;
- planning the development of people;

- taking action on development in relation to objectives; and
- evaluating the outcomes of training and development.

Organisations must provide evidence of how they meet the four principles and the standard is awarded subject to external assessment. An initial assessment that identifies areas where the required standard has not been met is usually carried out, with a further assessment before the standard is awarded. Once an organisation has IIP status, it is subject to periodic review.

There is a charge for assessments so the total cost will vary depending on the size of the organisation, length of assessment etc. Given the nature of this model, charities are unlikely to seek IIP unless they have a significant staff or volunteer team.

Which model?

Model	What it measures	Who is it suitable for?
PQASSO	Across organisation	Small to medium voluntary groups
Business Excellence Model	Across organisation	Larger organisations, although a more low-key implementation may be appropriate for smaller groups
Customer Service Excellence	Customer services	All
ISO 9000	Quality management	Large groups
Investors in People	Training and development of people within the organisation	Medium to large groups with significant staff/volunteer teams
Service-specific models	Quality of service delivery	All, although much will depend on the model in question

Service-specific models

Trustees should also consider whether there are any quality assurance or management systems that are specific to the type of service that they offer.

For example, advice services may apply for the Community Legal Service's Quality Mark. In some circumstances, achieving a service-specific quality standard may be a condition of funding.

Benchmarking

We have looked at monitoring and evaluation as an internal exercise, with organisations considering performance against self-created standards and by measurement against an external, common standard. We have also considered external, independent evaluation. A further option is for organisations to compare themselves against other groups or businesses through benchmarking.

Benchmarking involves comparing different aspects of the work of a group of organisations. It can be a very flexible approach. You can compare services, products or processes; you can look at a wide range of issues or focus on areas of concern; and you can benchmark with similar organisations or take a cross-sector approach on common issues such as customer care. Benchmarking may take place as a one-off exercise or be an ongoing process.

Benchmarking should be a mutually beneficial relationship, with every organisation in the benchmarking group being able to learn and develop from the experience of others.

If undertaking a benchmarking exercise, be sure that all parties are in agreement as to the scope of the review and what will be done with the information – will it be confidential to those in the benchmarking group?

Directory

General reference

Adirondack, Sandy & Sinclair Taylor, James (consulting eds)
The Voluntary Sector Legal Handbook (Russell-Cooke Solicitors,
Directory of Social Change, 2009) (3rd ed)
Adirondack, Sandy *Just About Managing? Effective management for
voluntary organisations and community groups* (London Voluntary
Service Council, 2006) (4th ed)
Claricoat, John & Philips, Hilary *Charity Law A–Z, Key Questions
Answered* (Jordans, 1998) (2nd ed)
ICSA Best Practice Guide *Guide to Companies Limited by Guarantee*

For up-to-date information on the proposed changes in charity law and
the new forms of incorporation for not-for-profit organisations check the
voluntary sector press, particularly:
Wednesday's *Guardian:* www.SocietyGuardian.co.uk
Third Sector: www.thirdsector.co.uk
Charity Finance: www.charityfinance.co.uk

Charity Commission

The Charity Commission makes its guidance booklets available on its
website, www.charity-commission.gov.uk. The most relevant are:

CC3	*The Essential Trustee: What you need to know*
CC4	*Charities for the Relief of Financial Hardship*
CC6	*Charities for the Relief of Sickness*
CC9	*Speaking Out – Campaigning and Political Activity by Charities*
CC11	*Trustee expenses and payments*
CC21	*Registering as a Charity*
CC23	*Exempt Charities*
CC47	*Complaints about Charities*

The Commission has been conducting a review of the register of charities, considering issues such as the different charitable purposes. A range of review documents are available, including:

RR7   *The Independence of Charities from the State*
RR8   *The Public Character of Charity*

Companies House

GBF1   *Company Formation*
GBF2   *Business Names*

Trustee responsibilities

Health and safety

Eastwood, Mike *The Charity Trustee's Handbook* (Directory of Social Change, 2010) (2nd ed)
Hinde, Al & Kavanagh, Charlie (Jill Barlow, ed) *The Health & Safety Handbook for Voluntary & Community Organisations* (Directory of Social Change, 2001) (2nd ed)

Charity Commission

CC3   *The Essential Trustee: What you need to know*

Companies House

GBA1   *Directors and Secretaries Guide*

Health and Safety Executive

An introduction to health and safety
A Guide to the Reporting of Injuries, Diseases and Dangerous Occurrences Regulations 1995
Tackling Stress: The Management Standards Approach
Health and safety regulation: A short guide
First aid at work: Your questions answered

Marketing

Ali, Moi *The New DIY Guide to Marketing* (ICSA Publishing Ltd, 2001) (2nd ed)
Bruce, Ian *Charity Marketing* (ICSA Publishing Ltd, 2011)

Risk management

ACEVO *Essential Guide to Risk Management* (2009)
ICSA Best Practice Guide *Managing Conflicts of Interest in the Not-for-profit Sector*

Planning

Lawrie, Alan *The complete guide to business and strategic planning for voluntary organisations* (Directory of Social Change, 2007) (3rd ed)

Data protection

Ticher, Paul *Data Protection and Freedom of Information* (Directory of Social Change, 2008) (3rd ed)
Cudmore, Lee *A Practical Guide to Data Protection* (ICSA Publishing Ltd, 2002)

Campaigning

Latimer, Mark *The Campaigning Handbook* (Directory of Social Change, 2000) (2nd ed)
Gray, John F & Elsden, Stephen *Organising Special Events: For Fundraising and Campaigning* (Directory of Social Change and Charities Aid Foundation, 2000)
Reason, Jacki & Hayes, Ruth *Voluntary but not Amateur* (London Voluntary Service Council, 2004) (7th ed)
Tingham, Tess & Coe, Jim *Good Campaigns Guide for the Voluntary Sector* (NCVO, 2005)

Recruitment, appointment and induction of trustees

Akpeki, Tesse *Getting on board: Strategies for finding and supporting trustees* (NCVO, 1997) (2nd ed)

Akpeki, Tesse *Recruiting and supporting black and minority ethnic trustees* (NCVO, 2001)

NCVO *Trustee Bank Directory of Trustee Services* (available free online)

Nunan, Kevin *The Good Trustee Guide* (NCVO, 2008) (5th ed)

ICSA Best Practice Guides (available free online)

The Appointment and Induction of Charity Trustees

ICSA Model Code of Conduct for Charity Trustees

ICSA Model Role Description for Charity Trustees

Charity Commission

Finding New Trustees – What Charities Need to Know

CC11   *Trustee expenses and payments*

CC24   *Users on Board: Beneficiaries who become trustees*

RS1   *Trustee recruitment, selection and induction*

Board of Trustees

Adirondack, Sandy *Good Governance Action Plan* (NCVO, 2002)

Balkam, Steve *Assessing Your Board's Performance: A DIY guide to board self-evaluation* (NCVO, 1995)

Belbin, Meredith *Management Teams – Why they succeed or fail* (Butterworth Heinemann, 2010) (3rd ed)

Belbin, Meredith *Team Roles at Work* (Butterworth Heinemann, 2010) (2nd ed)

Comer, Lee & Ticher, Paul *The Minute Taker's Handbook* (Directory of Social Change, 2002)

Hudson, Mike *Managing Without Profit: The art of managing third sector organisations* (Directory of Social Change, 2009) (3rd ed)

Morgan, Gareth G. *The Charity Treasurer's Handbook* (Directory of Social Change, 2012) (3rd ed)

ICSA Guidance Notes (available online)

ICSA Model Role Description for Chair of the Board of Trustees

ICSA Model Role Description for a Charity Treasurer

ICSA Model Role Description for the Secretary of the Board

ACEVO publications

Essential Guide to Duties of the Company Secretary

Meetings and governing documents

Charity Commission

CC22   *Choosing and Preparing a Governing Document*
CC36   *Changing your Charity's Governing Document*
CC48   *Charities and Meetings*
GD1   *Charitable Companies: Model Memorandum and Articles of Association*
GD2   *Charitable Trust: Model Deed*
GD3   *Charitable Associations: Model Constitution*

Companies House

GBA7   *Resolutions – Companies Act 2006*

People management

Akpeki, Tesse *Setting Chief Executive Remuneration* (NCVO, 2001)
Cook, Tim & Braithwaite, Guy *A Management Companion for Voluntary Organisations* (Directory of Social Change, 2000)
Harris, John The Good Management Guide for the Voluntary Sector (NCVO, 2002)
ICSA Best Practice Guide *Establishing a whistleblowing procedure*
NCVO *Flexible Working Solutions* (NCVO, 2000)
NCVO *The Good Guide to Employment* (NCVO, 2010) (6th ed)

ACEVO publications

Essential Guide to Recruiting a Chief Executive, Chair and Trustees
Essential Guide to Contracts of Employment
Essential Guide to Reward for the Chief Executive and Management Team
Essential Guide to Staff Handbooks
Leading the Organisation: The Relationship Between Chairs and Chief Executives

Charity Commission

CC10   *Hallmarks of an Effective Charity*

Financial management and control

ACEVO *Essential Guide to Setting up a Trading Company*

Morgan, Gareth G. *The Charity Treasurer's Handbook* (Directory of Social Change, 2010) (3rd ed)

NCVO *VAT for voluntary organisations: A step by step guide* (NCVO, 2005) (6th ed)

Poffley, Adrian *Financial Stewardship of Charities* (Directory of Social Change, 2002)

Sayer, Kate *Practical Guide to Charity Accounting* (Directory of Social Change, 2008) (3rd ed)

Sayer, Kate *Practical Guide to Financial Management for Charities* (Directory of Social Change, 2007) (3rd ed)

Sayer, Kate *Practical Guide to VAT for Charities and Voluntary Organisations* (Directory of Social Change, 2008) (3rd ed)

Charity Finance (monthly journal) is useful reading. See also the website www.charityfinance.co.uk.

Charity Commission

Accounting and Reporting by Charities: Statement of Recommended Practice (Revised 2005)

Annual Return Charities and Risk Management (2007)

CC8   *Internal Financial Controls for Charities*

CC12   *Managing Financial Difficulties and Insolvency in Charities*

CC13   *The Official Custodian for Charities' Land Holding Service*

CC14   *Investment of Charitable Funds: Basic Principles*

CC19   *Charities' Reserves*

CC28   *Disposing of Charity Land*

CC33   *Acquiring Land*

CC35   *Trustees, Trading and Tax*

CC42   *Appointing Nominees and Custodians: Guidance under s.19(4) of the Trustee Act 2000*

CC61   *Charity Accounts: The framework*

CC63   *Independent Examination of Charities*

CC64   *Receipts and Payments Accounts Pack 2001*
CC65   *Accruals Accounts Pack Based on SORP 2000*
CC66   *SORP 2000: Example reports and accounts*

Companies House

GBA2 Annual Return
GBA3 Accounts and Accounting Reference Dates
GBA4 Auditors GBA5 Late Filing Penalties
GBA5 Late Filing Penalties

HM Revenue & Customs

Notice 700/1   *Should I be registered for VAT?*
Notice 70111   *Charities*
Notice 70115   *Clubs and associations*
Notice 742   *Land and property*
CWL4   *Fundraising Events: Exemptions for charities and other qualifying bodies*
Gift Aid Toolkit (Institute of Fundraising website)

Fundraising

Botting Herbst, Nina & Norton, Michael *The Complete Fundraising Handbook* (Institute of Fundraising and Directory of Social Change, 2012) (6th ed)

Brown, Harry *Community Fundraising: The Effective Use of Volunteer Networks* (Directory of Social Change, Charities Aid Foundation and Institute of Fundraising, 2002)

Clay, Anthony (ed) *Trust Fundraising* (Directory of Social Change 2011) (2nd ed)

The Fundraiser's Guide to the Law (Bates, Wells & Braithwaite and Centre for Voluntary Sector Development, Charities Aid Foundation and Directory of Social Change, 2000)

Gilchrist, Karen & Horsley, Margo *Fundraising from Grant-making Trusts and Foundations* (Directory of Social Change and Charities Aid Foundation, 2000)

Gilchrist, Karen *Promoting Your Cause: A Guide for Fundraisers and Campaigners* (Directory of Social Change and Charities Aid Foundation, 2002)

Gray, John F & Elsden, Stephen *Organising Special Events for Fundraising and Campaigning* (Directory of Social Change and Charities Aid Foundation, 2000)

Institute of Fundraising *Forms of Agreement and Model Contracts*

Morton, Valerie (ed) *Corporate Fundraising* (Directory of Social Change, Charities Aid Foundation and Institute of Fundraising, 2012) (4th ed)

Mullin, Redmond *Fundraising Strategy* (Directory of Social Change, Charities Aid Foundation and Institute of Fundraising, 2002) (2nd ed)

Passingham, Sarah *Tried and Tested Ideas for Local Fundraising Events* (Directory of Social Change, 2003) (3rd ed)

Wilberforce, Sebastian (ed) *Legacy Fundraising: The Art of Seeking Bequests* (Directory of Social Change, Charities Aid Foundation and Institute of Fundraising, 2010) (3rd ed)

Charity Commission

CC20   *Charities and Fundraising*
RS2   *Charities and Commercial Partners*

Institute of Fundraising

The Institute of Fundraising produces a wide range of Codes of Practice including:

Acceptance and Refusal of Donations
Charities Working with Business
Charity Challenge Events
Handling Cash Donations
House to House Collections
Legacy Fundraising
Outdoor Fundraising Events in the UK
Payment of Fundraisers on a Commission Basis
Raffles and Lotteries
Reciprocal Charity Mailings
Telephone Fundraising

Monitoring, evaluation and quality

British Quality Foundation *Assessing for Excellence: A practical guide for self-assessment* (British Quality Foundation, 1999)
VSNTO *How To Become an Investor in People: A Guide for the Voluntary Sector* (Voluntary Sector National Training Organisation, 2003)

Charities Evaluation Services

Ellis, Jean *Practical monitoring and evaluation: A guide for voluntary organisations* (Charities Evaluation Services, 2002)
First Steps in Quality (Charities Evaluation Services, 2002)
First Steps in Monitoring and Evaluation (Charities Evaluation Services, 2002)
Connor, Anne *Monitoring Ourselves* (Charities Evaluation Services, 1999)
Van Der Eyken, Willem *Managing Evaluation* (Charities Evaluation Services, 1999)
A range of discussion papers is also available.

Charity Commission

CC10 *Hallmarks of an Effective Charity*

Quality Standards Task Group publications

Excellence in View: A Guide to the European Foundation for Quality Management (EFQM) Excellence Model for the Voluntary Sector (NCVO, 2000)

Web resources

Association of Chief Executives of Voluntary Organisations (ACEVO)
The professional association for chief executives in the third sector in England and Wales.
www.acevo.org.uk

Belbin Consultancy Training

Details of Belbin's products and services.

www.belbin.info/

British Chambers of Commerce

www.britishchambers.org.uk

British Quality Foundation

For information on the EFQM Business Excellence Model. See also the European Foundation for Quality Management below.

www.quality-foundation.co.uk

British Standards Institution

Information on ISO 9000.

www.bsigroup.com

Broadcasting Support Services

For the Broadcast Appeals Consortium Code of Practice.

www.bss.org

Business in the Community (BITC)

Encourages corporate social responsibility and business involvement in local communities, including employee volunteering.

www.bitc.org.uk

Business Link

Information on Business Link, the national business advice service. The website includes information and factsheets on benchmarking and different quality models.

www.businesslink.gov.uk

Charities Evaluation Services

Provides monitoring, evaluation and quality services to the voluntary sector, including consultancy, training, literature and PQASSO.

www.ces-vol.org.uk

Charity Commission

The statutory organisation that regulates charities in England and Wales. Provides guidance and advice to charities through its extensive range of publications, available free via its website.

www.charitycommission.gov.uk

Charity Finance Directors' Group

Helps charities to manage their accounting, taxation, audit and other finance related functions and promotes good practice.
www.cfdg.org.uk

Chartered Quality Institute

www.thecqi.org

Compact Law

Provides easily accessible information on employment law.
www.compactlaw.co.uk

Companies House

The statutory body responsible for regulating the incorporation, re-registration and striking-off of companies and the registration of documents to be filed under company legislation.
www.companieshouse.gov.uk

Customer Service Excellence

www.cse.cabinetoffice.gov.uk

Department for Business Enterprise & Regulatory Reform

Information on changes to company law and requirements in relation to company secretaries. See also BERR's *From Quality to Excellence* website which provides a range of information on quality improvements.
www.berr.gov.uk

Directory of Social Change

Provides information and training.
www.dsc.org.uk

Ethnic Minority Foundation (EMF) and the Council of Ethnic Minority Voluntary Organisations (CEMVO)

Maintain a trustee register.
www.emf-cemvo.co.uk

European Foundation for Quality Management

www.efqm.org

Federation of Small Businesses

Provides advice on tax and VAT issues.
www.fsb.org.uk

Financial Reporting Council
www.frc.org.uk

Financial Services Authority
Information on different investment products and regulation.
www.fsa.gov.uk

Gambling Commission
Requirements for regulating lotteries, bingo or other gaming events.
www.gamblingcommission.gov.uk

Health and Safety Executive
A wide range of useful leaflets are available free from the HSE.
www.hse.gov.uk

HM Government
Strategy Unit's *Private Action, Public Benefit* report can be found at:
www.cabinetoffice.gov.uk

HM Revenue & Customs
Useful publications and details of local VAT advice centres.
www.hmrc.gov.uk

Industrial Common Ownership Movement (ICOM)
The umbrella body for co-operatives.
E-mail: icom@icom.org.uk

Information Commissioner
Information on data protection principles.
www.dataprotection.gov.uk

Institute of Chartered Secretaries and Administrators (ICSA)
In addition to a number of useful publications and guidance notes,
the ICSA offers a trustee brokerage service through its trustee register.
www.icsa.org.uk

Institute of Fundraising
www.institute-of-fundraising.org.uk

Investors in People
www.investorsinpeople.co.uk

Legal Services Commission
Information on the Community Legal Service Quality Mark.
www.legalservices.gov.uk/civil/how/quality-mark.asp

National Council for Voluntary Organisations (NCVO)
The umbrella body for the voluntary sector in England. Produces a wide range of publications including good practice guides, training manuals, research reports.
www.ncvo-vol.org.uk

Northern Ireland Charity Commission
The statutory organisation that regulates charities in Northern Ireland.
www.charitycommissionni.org.uk/

Northern Ireland Council for Voluntary Action (NICVA)
www.nicva.org.uk

Office of the Scottish Charity Regulator
The Office of the Scottish Charity Regulator is the independent regulator and registrar of Scottish charities.
www.oscr.org.uk/

The Pensions Regulator
Details of stakeholder pension providers.
www.thepensionsregulator.gov.uk

Recruitment agencies include:
CF Appointments: www.cfappointments.co.uk
Charity Connections: www.charityconnections.com
Charity Futures: www.charityfutures.com
Charity People: www.charitypeople.co.uk
Charity Recruitment: www.charityrecruitment.co.uk/home.html
Harris Hill: www.harrishill.co.uk

Scottish Council for Voluntary Organisations (SCVO)
www.scvo.org.uk

United Kingdom Accreditation Service
Details of accredited ISO 9000 certification bodies.
www.ukas.com

Volresource
Lists recruitment consultants specialising in voluntary sector appointments.
www.volresource.org.uk/workopps/recruit.htm

Wales Council for Voluntary Action (WCVA)
www.wcva.org.uk

Index